Contemporary Policing

An examination of society in the 1980s

Edited by J.R. THACKRAH

Sphere Reference
30/32 Gray's Inn Road, London WC1X 8JL

Sphere Reference
30/32 Gray's Inn Road
London
WC1X 8JL

First published 1985

Phototypesetting by
The Word Factory, Rossendale, Lancashire.

Printed and bound in Great Britain by
Cox & Wyman Ltd, Reading

Contents

Publisher's Foreword

The idea of publishing a collection of essays and articles designed to explain the current state of policing and police management in the United Kingdom was conceived by Richard Thackrah and myself in the Autumn of 1982.

In pursuit of this aim I attended meetings at the Police Staff College at Bramshill and had discussions with various members of the Bramshill staff, both acedemic and administrative.

As a result of these discussions we decided that the project should be published as a commercial venture with members of the academic staff at Bramshill being commissioned to write articles expressing their own views about the areas of policing and police management in which they specialise.

The result is *Contemporary Policing — an examination of society in the 1980s*, ten essays covering areas of concern to the police, police management, students and the general public.

The essays were written during the latter half of 1983 and this should be born in mind whilst reading them.

All the views expressed in the essays are the views of the individual contributors and should not be taken to represent the official views of the Police Staff College, the Home Office or the police service.

James Tindall
Sphere Books,
January 1985

Introduction

The student of police history is well aware that the establishing of a modern law enforcement agency was not achieved without considerable debate of that most fundamental apprehension which occupied the minds of both proponents and opponents of a police force — and which was best expressed in the words of the select committee of 1822 when members found 'it difficult to reconcile an effective system of police with that perfect freedom of action and exemption from interference which are the great privileges and blessings of society in this country'.

That statement, made several years before the setting up of the first police force in Britain, reflected the deep-seated mistrust of any potential infringement of personal liberties, yet recognised the need for a formal agency of social control. It was little wonder that Peel, when setting about the appointing of the first Commissioners of the Metropolitan Police, Rowan and Mayne, felt the imperative need to harness the co-operation and consent of the public and to create a policing system in which the police did not appear to be set apart from the people.

The objectives of that police service were adumbrated by Sir Richard Mayne — 'the prevention of crime, the detention of offenders and the maintenance of public tranquillity'. In his use of the latter phrase Mayne was keenly aware, like Peel, of public tranquillity as an indicator of public acceptance of the police, of the willingness of citizens to obey the law as it was physically embodied in the person of the police officer. It is interesting that over a hundred and fifty years passed before those words of Mayne were to be given a fresh significance by Lord Scarman.

In the meantime, British policing had established itself amongst the people and earned a reputation, international in character, for the humane and caring application of the law. It had developed a tradition of service to the community and, from the principles established by Peel and his contemporaries, a law enforcement system which was supported and approved by those policed. Unlike many other countries the police were not an executive arm of government: neither were they an agent of the people.

It is a matter of considerable concern, therefore, when our society reaches a stage in its development in which many responsible critics of police feel that those principles and traditions of British policing are in some way being comprised.

The reasons for this situation coming about are complex and are, at least in part, the subject of examination by the contributors to this book. It is not my intention to analyse them at this point, nor indeed to delineate the nature of the police response; however, it is important to stress that the pressures upon policing are of a magnitude forces have not experienced before and create dilemmas for police organisations.

Such a dilemma is seen, for example, in the present emphasis upon a community policing strategy which is endeavouring to re-invigorate, even in some areas to restore, the police-public relationship. Undoubtedly this will be an appropriate means of meeting some of the demands which sections of the public are making upon police. Yet too hasty a move in that direction may appease the few at the cost of offending the many: law enforcement cannot be something which is selective in its operation, as police have to be accountable to society at large.

Whilst attempting to tailor law enforcement to public demand, the Police Service is well aware that economic constraints are of such an order that there will be little, if any, growth in resources; the phenomenon of growing demand and static resources places strains upon organisational structures and policies and is likely to do so for some time to come. The push is now toward more efficient use of existing resources and to liaison with other agencies in the field of crime prevention.

The overtly critical climate in which policing now takes place makes each and every police activity a matter for close scrutiny. The move toward a localised police response may well be welcomed in some quarters but others see the stresses and strains of modern living requiring a well equipped and more centrally directed policing response. In much the same way the citizenry may want greater value for money in the form of increased police efficiency, but it does always appear to welcome the outcome when police are seen to act far more effectively, for example, in defusing public disorders.

The truth underlying the police debate is that society does not really know what to ask of its law enforcement agency in any precise manner. For the police, hostility to many of their actions over a decade or so seems to have engendered the feeling that they, themselves, are an opposed minority, outside some communities rather than within them. The police feeling also appears to be that too often are they the convenient whipping post for the failures of governments and politicians to solve the problems of economic recession, of discrimination and of deprivation.

It has been argued that the police have supplied ample ammunition to their critics especially in not consulting their communities as often as they should have done and in not being more open about many aspects of police operations. The public image of the police has suffered in consequence at a time when more sophisticated technology could lead to threats to personal liberty of a very invidious nature: a prime example of this is the computer and the facility it offers for data collection.

If society is uncertain and ambivalent about the role of police then the same uncertainty and ambivalence transfers itself to police themselves and one can sympathise with any organisation which has to more precisely state its objectives when its clients' demands are, on many occasions, contradictory. On the other hand the police service has not re-examined, one suspects, those objectives set by Mayne a century and a half ago; intellectually the leaders of the service have remained somewhat aloof from this vital area of managerial responsibility.

The outcome of the events and deliberations of the recent past has been to raise the issue of police accountability to a position of some considerable pre-eminence. Within this is constantly reiterated the police belief, which many public opinion polls still substantially endorse, that this country enjoys a policing structure which is the most accountable in the world; certainly it is felt that no other public servants in Britain are made so responsible for their actions.

To this could be added the mildness of British policing but especially the progress already made both in the area of accountability itself and in the sphere of police training. Consultation committees are rapidly becoming a fixture of all forces, lay visitors' schemes open up police premises to public inspection, the complaints procedure is in course of revision; probationer training has been increased to 14 weeks and the development of professional skills has gradually placed greater emphasis upon the handling of street encounters.

The *Police and Criminal Evidence Act*, contenious though some find it to be, has placed accountability as a paramount concern and a major part of it is also devoted to the improving and safeguarding of the rights of the individual. The parliamentary debate which has surrounded it echoes the apprehension of the select committee of 1822 — the equating of the need to protect liberty with the need to secure social order.

For those whose interests in policing are very much of an intellectual order, a fruitful outcome of the policing debate has been the more significantly legitimate place which the social sciences now occupy in police thinking. The service has been forced to face the need for research data to effectively underpin the knowledge base required by modern management systems. In so doing a growing relationship is emerging between police organisations and research institutions; the Policy Studies Institute report on the Metropolitan Police is an excellent illustration of this; more importantly, perhaps, so is the Police Research Foundation.

Whilst this collection of essays has not emerged from a research institution per se the Police Staff College encourages studies of police organisations and draws widely upon social scientists for its directing staff. The contributors, therefore, are uniquely placed to comment upon problems and developments in law enforcement and bring to their perspectives a close association with officers at all rank levels from Sergeant to Chief Constable.

The aim of this book is to interest policemen, and concerned laymen, in many of the issues which are now part and parcel of the law and order debate. For too long the police and social order have been taken for granted; but in a rapidly changing society law enforcement and the securing of the Queen's Peace become more complex matters, especially when society seeks to maintain individual freedom and restrict restraints upon them in pursuit of its liberal democratic ideals.

The range of contributions is indicative of the width of approach now adopted in the higher education and training of senior police officers. Although limitations of space involve selectively in what is finally presented to the reader, there are certain policing issues around which the chapters may be seen to aggregate themselves.

- (i) The nature and purpose of policing, its relationship to central and local government and the reconciliation of law enforcement with the desire to protect personal liberty.
- (ii) The nature of the police officer, his psychological characteristics and his views of the policing tasks.
- (iii) The public dimension of policing as reflected in community and race relations, the impact of terrorism, economic constraints and the pressures placed upon police managers.

At no stage in this book are statements made which are other than the writers' own personal views. The contributors do not represent either an official Police Staff College, Home Office or police service policy.

Lastly, I wish to thank the following for their advice and comments: the Home Office and colleagues at the Police Staff College, in particular David Pope, Ivor Ellis and Ian Stuart, and Dennis Brett until recently the Police Staff College Librarian. For his forebearance and faith in the project, sincere appreciation is extended to James Tindall of Sphere Books.

Richard Thackrah
Bramshill,
May 1984

Some reflections on Economics and police management
I. STUART

The purpose of this article is to describe certain areas of police management which have caused me a little concern during fifteen years' teaching at Bramshill. I admit that although the function of Bramshill's staff is to explore and discuss objectively — and, one hopes, help to improve — police management, my views must indicate to some degree my personal preferences, perhaps even prejudices.

I assert that a study of economics is appropriate for police managers and can help in examining the great difficulties, even possible contradictions, which seem to arise in the deployment of police resources. I am certainly not claiming that Economics is more important than other social science disciplines in a police management-development syllabus or that, in itself, Economics is a surgical tool for the precise resolution of managerial difficulties — we are all aware that Economics as a subject has its 'problems'. Police management — and therefore training provided to police managers — is a problem, not a puzzle; puzzles by definition have clearly best solutions but problems do not. Economics can, however, provide a partial framework of analysis, a 'mode of thinking', which can often help managers by suggesting some of the questions germane to their resource deployment problems.

I believe that the most senior managers, since they are responsible for long-term resource-deployment decisions, have an obligation to:

    define their industry;
    ensure that their resources are used effectively and efficiently;
    weigh the costs and benefits of any public programme they wish to introduce;
    anticipate possible changes in the broad economic climate in which they operate so that resource difficulties, if they occur, will not be a complete surprise.

THE POLICE INDUSTRY

Many years ago, it is rumoured, British Rail woke up and discovered it was not in the railway industry but in the transport industry; in other words, they had competition. The police have come to a similar healthy conclusion about themselves, although perhaps the full implications of such a conclusion are still elusive for anyone in or connected with the police. The genuine difficulty for police (and police trainers) is that their industry is much more complex than selling transport or canned beans. Of course the police have 'competition': clearly from the huge private security industry (whose services they themselves employ) and from, say, traffic wardens. But in the wider area of social regulation and control, other institutions play an import part: the Church, the family, schools, the workplace, the media and so on. It is impossible to attribute accurately the contribution of each to what we accept as being an orderly (but free) society.

Objectives for the police were defined in 1829 and have been added to since, although not in any fundamental or significant way. These definitions have been inadequate as a guide for police strategy or tactics. Nothing is specified to show priorities or methods of achieving them, except perhaps in the haziest sense. In the British context of policing this has been understandable, if not always helpful to the police or those to whom they are accountable. Given this, and the operational autonomy of Chief Constables, police forces in their differing ways have decided their own priorities and policing styles (which provides flexibility but also confusion at times) against a supposed background of 'policing by consent'. I feel that the police do in the main police by the consent of the public, but it is to some extent misleading when they cite evidence to show that, next to the Monarchy, they are the most popular institution in the land: they *are* popular for what they represent — for example, traditional values, public tranquillity, etc. — but not necessarily at times for the methods they employ or the priorities they select.

It is legitimate of society to have certain expectations of the police; it is legitimate of government to have certain expectations of police; research and reflections on police should at least be listened to; the police have a right to make decisions based upon their undoubted professional expertise. What is lacking is any consensus on these matters. No industry will succeed unless it is customer-oriented, unless it continually examines critically the relationship between what it produces and those who 'buy' the product. At times, and in various places, the police have imposed their solution upon society without doing the appropriate 'market research' to discover how best to fit their multi-produce business to their different kinds of customers. Although the operational autonomy of Chief Constables should, in my view, remain, the customer must be consulted and has a right to have his anxieties allayed or at least understood and acknowledged.

THE EFFECTIVE AND EFFICIENT USE OF RESOURCES

It is, one hopes, a truism that corruption represents a form of resource misallocation; and I shall say no more on that.

6

Unless the police, in consultation with the customer, have successfully defined their industry, they cannot hope to deploy their resources in the best way. The police, understandably, tend to make a great display of being 'effective' — that is, whatever the cost, the job gets done. (This could mean, for example, that there are ten times as many officers attending a demonstration as demonstrators.) But 'effectiveness' and 'efficiency' are different things: efficiency envelops effectiveness. Efficiency, for the economist, means doing successfully and with the least resources a task that society wants to be done, a job for which there is a reasonable demand.

One matter that Economics highlights is that police activities (sales of services to the customer), like any other product, are subject to 'diminishing returns'. Thus public satisfaction derived from the consumption of a particular good falls per unit as more is provided, whilst the cost per unit of that good rises as more is produced. Sooner or later, cost will exceed satisfaction. One might imagine the effect of the police concentrating all their resources on catching parking offenders. And some Chief Constables seem to think that, as well as being custodians of the public tranquillity, they have a duty to safeguard the private moral tone of society, even when the clarity of the law is not perfect and citizens do not seem to be especially interested in this particular form of police vigour.

In the qualitative world of policing, returns on 'sales' can only rarely be measured totally in terms of money; we need the still elusive concept of 'public benefit' to measure the consequences of what police do. Economics says that an activity should continue up to the point where the value of, or satisfaction with, the marginal output is equal to its marginal cost. Indeed, this should be true of all activities, otherwise society will not be attaining optimal satisfaction from the resources available at any one time. In policing, this notion is impossible to apply with precision. But, together with the concept of diminishing returns, it implies that the police — given their resources and assuming that they are doing the things for which there is a public demand — are not wasting manpower and equipment by failing to see that the latter would yield higher public benefit by being employed in some other department of their multi-product industry. This, of course, requires very sensitive judgments about public concern, a concern that will vary in different places and at different times, and amongst different social and ethnic groups.

This problem for police in deploying their resources in an optimal way is sometimes connected with the issue of 'empire-building', which is believed to occur in the private-commercial as well as in the public-non-commercial sector. Because the idea that managers would wish to build empires for themselves appeals to common sense, economics is on safer ground in attempting to give an explanation for this phenomenon. Managers of departments within the larger organisation will usually find an excuse to retain or expand their staff because the relationship between effort and rewards will seldom be immediate or precise — except, perhaps, where the one-man business is conerned. If a person does not receive an almost immediate promotion or bonus for a job well done, he may try to reward himself by seeking (and 'justifying') extra staff; thus gratification occurs by self-aggrandisement, which could lead to promotion later on. But one of the important tasks of the senior manager is to ensure that resources are continually examined to see whether they can be gainfully switched among different activities so that profit, or public benefit, is at a maximum. Empire-building will be a constant hindrance to this duty. Police specialist squads may present an example of this problem: it is often difficult (except in cynical terms) to understand how their size and duration are determined.

The results by which police efficiency is considered should not, however, neglect the important dilemma where efficiency seems to be at odds with fairness, or equity. Efficiency and equity are not, of course, incompatible in the broadest sense, and this dilemma is by no means confined in the public sector to the police. The problem — so frequently recurring in the non-commercial service sector — is that of measuring public benefit. In education, results measured purely by examination successes indicate that the bulk of resources should not be directed towards the working class. In medical care, the elderly and the mentally ill should be relatively neglected. In policing, it might be better almost to abandon those sections of the population whose support for the police seems less than wholehearted. (Already there are the beginnings of a systematic discrimination in the use of police resources virtually to ignore certain sorts of crimes.) To pursue these kinds of policies would be monstrous, of course. The balance can only be found by the use of compassionate judgment. Economics does not help very much, beyond drawing attention to the problem.

In the now keen search for police efficiency, I feel that a change in the way in which police accounts are presented should help. At the moment, police accounts are very bland, cloaking important detail; the various activities of police are seldom costed overtly. Some time ago, 'planning, programing and budgeting systems' was introduced in an attempt to meet this problem but it was not altogether successful; in trying to shed light on the cost of the main police efforts, it relied upon the classification of an officer's duties according to whether he was in the traffic department, or in C.I.D. and so on. But these so-called discrete classifications often greatly overlapped and the exercise attracted much criticism. When police activities come to be more openly costed — for example, revealing the average cost of answering a call, of giving evidence in court, etc. — then it should become a little easier for police to examine whether they are giving value for money. And such accounts, if available to the public, might add an interesting element to the discussion on police accountability.

As in medical care and education, where the cost of a service to the individual is zero, the police face an almost unlimited demand for their services, which they can never meet. Discretion and discrimination in the use of resources is inevitable. Since resources are by definition limited, society demands good value for money — even when, as in the recent past, governments were fairly benign towards the public sector.

WEIGHING THE COSTS AND BENEFITS OF PUBLIC PROGRAMMES

If the police can define their industry, then they will be better able to fix their objectives and apply sensible measures of efficiency — even though some of these measures might have to be rather more subtle than current clear-up rates for reported crime. If this can be achieved the door is open wider for an improved evaluation of public programmes such as, for example 'neighbourhood watch' (an American innovation) and 'case-screening' (another American innovation), the former concerned primarily with crime prevention and the latter primarily with better detection rates. It is in this kind of area that 'Cost Benefit Analysis' (CBA) can help.

Economics can help a manager generally to ask more of the relevant questions to resolve a problem than might otherwise be the case. Although CBA does not necessarily cause good or better decisions to be made, it too can widen the agenda of inquiry, assisting in more specific — that is, programme — areas. CBA, which has been widely applied in various parts of the public sector, is an interesting off-shoot of Economics but economists are by no means the only social scientists to employ it. As its name suggests, it is a process of inquiry which attempts to focus more sharply on those costs of a programme which are real costs to society — that is, 'opportunity costs', where society actually has to forgo other worth-while goods and services to pay for a programme — and those which are transfers, where resources are merely redistributed. This distinction is not always easy to make (robbery, of course, is not a pure transfer of wealth because, amongst other things, without paying for the protection of property rights our kind of society could not endure). CBA also helps to identify the 'psychological costs' incurred in certain kinds of human interaction which cannot be measured accurately if at all, for example, the anguish caused by having one's home broken into. And as regards the benefits inherent in a programme, the same kinds of notions apply as well.

As the police refine the concept of their industry and as the pressures for efficiency increase, I foresee greater innovation regarding programmes such as neighbourhood watch and a wider involvement than just police in their detailed evaluation. Economists will undoubtedly play some part in such evaluation; but it would be useful if police managers could keep a knowing eye on what they are up to.

THE ECONOMIC CLIMATE

Just a few years ago, police officers were relatively badly paid, given their responsibilities. Recruitment was poor and morale was low. Fortunately, this has changed: pay has improved greatly and all forces are at about full strength. If ever there was a 'golden age' for policing, it must be now. But it is also true that things are changing once again, the shiny picture is beginning to tarnish. This was inevitable and should have been anticipated earlier. The issue of what share of public resources should go to the police is now being discussed in terms less favourable to them. The 'crime-wave' scare — so stridently voiced by the press — whose theme was that, without increasing police resources, the country would be engulfed by an inexorable tide of lawlessness and sin, has now largely disappeared. Indeed, the police are at the heart of economic affairs in Britain and have been for many decades, perhaps longer; but this is only in small part due to their competition for public resources.

Let us take the present (Conservative) government's economic policy as an example; but this government, although perhaps more 'law-and-order' inclined than usual, is no different from any other government — left, right or centre — in facing certain inescapable economic difficulties. These difficulties are how to achieve simultaneously four basic economic objectives: full employment, expansion of the economy, a healthy balance of payments and control of inflation. Few governments since the war have faced these issues honestly.

The present government has decided — conveniently or rationally — that the key to successful macro-economic management is to concentrate first on controlling inflation then all else will follow. To try to attain all four objectives at the same time is a hopeless task (only the Japanese seem able to do this, and the British apparently feel that to become like the Japanese is too high a price for such a success). But how to control inflation, which, if too high, is said not only to jeopardise the other three objectives but also to sow the seeds of malignant political and social change? If an overt incomes policy is ruled out — because allegedly it will distort (an already distorted) labour market — then the government must tackle the 'money supply'. If the government itself is the principal culprit in causing the quantity of money in the system to grow faster than output at constant prices, then it should reduce the non-borrowed part of the budget deficit, at the same time, some would prefer, curbing the powers of trade unions to achieve inordinate wage increases during times of monetary constraint, as this would aggravate the problem. (Unions can be expected to resist such changes, which is why police are, in effect, at the

10

expected to resist such changes, which is why police are, in effect, at the heart of economic policy, because then it becomes a matter of social control as well.) But how to cut the budget deficit? By raising taxes? — but that would discourage effort, it is claimed. By reduced public expenditure? — surely that is the answer, especially if, with improved efficiency, the effectiveness of services need not fall a great deal.

A policy of trying to reduce public expenditure, despite the large number of unemployed and old-age pensioners relying on state benefits, enjoys some public support — but only up to a point, perhaps. Increased efficiency in the provision of public services is always possible, of course. But it is quite likely that much of the electorate is against large reductions in spending on, say, the health service and education. Defence claims a large part of the budget but our commitment to NATO is currently very strong and our forces require expensive re-equipment. What about the police? Surely they have fared rather well of late; and are they all that efficient anyway?

It is thought that, despite rising demands upon police, their share of public resources will not rise in real terms for some time to come; indeed, that share might even fall. If this is so, the best that society (and government) can expect of police is that they become more efficient. Which brings me back to the beginning of this article.

I have no doubt that, by a broad range of criteria, the British police service stands very high amongst those of other advanced countries. But changes in the nature and style of police management have already begun and will continue. Gone, I hope, are the days of certain senior officers who were best described as 'great characters'. The need for leadership and courage is as great as ever, but other qualities are needed besides. Difficult to teach and dismal though it may be, Economics has some small part to play in developing the new kind of police manager.

A plea for applied ethics
N. RICHARDS

INTRODUCTION

As the title suggests, the main object of this paper is to recommend that applied ethics be given more attention within the police service. The social sciences have an established place within police training and education, so much so that police experience is often expressed in their language. It is a language which is much taken up with accurate observation, conjectures resting upon significant correlations, and prediction. When applied to police the emphasis is typically on how officers do or will act in various situations. However, there is a tendency to set aside questions of how officers *should* act, particularly in problematic or conflicting circumstances. It is the business of ethics to consider just such questions and to provide the conceptual framework with which to do it.

I believe, however, that the promise of applied ethics goes further than this. Such an approach enhances the possibility that moral problems will be more fully understood, analysed more carefully and made more tractable. It also raises questions about the values served by an occupation and focusses upon how those ends are to be legitimately achieved. Logically it demands, therefore, that policing's key concepts, such as 'authority', 'consent', 'impartiality', 'discretion' and 'professionalism', are carefully unravelled and defined so that value commitments and moral requirements are made explicit. The application of applied ethics to an occupation also encourages reflection on one's personal obligations, on the rights and obligations of colleagues and upon the virtues which it is appropriate to cultivate as a police officer and within society at large.

But why should applied ethics be of particular importance for the police? The police are invested with the authority, which includes a virtual monopoly of legitimate coercion, to deal with a wide range of emergencies which include relatively minor domestic disputes, criminal activities, road traffic accidents, natural disasters and public disorders. They are also granted wide discretionary powers that afford them the scope and opportunity to respond to such emergencies in a flexible and appropriate manner. In other words, public trust in and dependence upon the police is considerable and conditional. They are expected to justify that trust by maintaining not only commitment and capacity but also the highest standards of conduct. Applied ethics has an important part to play in securing this last condition.

This paper is divided into five sections. The first presents a review of recent policing developments with particular emphasis upon those which have been inimical to the police-public relationship together with some indications of the circumstances in which they arose. The following section seeks in simple, but I hope not too pedestrian terms, to make explicit the relationship between policing, morality and the liberal democratic state. Here the focus is upon the moral conditions of that relationship. The third section deals with the part which a concern for moral values and standards must necessarily play in the leadership and management of a public service. The next section identifies some of the moral dilemmas of police. It does not attempt solutions but seeks rather to point up the conceptual difficulties and moral choices which are centred upon their occupational functions. Finally, a section is devoted to a more detailed discussion of what a greater emphasis upon applied ethics might be expected to achieve for police together with some suggestions for its implementation.

TRUST AND CONFIDENCE

The British police service, which was diffidently introduced into a libertarian political and social climate, has, throughout the one hundred and fifty years or so of its existence, managed to combine a high order of public acceptance with the discharge of its duties. Indeed, from its beginnings, its relationship with the public, that vast and amorphous body, has been governed by the principle that only by gaining its co-operation and trust could it hope to secure the objective of helping to uphold social order. That it has generally managed, in pursuit of this objective, to police in a mild and unaggressive way says much for both police and public. However, during the past twenty years there have been considerable social changes in British society which have affected all sections of it and hence both parties to the police-public relationship. Many of them undoubtedly made the task of the police in seeking the support of the public more difficult.

A brief retrospective of some of the changes most affecting police will highlight the challenges they faced. The number of laws unpopular with sections of the public, such as those relating to traffic, drugs and pornography, and which police have been required to enforce, has increased. Protest marches and public demonstrations have become a regular occurence; welfare agencies have arisen which have a social regulation function, thus reducing the number of services which used to be performed by the police (Richards, 1982a). A public has emerged which is better educated, is less ready to defer to authority without reasons and has an increased awareness of its legal rights. Demands for economic and social justice have often been expressed through political and industrial action. The changes brought about by the *Police Act*, 1964, combined with the effect of amalgamating police forces to form larger units, have weakened democratic control generally (Critchley, 1973, p.36). Until recently, when the trend was reversed, police strategies have tended to increase crime response efficiency at the cost of greater remoteness from the public. The growth of ethnic minorities has contributed to increasing social pluralism. The increase in pay and status has tended to distance them socially from some of the public whom they police while bringing them closer to others.

Such changes serve to emphasise that favourable public attitudes cannot be entirely earned. They are the product of complex social forces, many of which are beyond the control of the police. What they also illustrate is a period when social norms and values were being challenged, when class and status underwent a process of redefinition (Dahrendorf, 1975) and individuals experimented with different styles of life and demanded the freedom to do so. As upholders of the *status quo*, the police lagged behind in reflecting this process; but reflect it they eventually did. Conditions of service improved, a predominantly directive style of leadership and management became gradually more consultative and both the discipline code and informal practice allowed for a more permissive distinction between the public and private morality of police officers. In operational terms the police found themselves working to a social contract whose terms were often being re-evaluated by members of the public, when they were not being challenged and tested through action. And they found themselves, like other public institutions, subjects of the greatest critical scrutiny and controversy since that of the years of their origins in the 1820s and 1830s.

From the mid 1960s onwards incidents, investigations and inquiries cumulatively began to erode public confidence in the integrity and competence of the police service in general, and the Metropolitan Police in particular. There were remarkable achievements, such as the successful resolution of the Spaghetti House, Balcombe Street and Iranian Embassy sieges, and the impressive successes against organised crime, all of which took place against a background of unspectacular but effective daily peace keeping. Conversely, *The Times* inquiry, the Soho pornography scandal, Operation Countryman, the riots of Summer 1981, the Yorkshire Ripper investigation and inquiry, Michael Fagan, Grunwick, Lewisham, Southall and Blair Peach and similar happenings lent credibility to the growing accusations about abuse of suspects while in custody, racism, corruption, the excessive use of force in effecting public order, and scepticism about police effectiveness and efficiency in dealing with crime.

Reference has already been made to the weakening of democratic control. This could not have come at a less opportune time as the constitutional accountability of the police, with its tripartite arrangements of Chief Constable, Home Office and police authority outside London, and Home Secretary and Metropolitan Police Commissioner for London, was called into question with demands for greater accountability. The coincidence of diminished democratic control and the events inimical to the reputation of the police gave a fresh urgency too to the quest for a means of dealing with complaints against the police that were acceptable to both police and public. It is worth adding that the inquiries and measures initiated to reform police procedures, alay public disquiet and redress grievances themselves, perhaps inevitably, served to keep the informed public eye upon police short-comings. In this respect Sir Robert Mark's purge against corruption, Lord Scarman's various reports and the Royal Commission on Criminal Procedure, which was instituted to consider the vexed issue of police powers, their proper extent and the safeguards over their exercise, may be instanced. More recently the four Policy Studies Institute reports published in November, 1983, under the general title, *Police and People in London*, present a generally uncomplimentary view of police performance, behaviour, attitudes and management.

Although the circumstances which gave rise to these developments are complex, there are a number of factors which help to explain them. Three have already been mentioned. As the people within our society have become freer, better educated and informed than ever before so their expectations of public services, including the police, have risen. With regard to the police in particular they would seem to expect a heightened awareness and understanding of the dignity and rights of the individual. Overall they are more likely to criticise and complain about police behaviour which, in the recent past, would have been thought unremarkable. It is also the case that if wide-spread changes offer opportunities, they also create a climate of uncertainty as the *mores*, conventions, rules and usages, which pattern human relationships, are reformed, revised, developed or discarded. Within such a climate the police, in their role as upholders of law and order, can be put under considerable strain. In seeking for certainty in the face of pressing practical decisions they may assume functions which go beyond those with which they have been entrusted. They may also sometimes over-react towards those sections of society for whose causes they have little sympathy or whose motives they do not understand. Again, uncertainty about the moral basis of law, as is the case to some extent with pornography, soft drugs and some driving offences, when combined with high monetary profitability provides necessary, if not sufficient, conditions for some police corruption. In addition to those factors, prior to the Edmund Davies pay award many police forces were under-manned and there was considerable loss, through resignation, of experienced constables. The quality of recruits was also lowered, in-service probationary training was starved of the appropriately experienced tutor-constables and the time allowed for it was often skimped. More importantly, this factor exacerbated all the pressures mentioned so far.

POLICE, MORALITY AND THE LIBERAL DEMOCRATIC STATE

The circumstances, responses and explanations outlined above all serve to illustrate three fundamental points. Firstly, the truth of the often overlooked fact that policing a liberal democratic state is a demanding and delicate activity. Secondly, that there is a continuous need for police at the supervisory levels to possess high qualities of leadership and management and to seek to develop them. Lastly, that the changes and developments within the police service, which have grown symbiotically with social change, often make it difficult to get by with habitual moral practices, vague moral perspectives, and intuitively applied values. Tried, and still valid, ethical principles have to be understood and interpreted afresh, and then applied to some very problematic situations. For my purposes, it is this last point which serves to show the relationship between the first two. Ethical problems are unavoidable and pervasive and they are necessarily bound up with practice. Without a thorough grasp of the values which it serves and the means which may be legitimately employed to realise them, no public service can properly understand its role or purpose within society.

It is one of the remarkable achievements of the modern liberal democratic state that it facilitates a wide range of human goals and enterprises in a manner which satisfies, if imperfectly, the demands of morality. By morality here is meant a system of social control which is effected through principles whose main purpose is to protect the interests of other persons, as well as the individual, and which present themselves to the individual as checks on his natural inclinations or spontaneous tendencies to act, where those are purely self-interested. In Britain, there is a high degree of public order because social control is effected voluntarily by a people who generally adhere to moral principles and are prepared to make the sacrifices of personal self-interest which such adherence requires. This same people, through its democratic political arrangements, bring into existence rules which are enacted by the Queen-in-Parliament and upheld by the courts; in short, the law. Such laws are both substantive and procedural and one of their functions is to reinforce, with an elaborate battery of sanctions and penalties, some of those moral principles which are central to social control.

Under these same political arrangements the police service as a public body is entrusted, in the interests of citizens, with upholding the rule of law, preventing crime, protecting life and property and preserving public tranquillity. For this purpose, individual police officers are invested with rights and duties which prescribe their role, give them authority and provide them with the necessary powers to carry out their duties. Moreoever, in a liberal democratic state to say that the police enjoy the trust, confidence and respect of the public is often summed up by the notion of policing by consent. It is also to claim that the values served by both police and citizens are the same. So, in British society the police act with consent and are legitimately in authority if, and only if, the generality of citizens consent to the constitutional provisions — rules, usages, conventions — which determine their office.

As with all models, this represents an idealised abstraction which merely serves to show, in bald terms, the relationship between police, morality and the democratic state. Nonetheless, it supports the contention that, to the extent that the police service has managed to combine a high order of public acceptance with the discharge of its duties, it has enjoyed such a relationship in part because it has been recognised as pursuing worthwhile ends in a morally acceptable manner. Both the worthwhile ends and the morally acceptable manner present dilemmas for police, a line of argument I shall develop later. For the moment what this characterisation of the police-public relationship identifies is the social interface position of the police and the high expectations which their public have of them. Somehow the police have to serve the public by upholding individual rights and liberties while exercising their lawful powers for the well-being of society. They are required to strike a balance between preserving fundamental freedoms and containing crime and disorder. When it is remembered that majorities can be tyrannous on occasions, acquiesing in questionable police practices in the interest of detection and conviction, then the moral burdens placed upon the police are readily apparent. These must surely be prominent amongst the demands which make policing a democratic society such a difficult and delicate activity.

LEADERSHIP AND MANAGEMENT

That the modern police service needs effective and efficient leadership is a truism. What is not nearly so obvious is the importance of ethical standards for the achievement of this objective. Most leadership and management models give prominence to the setting, maintaining and reassessing of those practical standards and principles which have to do with ensuring that an organisation has the capacity to fulfil its objectives (Adair, 1972: Hodgkinson, 1983). But those standards which concern ethical practice are often given either cursory treatment or neglected altogether. For the police service, as I have already indicated, this area is of vital importance and to view it from the leadership/management perspective should throw new light upon it.

In our society the relationship between law and morality is complicated. There are laws which refine and clarify moral precepts while others are open to ambiguous moral evaluation. Indeed, the borderline between law and morality is often blurred. For many, and this includes some police officers, being moral is simply doing that which the law requires and their sole motivation is fear of the penalties for not doing so. It is also the case that all too often the same people see obedience to the law as a kind of game, as a set of rules whose requirements the clever or cunning avoid whenever possible and especially when there is no chance of a penalty being incurred. This is one of the limitations which attaches to discipline codes and other instruments of quasi-legal regulation within organisations. Were such attitudes to be pervasive in a liberal democracy or its institutions it is doubtful whether it would long survive as such. Freedom exercised with responsibility is the touchstone of such a society and laws could not be enforced unless most people believed in the moral basis of law and were committed to it. The law does not tell us what we ought to do in most situations. At most it sets a framework which determines the minimum acceptable behaviour which a society will accept. Moreover, the requirements of morality go beyond those of law. Law does not require sympathy, kindness, altruism or civility.

There is, then, vast scope for the use of moral judgment and this is nowhere more so than within the police service. This presents an organisational problem for its command structure. Police officers are independent officers under the Crown and, as such, are personally responsible for their unlawful acts. They also are entrusted with considerable discretion in the performance of their duties and much of their activity is not directly supervised. It follows that they have considerable latitude in the way they effect their office, and how this is done will depend upon the attitudes of the individual. Of course, the setting of moral standards by police supervisors will involve reference to shared codes but what it also involves is the more complex process of fostering an atmosphere where moral dilemmas may be faced and shared and the cultivation of personal and occupational virtues is a possibility. In such a process example is as important as precept but in securing practice which is informed by the appropriate principles critical attention to the moral requirements is a necessity.

There is one closely related comment to add. Many police officers, perhaps the majority, have come to see themselves as professionals offering a professional service. If by 'a profession' is meant a body which provides a service deemed both essential and worthwhile by its clients, exercising skills resting upon a systematic body of knowledge and governed by concern for the principles and values which sustain both the commitment of members to each other and their clients, then the police service is clearly a good candidate for professional status (Greenhill,

1981). However, an explicit occupational ethic, and a commitment to it, is a logical requirement of professionalism in the above sense and it is through making such a commitment that a body satisfies one of the main conditions of professional status.

SOME MORAL DILEMMAS OF POLICING

Thus far I have been arguing that greater emphasis upon applied ethics in the training, education, leadership and management of police would be beneficial both for them, as individuals and in terms of their occupation, and for the public they serve. What I have not done is show the sorts of problem which such an emphasis might be expected to ameliorate. This I shall shortly remedy with what I believe is a representative sample of the types of moral dilemma which regularly confront police officers. Some of them highlight the difficult choices facing police and may well excite sympathy, but others focus upon those, the unsuccessful resolutions of which, are impediments to good police-public relations.

However, before proceeding further it is appropriate to consider a notion which is inseparable from any consideration of police action: discretion. Discretion, the liberty or power of deciding, or of acting according to one's own judgment or as one thinks fit (Concise Oxford English Dictionary), used to be referred to *soto voce* by police administrators (Goldstein, 1976). This is because of their concern with the control of the police and the recognition that impartiality as well as discretion is a condition of police action. A marriage between discretion and impartiality *is* possible, but only if there are uniformly applied rules which govern the exercise of discretion. To fulfil this requirement would tax the ingenuity of administrators to breaking point given the myriad situations for which rules would be needed. It would burden police with extra rules, when they already have enough to cope with in knowing the law and keeping abreast of developments within it and would mean getting involved in regressive procedures. This is because discretion would still be required to apply the discretionary rules. The exercise of discretion by police officers is inevitable: it is logically impossible for laws to be deductively applied without intermediate inductive judgments; the whole body of the law cannot be applied on practical grounds and the police are expected to exercise discretion in order to realise the 'spirit' rather than the letter of the law.

Morality and discretion are intimately connected. Because police officers are expected to use discretion when making peace keeping choices the moral space, so to speak, within which they act is quite extensive. I mention this because it is contrary to first appearances. Although police officers are independent officers under the Crown they are bound by law, police discipline regulations, force orders, the Judges' Rules and

Administrative Directions as well as the pressures of a disciplined service. In terms of individual motivation this suggests that prudential considerations might be very much to the fore, and, no doubt, with many they are. However, this does not affect the fact that they exercise discretion in countless ways and are expected to do so. A few examples and one quotation will serve to support this contention. Discretion is used in the selection of suspects, in deciding which offences to 'notice' and which laws apply. Police must decide whether to caution or charge formally, and determine at which point, after arrest, to apply the provisions of the Judges' Rules and make decisions about the extent of seizure and search and prosecution and bail. Lord Scarman wrote in his report that:

'...discretion lies at the heart of the policing function... The good reputation of the police as a force depends upon the skill and judgment which policemen display in the particular circumstances of the cases and incidents which they are required to handle. Discretion is the art of suiting action to particular circumstances. It is the policeman's daily task.' (Scarman, 1981)

I suggested above that public acceptance of and trust in the police has been continually secured because, in part, they have been recognised as pursuing worthwhile ends in a morally acceptable manner. To take worthwhile ends first, I shall assume for the sake of argument that the traditional ends of policing, upholding the rule of law, preventing crime, protecting life and property, maintaining public order and preserving public tranquillity, as understood within a liberal democracy, are morally worthwhile. But even allowing for this assumption, the scene is still set for a classic conflict between *prima facie* duties. Nowhere has this been better exemplified than by Lord Scarman in his most recent report (Scarman, 1981, p.62). According to him the choice for the police of Brixton on the eve of the riots was between upholding the law or preserving public tranquillity. In the event they chose to uphold the law. Lord Scarman argues, according to what looks very much like utilitarian moral logic, that they were wrong to do so; that under the specific conditions which prevailed in Brixton on the eve of the riots the police had the duty to preserve public tranquillity. But whether the police ranked their prima facie duties correctly or not on this occasion they were posed with a very tricky moral dilemma. This situation also provides a nice reminder that moral reasoning is dependent upon beliefs as to fact. Had the Brixton community been less tense then the actions might have been judged the right ones.

Less dramatically, and on a day-to-day basis around the country, the same dilemma is faced by police officers engaged in case conference consultations with other social agencies which have a social control aspect to their work. Police often have to decide whether to initiate judicial proceedings or to allow other agencies to effect a possible reform of criminality by extra-legal or quasi-legal methods. Another instance is that of police in pursuit of motorised criminals. Police drivers clearly run the risk of endangering life and property in the interest of law enforcement. The reader can probably think of further examples.

I now wish to look at the dilemmas which are posed by policing in a morally acceptable manner. It is both a moral and legal requirement that the police should apply the law impartially. It is also the case that some police officers allow their prejudices, interest and strong personal moral convictions to outweigh their commitment in this respect. More subtly, police interest groups also, on occasion, undermine impartiality in this way. However, although these constitute problems enough, they are not the main concern here. Put formally the principle of impartiality requires that each person should be treated equally unless there is a relevant reason for doing otherwise. This implies not only that people should be treated equally with respect to something, such as goods or opportunity, but, negatively, that on occasions people should be treated differently. Now, *prima facie*, this presents no problem for police officers. In their capacity as upholders of the law they are required to apply to everyone what the law allows. And there are 'legalists' within the service who try to conduct themselves strictly according to the letter of the law. But if, as many police officers believe, they are required to take account not just of the letter but also of the spirit of the law then more is demanded of them. This is certainly so if their comprehensive peace keeping role is stressed. In fact they exercise a judicial function. They are in the business of taking account of other considerations beside the strict prescription of laws. The main candidates here are entitlement, need, and morality. The following examples will give some idea of how these considerations find their way into practice.

The impartiality principle requires that all motorists be treated equally in respect of speed limits, but a father's plea of a special entitlement to exceed the limit on his way to a sick child would probably count as a relevant reason for unequal treatment by a police officer. Again, it is well known that police regularly exercise discretion over the prosecution of shoplifters with social and mental needs counting as the relevant grounds for unequal treatment. Protestors who, acting in accordance with their declared moral convictions, break the law in minor ways, are sometimes treated sympathetically. Whether such reasons for unequal treatment are relevant in these sort of cases is not at issue here. What, hopefully, they show is that difficult moral dilemmas are posed in the exercise of impartiality. Such dilemmas are complicated further by what might be called the third person problem; police are usually subject, either directly or indirectly, to public scrutiny in what they do and the need to be seen as acting impartially, and hence credibly, exerts its own pressure. This is particularly so if it is conceded that we live in a society where consensus is lacking over how different substantive concepts of impartiality and justice are to be accommodated to each other (MacIntyre, 1981, Chpt.17).

Conceptual difficulties too lie at the root of the failure to take sufficient account of the differences between the notions of discrimination, prejudice and impartiality. Clearly if it is a case of to each what the law attributes to him then criminals have no grounds for complaint when they flout the law and are duly apprehended by the police. The police have discriminated between them and non-criminals and acted accordingly. And this too is completely unremarkable since discrimination, the making or observing of differences that are there to be made or perceived, is an essential precondition for such human action. Difficulties arise for police in this area because they have a duty to prevent crime. Whenever possible they must anticipate criminal activity and counter criminogenic situations. What then of sub-cultural groups who, experience shows, are regularly associated with particular sorts of crime? For police officers to engage in what might be called professional discrimination and the corresponding crime preventative measures towards such groups would seem not unreasonable and to meet the requirements of impartiality. Of course, the reality of such responses is not so straight forward. Professional discrimination can all too easily degenerate into prejudice. Criminal dispositions are conflated with other characteristics, such as those of race or dress or manner, within the habit of practice and people are treated differently solely on the basis of such differences, which is irrational, immoral and partial, that is, prejudiced. For police here is yet another moral dilemma.

When considering pre-trial procedure two dominant perspectives are discernable which, when they conflict, produce some of the most acute moral dilemmas in policing. The first perspective lays emphasis upon what is referred to as 'due process'. It gives prominence to the need to control governmental interference in peoples' lives. It claims that abuse is especially frequent by those who uphold the law and those who apply it. Thus, it stresses the need for clear and narrow guidelines regulating the use of confessions, the conduct of searches and arrests, the availability of legal aid and advice to people accused of crimes and the protection of individuals against self-incrimination. It argues most strongly that it may be necessary to support those guidelines by letting guilty persons go free, as a price for upholding the principles of judicial procedure. It also supports this view by maintaining that there are values in society, such as freedom, privacy and the integrity of the law, which may rightly override the minimisation of crime. The second perspective, which has been labelled the 'crime control' perspective (Packer, 1968), simply takes as its objective the streamlining of pre-trial procedure so as to facilitate a greater number of convictions and so deter crime through securing a higher conviction rate. This perspective is less sensitive to the rights of the individual in relation to the state largely because it is more trusting of governmental powers and believes them to be used, on the whole, for the general good. It is worthy of note that the most recent Royal Commission on Criminal Procedure wrestled to achieve a balance between these two perspectives and clearly found the task very demanding. I should add that, although it is being erroded, the rules of the English pre-trial procedure still reflect the strong libertarian outlook which predominated for the two centuries preceding the growth of the modern welfare state.

Police officers, because of their occupational orientation, tend to have a predeliction for the crime control perspective and it, or its implications, are a recurrent feature of their justifications for nominally immoral behaviour. Here I want to concentrate upon one aspect of that behaviour: deception. Sissela Bok (Bok, 1980, p.76) notes that the reasons most commonly used to defend deception appeal to four principles: that of avoiding harm, that of producing benefits, that of fairness, and that of veracity. Nor is such a procedure peculiar to police officers. Within conventional morality deception, either by commission or omission, is both practiced and justified in terms of such moral principles which are seen as overriding the requirement to be non-deceptive. Four illustrations, which employ each of the four principles in turn, will serve to expand this theme.

Firstly, detective officers who practice elaborate deceptions when questioning a person suspected of sexual assault, for example, will argue that the innocent suspect suffers no harm but that to omit such 'regularly successful techniques' would be to risk the possibility of releasing the sort of offender who would be likely to repeat the offence. Secondly, the officer who perjures himself in court, because he swears to having administered a caution when he did not, might well argue both for the relative lack of significance of the caution in the pre-trial procedure, and hence the triviality of the harm done, and the benefits of getting a conviction which might otherwise have been lost on a technicality. Moreover, an officer might justify including in his testimony before the court things that are 'not quite true' (Cain, 1976, p.175) partly for the practical reason that otherwise it would lack coherence and credibility but also on the grounds that the adversarial procedures of the court could not be relied upon to secure a just or fair outcome. Lastly, police are not merely regarded by those they serve as being *in* authority but as being *an* authority; as having knowledge that and knowledge how, which they are able to put at the disposal of the public in their peace keeping role. And public confidence in this capacity time and again contributes to the outcome of police interventions in a self-fulfilling way. Because people do have such confidence in the police when they are on the scene of a serious traffic accident, for instance, panic and confusion does subside, belief in some restoration of a normal state of affairs is bolstered and things tend to go better as a result. A police officer may therefore, in some situations, pretend to knowledge he does not have and simulate confidence which he does not possess. And his justification is that the truth of police trustworthiness is preserved through his deception and that things will go better if this is so.

The dilemma posed in this last illustration is to be found writ large in the police service, largely as a result of technological and research developments, and officers are usually fully aware that they risk the accusation of being manipulative. Victorian police did not have to concern themselves much with crime statistics or clear-up rates; a very imperfect measure of police effectiveness since they reflect only a part of the police function. Moreover, it seems to me that the police have to be effective enough to support the assurance of the generality of people that an uncertain world is free enough from risks and hazards for the normal pursuits of life to be possible. So, effectiveness is relative to different conditions of, and within, society; assurance will vary with regard to both time and place within society and the different climates of opinion of society as a whole. The problem for police, and chief officers in particular, is how far they should go through their reports and publicity to foster such assurance and how far they should go in presenting the statistically based 'truth'.

Conflicts between claims to rights constitute further dilemmas for police. What follows is a familiar and fairly typical example of such a conflict. A racist organisation wants to have a march and, as it is required to do by law, it notifies its proposed march route to the police. The route would take the march through areas largely inhabited by ethnic minorities. It is also virtually certain that political groups opposed to the racist organisation will mount counter demonstrations, which will, on past experience, probably be violent. The police are aware that certain rights are at issue and in conflict and that their decision will determine which right or rights prevail. They have to take account of the right to demonstrate peacefully, the right of minorities not to have hatred preached against them and the general public's right to be protected against outbreaks of violence. There may be others.

At a more private level, police officers often find themselves in the painful position of having to choose between vocational and family commitments. Most officers develop a vocational commitment to policing; they accept the responsibility for developing their police knowledge and upholding the principles and values of their office. The police, however, provide a twenty-four hour service which operates a demanding shift system in which contingent happenings requiring immediate attention continually occur. This places considerable demands upon wives or husbands and families and the choices involved in them are often moral choices.

The dilemmas which cluster around loyalty within the police service are the subject of my final example in this section. As with any other fairly abstract concept, the notion of loyalty is not at all easy to pin down. Ordinary usage indicates that it takes its place with such notions as faith, trust, devotion and, even, reverence. In the interest of clarity, I will content myself with a stipulative definition which captures well enough the meaning in general use. A person is loyal if he has a disposition to act in such a way that the relationship into which he has willingly entered with another person or persons is upheld. Although, ideally, feelings of affection or devotion often attend such a disposition, they may not necessarily do so, even if a sense of purposiveness does. From this definition it follows that loyalty is to be valued instrumentally: it takes its value from the ends which it serves. It also admits of degree; a person may be more or less loyal.

Because comradeship and loyalty are inculcated by the service the individual may often be motivated to sacrifice his own narrow self-interest to the interests of his fellow officers and thus to the many policing situations where it is imperative that concerted action be taken. Where loyalty is absent from such collective activities hurt and failure are often the outcome. This is so with public order, kidnap and armed fugitive incidents, for example. Incidents are 'winnable' for so long as ranks are closed. This partly explains, and characterises, one of the salient features of the police sub-culture. Unfortunately, loyalty is sometimes misplaced and the same disposition is tolerant of, or supports, corrupt or irregular practices. Looked at from the viewpoint of one committed to the values and ideals of the service and only concerned with strictly professional relationships, there is little problem with misplaced loyalty. His loyalty is directed towards sustaining a professional relationship and the corrupt, by abrogating the principles and rules which prescribe their office, and hence their professional relationships, forfeit their claims to his loyalty. However, because loyalty is inculcated and, consequently, directed intuitively, there tends to be a reluctance to be disloyal towards those who are undeserving of it. Indeed, where loyalty is reinforced by the ties of friendship and comradeship, the dilemmas are often felt even more keenly. Such dilemmas are a recurring experience for a service in which loyalty upwards, sideways and, for those with rank, downwards is given prominent emphasis and strongly influences practical expectations.

APPLIED ETHICS

In my introduction I sketched out the benefits which I believe would acrue to the police service through its paying more attention to applied ethics.

The implied recommendation is a response to events and circumstances and in what followed I indicated what those were, the practical demands which they make and the particular sorts of dilemmas which a concern for applied ethics might be expected to ameliorate. In this section I shall outline further what applied ethics is, what it could be expected to achieve in the policing context and some suggestions for its implementation.

It seems to me that an occupational code is a necessary, if not sufficient, practical step on the way towards the emphasis I am suggesting. At the time of writing the Metropolitan Police, on the initiative of the Metropolitan Police Commissioner, Sir Kenneth Newman, is on the eve of promulgating a new code of police ethics (Police Review, 1982, p.1957 : Evens, 1983 : Kettle and Shirley, 1983). But what is the practical purpose of such a code and what is the theory behind it?

Moral conduct requires the possibility of choice, that there be alternative courses of action open to the individual, but it does not require that conscious choices be made on every occasion. It may be practised habitually once acquired as a skill. The same point is made differently with the contention that we regulate our lives by the application of intuited moral principles. Principles which urge us to keep our promises, make reparation for past wrongs, care for our parents and children, act with honesty, respect the rights of others, and so on. Moral principles structure our experience: not only do they prescribe how we ought to behave but, because they have a descriptive content, they indicate what it is we should attend to. We learn of them in a complicated and largely informal way in childhood from parents, teachers and other adults, and, more often than not, in the context to which they have application. They often appear as the abstractions of practice, from such a viewpoint. Indeed, so habitual does the application of such principles become that they may be said to inform our perceptions and we are not aware of 'applying' them at all.

The British police service, with its long and creditable tradition, has evolved a body of practice, a way of going about things, which is generally responsive to the society which it serves. The individual police officer is initiated into this practice and learns much of the substance of his work through a process of apprenticeship in which good conduct is understood as appropriate participation in the activities of policing. The rules, formal and informal, which guide his practice are gradually assimilated into his outlook and help form his actions. Many of these rules are not so much the product of design but the product of countless, long-forgotten choices which encapsulate suggestions of how to achieve practical results. Others are those which relate to the prudential arts of the job: those which embody the hints, tips and clues which prescribe the sort of officer who is acceptable to his colleagues of all ranks. There are also formal rules, embodied in the Discipline Code, the Judges' Rules and other quasi-legal instruments which, together with the law, establish a pattern of organisational accountability and requirements. The 'good conduct' referred to above, as sustained by those various rules, has generally enabled the police to satisfy the public's expectations as to their capacity, commitment and way of fulfilling their role. But, as I endeavoured to show in the first section, there has arisen a dislocation — crisis is too strong a word — in the police-public relationship and the police themselves have both recognised it and are in the process of responding to it. Part of that response is a code of police ethics (Richards, 1928b).

How, then, might such a code be expected to help mend the dislocation? It is suggested by G. J. Warnock (Warnock, 1971, Chpt.2) that the primary purpose of morality, in a world where human wants, needs and interest are likely to be frustrated by the limitations of resources, information, intelligence, rationality and sympathies, is to counteract the limitations in human sympathies. I believe that this is so, with the qualification that limitations in intelligence, rationality and information are also counteracted by morality to a more modest extent. This accepted, the purpose of morality can be extended, by analogy, to an occupational code. Such a code, when developed for police, would function to help counter those limitations to good policing which are rooted in limited sympathies, rationality, intelligence and information. Besides prescribing responses to situations and recommending dispositions, it would also identify the appropriate loci of attention — some of which are specified in the section on moral dilemmas above. This type of code would be made up of principles arrived at in a number of different ways. One major source would be the tradition of the police service itself. It would seek to make explicit some of the principles which have served it so well, such as those which prescribe impartiality and treating the public with civility. Another source would be the human rights provisions of such bodies as the Council of Europe (Declaration on the Police, 1979). A third way of proceeding would be to take account of those practices which tend to undermine public confidence and trust in the police and frame countervailing principles. A code of this sort should enable officers to form clearer expectations concerning ranges of permissible behaviour regarding each other and the public.

Important though such a step would be, however, something more is required: applied ethics. A police code, in terms of its possible influence upon practice, stands somewhere between applied ethics and habitual morality. It provides a set of principles which act as a reference point for guidance for a great many regularly recurring situations, and in a fairly straight forward manner. Nonetheless, they still have to be applied, and applied with understanding, sensitivity and consistency. Only thinking in general terms about priorities, as well as how to apply them, would promote such an outcome. And this links in another argument. It was indicated, in the fourth section above, that the police are expected to exercise discretion and to do so with skill and judgment which relates to the particular circumstances which they are required to handle (Scarman, 1981). One of the necessary conditions which must be fulfilled, if this demand is to be met, is that police officers act with autonomy. Put simply, they must be able to think for themselves, and think well. I have already referred to the process whereby intuitive moral principles are inculcated and one of the points that emerges is that we do not reach adult life with open minds about morality. Our responses, all too often, are simply the result of childhood conditioning and this is compounded by our unthinking acceptance of occupational *mores* and the adoption, in an unreflective manner, of views which are the products of society's whims and fashions. We advance in an autonomous direction and avoid such manipulation to the extent that we are able to subject such processes and influences to critical thinking. Applied ethics provides one of the tools for that purpose in a very important area of our lives.

Intuitive moral principles need to be considered again in order to show the part played by applied ethics in more detail. Such principles fall into four broad categories: those which require us to avoid harming others, those which prescribe sympathy and benevolence, those which require that we act honestly and avoid deception and those which prescribe fairness (Warnock, 1971, p.86). But, as was shown with the moral dilemmas which confront police officers, there are many situations within policing when moral principles conflict and it is difficult to decide which should guide action. When we remember that there are many such principles and they give rise to rights, duties and obligations then there is a problem of selection too. It is also the case that they must be simple enough to be learned and able to refer to a fairly wide number of situations. In other words, they must be general. But what is often required are principles which relate to specific situations. For example, there are certain situations where we would wish to make an exception to 'Never kill people' to allow for self-defence. What is required is the more specific principle, 'Never kill people except in self-defence'. So, although our moral practice is guided well enough by intuited principles for much of the time, we would seem to require some way of selecting between them, rendering them more specific and resolving conflicts between them on certain critical occasions. I should add that a code of police ethics is also subject to these problems.

What all this means, when translated into attitudes, is that the habitual application of intuitive moral principles often leads people to dig their heels in when convinced of what they believe to be their duty, fair, impartial, right, and this often results in disagreement, dissention and unnecessary misery. If this sort of predicament is to be avoided what is needed is a commitment to think critically. That is, a willingness on the part of people to criticise their own intuitions, as well as those of others, and a preparedness to acquire the appropriate conceptual apparatus to do so effectively. For much the same reasons, it is not enough just to be well-meaning; it is not for nothing that the old saying, 'the pathway to perdition is paved with good intentions', has a ring of truth.

For all these reasons what is required is the application of a normative ethical theory. In fact, some theoretical position is an integral part of taking a stand on issues. If I were to recommend an increase in the use of police discretion, for example, I should implicitly commit myself to some theoretical position about the benefits this would bring as well as to a view of current circumstances. It is surely far better to know what one's theoretical position is. Engaging with an ethical theory would suggest ways in which intuitive moral principles might be ranked, selected and arbitrated when moral dilemmas arise. It would also, ideally, satisfy rational criteria: it would not be arbitrary in the ultimate principle or principles which it set and the reasons given for adopting it, or them, would be, at least, plausible. It would demand clear conceptualisation; much founders on a lack of conceptual clarity in the practical domain. Earlier, when discussing dilemmas, I endeavoured to show, but in a way which was far from exhaustive, the importance of defining terms. Too often discussion and action proceeds as if it were obvious what was being talked about or what was required. Conceptions of critical notions, such as fairness or the morality-law relationship, are allowed to pass unexamined when important practical outcomes hang on a clear understanding of their meaning(s). The theory would also give an account of moral reasoning: of how moral principles and factual beliefs contribute to moral judgments and resolutions. Finally, it would require resolute critical thinking of the order which is needed if the moral dilemmas which regularly confront police officers are to be resolved satisfactorily. For this is the sort of rehearsal which makes for effective practice in this area.

The theory which I believe to be by far the most plausible, and to meet the requirements outlined above, is utilitarianism, 'the creed which accepts as the foundation of Morals, Utility or the Greatest Happiness Principle, holds that actions are right in proportion as they tend to promote happiness, wrong as they tend to produce the reverse of happiness. By happiness is intended pleasure and the absence of pain, by unhappiness, pain and the privation of pleasure' (Mill, 1962), although not in quite this form. But it is not for this reason that I recommend it here. From the point of view of individuals coming to ethics for the first time, and training/education courses where topics vie with one another for time on the curriculum, this theory is readily understandable, if difficult in application. It is also probably the most influential moral theory in British society today, albeit at a subterranean level for most of the time. Most people would probably not claim to be utilitarians if asked, and yet many also behave and reason as if they were. Utilitarianism is unconsciously taken for granted. This provides the considerable advantage that, as a theory, it links with intuitive convictions and makes explicit some elements of conventional moral reasoning.

For the police as a public service utilitarianism has the related advantage that whenever civil servants, those involved professionally in politics and in public administration talk about what they do, often the underlying assumptions are utilitarian in character so that insights are incidentally gained into aspects of public life. Further, many of our social, legal and institutional arrangements presuppose utilitarianism, a fact hardly surprising given that it has been with us for 150 years or so in one influential form or another.

Nor is utilitarianism put forward in any exclusive spirit. There is no shortage in the literature of arguments against utilitarianism. Indeed, rival theories and outlooks often use it to point up their own merits (Brown, 1983). Objections are raised against the difficulties of utilitarian calculation. The problems of predicting the consequences of actions; of comparing different people's happiness, and even of measuring happiness at all. There are also moral objections which suggest that the utilitarian is prepared to sacrifice other values — honesty, fairness, mercy, beneficence — to utilitarian ends. All this has the considerable advantage of engaging individuals in the process of considering arguments for and against utilitarianism and other rival theories. From my own experience, where moral dilemmas are encountered, or presented in the form of case studies, say, the application of utilitarianism is a reasonably direct affair which, for the non-utilitarian, acts like a catalyst in making explicit some of the thinking behind otherwise repressed intuitions. And this, after all, is certainly the beginning of what I am concerned be achieved.

To conclude briefly, if, as I have argued, the police, in order to enjoy the trust and confidence of the public, need to police towards worthwhile ends in a morally acceptable manner, then applied ethics, as well as such instruments as police codes, are a necessary requirement for officers.

REFERENCES AND BIBLIOGRAPHY

Adair, J. (1973), *Action Centred Leadership* (Macgraw Hill).
Barrow, R. (1982), *Injustice, Inequality and Ethics* (Wheatsheaf).
Benn, S. I. and Peters, R. S. (1959), *Social Principles and the Democratic State* (Allen and Unwin).
Bok, S. (1980), *Lying. Moral Choice in Public and Private Life* (Quartet Books).
Brown, D. (1983), *Choices, Ethics and the Christian* (Basil Blackwell).

Critchley, T. A. (1973), 'The Idea of Policing in Britain: success or failure' in *The Police We Deserve* edited by J. C. Alderson and P. J. Stead (Wolfe Press).

Dahrendorf, R. (1975), *B.B.C. Reith Lectures* (Routledge Kegan Paul).

Downie, R. S. (1971), *Roles and Values* (Methuen).

Evens, R. (1983), 'Newman's code of ethics to cement contract between police and public' in *The Times* 31st October, 1983.

Glover, J. (1977), *Causing Death and Saving Lives* (Penguin).

Goldstein, H. (1976), 'Police discretion — the ideal versus the real' in *Public Order* Decision Making in Britain II edited by R. Finnegan and others. (Open University Press).

Greenhill, N. J. (1981), 'Professionalism in the Police Service' in *Modern Policing* edited by D. W. Pope and N. L. Weiner (Croom Helm).

Hart, H. A. L. (1960), *The Concept of Law* (Clarendon Press).

Hare, R. M. (1981), *Moral Thinking, Its Levels, Method and Point* (Clarendon Press).

Hodgkinson, C. (1983), *The Philosophy of Leadership* (Basil Blackwell).

Kettle, M. and Shirley, J. (1983), 'Revolution at the Yard' in *The Sunday Times* 6th November, 1983.

Mackie, J. L. (1977), *Ethics: Inventing Right and Wrong* (Penguin).

MacIntyre, A. (1981), *After Virtue. A Study in Moral Theory* (Duckworth).

Mill, J. S. (1962), *Utilitarianism* edited by Warnock (Fontana).

Morawtz, T. (1980), *The Philosophy of Law* (Macmillan).

Oakeshott, M. (1962), *Rationalism in Politics* (Methuen).

Declaration on the Police (1979), *Parliamentary Assembly of the Council of Europe*, Resolution 690, 1979.

Police Review (1982), 'Newman's Contract' 8th October, 1982.

Richards, N. W. (1982a), 'The Concept of a Police Ethic' Unpublished Paper, Police Staff College, Bramshill.

Richards, N. W. (1982b), 'Moral Choice and the Police' Paper given at the Manchester University Conference on *Ethical Issues in Caring* September, 1982.

Scarman, The Rt. Hon. Lord, (1981), *The Brixton Disorders 10–12th April, 1981.* (H.M.S.O.).

Warnock, G. J. (1971), *The Object of Morality* (Methuen).

The challenge of change — the police response

B. J. MASON

It might be prudent, right at the outset, to indicate what this article or essay is *not*. It is not intended to be a learned treatise nor a detailed thesis but rather a general view of the problems facing the police in a highly complex and rapidly changing society and of the nature of their suggested response. It is intended to be no more than some personal reflections[1] into the grey, uncertain and nebulous area of how best to meet the challenge of change.

Nevertheless, of some things there can be little doubt. There is no doubt, for example, that the police have a most difficult and comprehensive job because they have to operate at all levels of society with great and diverse problems and within certain constraints, both financial and practical. There is equally no doubt that many of these problems, particularly those highlighted by Lord Scarman's Report, are not new though some are growing in intensity and complexity. Finally, there is no doubt at all that it is the speed of change both within society itself and in all aspects of human activity which is the 'X' factor, tending to disrupt, to undermine and, to use the modern jargon, to 'de-stabilise'.

When to this mixture of complexity and rapid change is added a hierarchical organisational structure for a disciplined Service with 43 component and different Forces within it, the magnitude of the task becomes ever more obvious. Organisations anywhere are not often in the business of change but change, flexibility and adaptability are the essential ingredients in any response to the serious problems facing the police at the present time.

Yet these problems, it is encouraging to reflect, are no greater than the problems facing Government itself and it may be salutary to draw fairly detailed comparisons[2] with both Westminster and Whitehall, along the lines suggested by Sir John Hoskyns, the former head of the Prime Minister's Downing Street policy unit. In September 1983, in a speech to the Institute of Directors, Sir John made a far-ranging critique of the mechanics of power. After three years in Whitehall (he is now a Director of I.C.L.) he was convinced that the people and the organisation were wrong. 'The only person who can change things is the Prime Minister. If our present Prime Minister does not do it, I doubt if we shall ever have one who will. But despite having been so often right in challenging conventional wisdoms[3], there is no evidence that she sees the need to challenge this one. She is, in any case, surrounded by colleagues and by

33

career civil servants who, for the most part, *prefer things the way they are* (my italics). Debate outside Whitehall is, therefore, the only way to get fresh thinking started.'

In our direct analogy, I am not sure if the only person who can change things is the Chief Constable but someone or somebody within the organisation with the approval and encouragement of the highest ranks should be 'challenging conventional wisdom', should in fact be challenging the obvious, the accepted and the traditional to see if current needs are being met.

Sir John went on to urge change in 4 areas, for some of which one could read 'Police' instead of 'Government':

'An end to restricting the Prime Minister to the small pool of career politicians in Westminster in forming a government'.

'Whitehall must be organised for strategy and innovation as well as for day-to-day political survival'.

'Adequate numbers of high quality outsiders must be available to be brought into the Civil Service'.

'The workload on ministers must be reduced[4] (to facilitate thinking, planning etc.)'.

None, Sir John said, was particularly novel, nor were there options from which the least 'controversial' could be selected on traditional Whitehall lines. (The phrase has a familar and unwelcome ring about it and not merely regarding Whitehall!)

'They formed a minimum package necessary if government was (sic) to develop the competence needed to match its responsibilities'. They should, he said, form part of a larger agenda which should be examined as a whole... 'debate... was too often inhibited by a Catch 22 situation: no one was qualified to criticise the effectiveness of government unless he had first had experience of working in it. Yet once he had, there was a convention that he should never speak about it except in terms of respectful admiration... But, if his experience leads him to believe that Westminster and Whitehall are not up to the job, he has a duty to break with convention at the earliest opportunity'.[5]

After reviewing the massive problems facing the government which called for new and imaginative approaches, Sir John asked where all the planning and thinking for this were going on. His answer was 'nowhere'. 'The reason why the thinking is not done is that Whitehall is not organised to do it. Ministers cannot do this sort of thing in the odd day at Chequers. Such days, unsupported by training, method or organisation, simply waste time... In organisational terms, government is a creature without a brain. Westminster and Whitehall cannot change Britain if they will not change themselves.'

All this strikes unpleasant chords not only for our comparison with the police but in parts of commerce and industry, in business, and at the Town Hall, especially in some departments such as education, social services and planning. What followed, though, was equally thought-provoking, because Sir John 'had been struck by the fact that there was little sense of system, of dynamic processes. Solutions were discussed before there was agreement about the problem...[6] Most post-war governments had, like hamsters, gone round and round in a strategic box too small to contain any solutions.'

At another point, he argued that people often forgot that, like period houses, today's traditions were once innovations by bolder spirits. The sense of drama and romance in both central and local government was heightened by the rules of convention and secrecy which conveniently hid error and human frailty from public gaze. Open government was not a fashionable option, but a precondition for any serious attempt to solve Britain's underlying problems. 'My own experience is that teams of insiders and outsiders working together are much more successful at seeing the wood for the trees and proposing solutions than either would be alone.'

Of course, not all change or innovation is for the better. The concept behind Peel's Tamworth Manifesto in 1834 still holds good today. He pledged the Tory Party to conserve what was good but to be prepared to change what was out of date, irrelevant or simply inappropriate. Nor am I suggesting replacing policing with management science but simply stressing the need to look around for people who are not frightened of change.

To some extent, indeed, this willingness to change and experiment is evident now in many Police Forces not least in London itself where Sir Kenneth Newman is currently engaged on a massive programme of change. Researches into police experimentation have been undertaken by many groups of students on Command Courses at the Police Staff College who have been invited by several Forces to look at specific problems and to put forward options towards possible solutions[7]. Several Forces have employed outside consultants to advise on particular problem areas and many organisational experiments have been made internally. It would appear, then, that more thought, planning and research are going on now than ever before but serious questions remain. How effective is all this activity? How universal? How well organised? How much is it accepted by the Force concerned and by all ranks within it? How much commitment is given by whom and for how long? How many officers are involved? (why not more? Why not all in one way or another?) How lasting is the change? Is it part of a long term strategy or simply for a particular problem? How much consultation and explanation has taken place internally within the department, station or Force or externally with relevant groups among the public (as appropriate)? How much agreement has been reached during this process of consultation, agreement without which even the best thought-out innovation is likely to colapse?

These, and other questions like them, point to many difficulties which are compounded not only by the constraints on the police but also by the hierarchical organisation required by a disciplined Service. Like the poor, this system (or some derivative) will always be with us but it is possible to devise methods and to create a climate for stimulating innovation and ideas without upsetting or impairing the needs of discipline and command, as is evidenced by several specialist branches of the Armed Services.

In addition, many, including Sir John Hoskyns and some senior military officers, would argue that these problems and difficulties are made worse by the lack of a 2-tier system of entry into the Service. There being little or no influx of external or outside management ideas at a middle ranking level, the argument goes, people and organisations tend to ossify or 'get stuck'. Sir John would prefer using outsiders working with insiders to reveal new ideas, insights and perspectives. Officers in the Armed Forces would advocate a direct 2-tier entry system (or even, possibly, a 3-tier one). In this context, police officers would want to consider the question of the recruitment and use of suitable graduates, the position and aims of the Special Course and the various schemes involving scholarship, bursaries, Fellowships and exchanges which seek to make the best use of the talents available. At the present time, the Special Course is under review while police officers generally would argue with considerable conviction that their Service is capable of providing its own leaders.

Whatever the merits or demerits of the contrasting views of these vexed questions, there is an over-riding need to encourage innovation, to seek for new solutions to old problems, to promote[8] new ideas and, especially if a 2- tier system is to be avoided, actively to foster the promotion of creative thinking by ensuring that training in creative thinking techniques and in some aspects of creative management is given to middle management. Those particularly talented in these respects should be identified, supported and carefully used.

Of course, new ideas — in any organisation — and 'ideas' men are threatening and thus often viewed with suspicion. 'Creative' people tend to be disturbing and potentially disruptive, although it depends, as Professor Joad would have said, on what you mean by 'creative'. In some business and educational circles, it has become a 'dirty' word. Yet most companies pay at least lip-service to the importance of innovation and creativity for their continued competitiveness. In some companies, appraisal forms may even include an assessment of the creativity of individual managers. Similarly, management courses often include sections of 'creativity' or 'creative problem-solving'. But paying lip-service to the role of innovation and creativity is not enough[9] according to the authors[10] of a recent article in *Management Today* (August 1982).

Initial cynicism on this matter of creativity is fairly widespread and, I daresay, natural. Some may even argue that it is inappropriate for a public service such as the police. Messrs. Rickards and Brown quote one managing director of a company in the pharmaceuticals industry saying recently, 'Come and talk to my people about innovation if you like, but we won't advertise it as creativity training. We've had enough of that for the time being'. Yet I would argue that precisely because the Services in the public sector lack the stimulus of competition and commercial rivalry, they are in at least as much need as private firms of stimulating creative thinking and creative problem-solving.

Unfortunately for the innovators, creativity has become discredited as a topic of management education because of the ambiguity surrounding the term and the inability to distinguish between the two widely different usages of the word. Most managers tend to talk about creativity as an exceptional gift and to quote outstanding artists and scientists such as Leonardo, Newton, Picasso and Einstein as examples of creative talent. This interpretation of creativity, according to managers, implies not only that creativity is an exceptional characteristic but, so Rickards and Brown aver, that 'management training will not produce a whole company full of Leonardos or Einsteins (which might not be desirable anyway). Anybody who attaches that meaning to creativity will quite understandably be cynical about the place of such a topic in a management course'.

A vicious circle operates in this respect because two of the main obstacles to creativity are the fear of looking foolish and an almost overwhelming inclination to evaluate ideas too quickly. Given this, it is hardly surprising that natural caution allied to the premature impulse to reject what is new, simply because it is new or different, ensures that the need for creativity, and also creativity training, is either rejected out of hand or accepted in name only. This is even more unfortunate since an essential pre-requisite for the ability to form balanced judgments, vital for managers everywhere, is the need to promote, in self and subordinates, thinking techniques creative.

To the trainer, however, creativity is *not* an exceptional gift appropriate only for an Einstein or a Menuhin or a Rutherford, but a characteristic shared by all human beings, half of whose brain is analytical in thought processes and half creative[11]. It is simply, as our authors record, the human capacity 'to change one's perception in a productive way. In this sense, the opposite of creativity is "stuckness" or habitual thinking. Everyone gets stuck in thinking from time to time; indeed it is by becoming unstuck, by moving from the stuck position, that new insights are obtained, and creativity is exhibited. Although creativity training may not turn out many Einsteins, it can help to cope with "stuckness" and it can teach people how to escape from that condition in order to find better resolutions to problems. The training can highlight common behaviour and assumptions that reinforce "stuckness" and offer procedures to escape from a mental rut or "mind-set".

'Give such a mind-set person all the creativity techniques in the world and he will not budge from his stuckness. His customary pessimism over the possibility for change is often accompanied by a negative attitude towards new ideas. After all, if you believe you cannot change anything, that becomes a self-fulfilling prophecy... some companies have senior managers who have a justifiable reputation for competence and soundness and yet who are essentially suspicious of new ideas. These managers have demonstrable value to the company as custodians of the "status quo" protecting the organisation from rash decisions. Not surprisingly, however, they can prove to be a liability when we demand imaginative responses to new circumstances.' To foster (and contain) creativity and planning, the organisational environment must be right in terms of reward, resources, support and implementation. Today, applied imagination is needed more than ever before, 'since one of the greatest constants of the era is change itself... we estimate, however, that only a very small minority of senior managers show strong psychological resistance to creativity training. Most managers can benefit greatly from:

1. An awareness that they can enhance creativity;
2. An awareness of the blocks to creativity;
3. Specific techniques which, in conjunction with (2), can actually enhance creativity'[12].

There are many of these techniques to spur on creativity and it matters little which a group, team or individual favours. They include morphological analysis, synetics, check lists — especially Osborne's General Check list — attribute listing and, of course, brainstorming, which is not only one of the most dramatic and effective means of producing creativity and change of attitudes but is also one of the most misunderstood and misused techniques for stimulating new ideas[13]. Experience teaches that, used properly, it rarely fails because it successfully smashes through the various barriers to creative thinking such as evaluating too quickly, the fear of looking a fool, conformity, the adherence to the 'right' answer and failing to challenge the obvious. It also actively teaches participants to suspend judgment until *all* ideas, however fanciful and exotic, are safely gathered in. It has the priceless asset of a rigorous evaluation procedure which is used at the end of the whole session or sessions and this, when allied to the even more rigorous system of reverse brainstorming, ensures that the ideas which are eventually accepted have been tested from every perspective and have stood up to attacks from those team members playing 'Devil's Advocate'. From the organisation's point of view, it has the equally priceless assets of involving and motivating a great many people who have a remarkable ability to produce some excellent ideas, many of which come from the most junior members of the group[14]. It should not be forgotten that constables, whilst junior in rank are the *experts* on their patch and in handling certain tasks for which senior officers have long-since lost their skills.

All these techniques, however, will fail if they are followed too slavishly. They all should provide a means to switch from one perception of the problem to another, which is the key to making technical, artistic, scientific, administrative or, indeed, any breakthroughs. They all should show that with any managerial problem or difficulty, there are various different ways of proceeding, various different ways of perceiving, leading to a whole variety of different options, each with their own advantages and disadvantages. The effective manager at whatever level should be aware of these different perceptions and be capable of making balanced judgments bearing all the options in mind. What is unfortunate is that, if trainers offer techniques as a substitute for this awareness, the consequences are predictable — more ammunition for the doubters or those irrationally opposed to creativity training. However, when these techniques are used in a properly prepared environment, they can make a valuable contribution to creative problem-solving.

In his book *Leadership in Management*, Barry Maude bemoans the lack of sufficient enterprising young managers prepared to 'strike out boldly in new directions'. He writes, 'I talked to scores of executives in a wide range of industries. Almost all agreed that there is no shortage of managers who are capable of doing the routine work — the administrative chores — but there is a real shortage of managers who are capable of exercising such decisive leadership via innovation, motivation, opportunity — grasping, that they actually make a significant difference to results'.

In the light of current demands for change in the Police Service and the conflict caused by the traditional opposition from within which often appears to frustrate genuine efforts to initiate such changes whether in policing or any other sphere, Maude's comments regarding opposition inside companies are instructive. 'Whole organisations, not only selected individuals within them, must learn to adjust. . . The history of innovation is full of opposition and scepticism. In every company, there are managers whose reaction to new work methods, new systems, new products and new participation schemes is, 'It's dangerous. It's doomed to failure'. The leader's job is to convince these conservatives that company sales and earnings will respond with alacrity to innovative projects which are carefully selected and subjected to stringent controls.' If organisations have a system of their own, namely, the weight and tradition of inertia, then the deck is stacked in favour of the tried and proven way of doing things and against the taking of risks or striking out in new directions. But particularly at times of rapid change, organisations need innovation as well as prudence.

Some of this is inappropriate in both language and concept to the police because it is written with the business world in mind but there are clear parallels with the Police Service. Although there is little room for a charismatic swashbuckling enterpreneur riding rough shod over all and sundry, there is a need for men and women who, by convincing argument, can get new ideas accepted in the first place and then by their own example, drive and enthusiasm ensure the full co-operation and commitment of all those necessary to achieve success. Ideally, as we have seen, many of these people should have been involved at the start of the whole creative process. The commitment could therefore be almost guaranteed, a most important consideration.

The management of change is thus bound up with the 'management of creativity'. Of course, new ideas and those who bring them forward are often viewed warily especially in a traditionally or practically oriented Service. Creativity has to be managed and managed sensitively. A difficult and nice balance must be struck between the needs of creativity and the needs of the organisation, practically and functionally. Ideas and 'ideas men' cannot control the organisation. The organisation must control them and yet not inhibit them or erect barriers to thought and innovation, still less barriers to creative thinking and training.

Certain management styles not only destroy creativity but create stress. Recently the A.C.P.O. Working Party on 'Stress in the Police Service' has been handed the results of the preliminary study conducted by a panel of medical specialists and police officers. In their comments, opinions and recommendations were some interesting observations relevant to our topic. For example, among the aspects of poor management highlighted as specifically affecting the performance and health of all officers, were unjust criticism/ scapegoating, lack of counselling skills, lack of concern for the individual, lack of communication and excessive autocracy/lack of consultation. All these would be fatal for initiating innovation, co-operation and imagination, i.e. they would destroy creativity and new ideas.

Among the recommendations were the following:

> In assessing officers for promotion, consideration should be given to such qualities as 'ability to innovate' and 'concern for individuals' as well as to the ability to maintain existing systems and to possess technical knowledge;
> The system should enable managers to respond to change. One of the ways it can do this is by stimulating consultation at all levels, providing support and making sure expectations are realistic in the selection, training, development and control of the officers in their care.

I would go further. Managing change is a slow, deliberate and, at times, rather a frustrating process because, to be done effectively, it really requires considerable and detailed explanation for, and consultation with, all those affected not only towards the top of the organisation, sometimes the most difficult place to 'sell' new ideas, but also in the middle management and especially at grass roots level but where the best laid schemes can founder if not properly and conscientiously implemented.[15] And founder they will if those directly responsible for their operation and supervision are uncertain, lukewarm, apathetic or even downright hostile. Here the effectiveness not only of the consultative process but also of the internal communication system of the organisation comes under severe test, an area where few organisations can, or would, claim permanently satisfactory results.

As important, if change is to affect the public at large, is the educative process which ought really to be as long, as deliberate, as inventive and imaginative as possible, and to employ any or all of the media resources open to the organisation wishing to institute change.[16] Additionally, as we have seen, there is a need to manage creativity (in both senses of the word). The requirement to provide, and support, creativity training, to help to stimulate new ideas and encourage innovation, to free minds which may be set or overburdened remains the prime concern but there may also be a need to manage a few people in the organisation who are even more creative than most. These people may not be Einsteins but they may well be radical and imaginative thinkers, people who question and probe, who bring new perspectives to old and complex problems. Very frequently, almost by definition, they are 'unmanageable' or at least, difficult to handle. Their abilities and personalities may not be as exciting, explosive and tempermental as, say, John McEnroe's but they sit uneasily in some organisations and are not happy with what they see as the routine or restrictive. They require firm but sensitive handling, exact job definition and specification, precise briefings, a little encouragement (but not too much) — in short careful control, for too much will kill or curtail the creative talent and too little will result in massively inappropriate or extravagant schemes.[17] Initially, however, the task is to identify the creative talent and then to manage it soundly. 'Managing creative people and creativity are won by recognising that special problems are manageable'[18].

All management is difficult.[19] The management of change is more difficult yet is vitally important in an era of rapid change. It is even more vital that the police response to the challenge of change is comprehensive and successful for, as has often been said before, the police are the upholders of the rule of law which is itself an indispensable part of a liberal democracy.

41

NOTES

1. Based partly on experience, partly on observations and partly on comparative studies. Such as it is, the experience has been gained from teaching at various educational levels from university, through colleges of higher and further education to comprehensive school, from the Services, especially the Royal Air Force Education and Training Branch, from the Civil Service and, latterly, from working at the Police Staff College.
2. The comparisons which follow are somewhat lengthy but they go right to the heart of the argument. If a detailed analogy with the Police Service (including both the posts and the organisation) is made at each level and in every sphere mentioned by Sir John, the nature and size of the problem facing the police becomes clearer and much better defined.
3. One of the essential ingredients of the creative response to change to which we shall return.
4. Though the use of 'high quality' outsiders may be more controversial and is a topic which will be discussed later in this article, there seems to be a clear requirement for Forces to be organised for strategy and innovation as well as for day-to-day survival. Equally clearly, the workload on certain officers (and/or departments?) could, with profit, be reduced. And from whom does the Chief Constable and his senior colleagues take advice? Whom do they consult? Is the sphere of consultation wide enough? There may be 43 different answers.
5. This may be held to be a somewhat dangerous precept for a disciplined Service but the principle underlying it need not be disruptive, far less subversive, if it is carefully structured and sensitively handled.
6. If true, a distressing point because another of the essential ingredients of the creative response to change and problem-solving is to agree an exact definition of the nature of the problem at all stages of the thinking process and certainly initially.
7. Topics covered within Forces are wide-ranging and groups have dealt with subjects as varied as the organisation of the C.I.D., victim support schemes, the policing of inner cities, the effects of unionisation on police operations, inter-agency co-operation, neighbourhood watch schemes, the effectiveness of internal communication procedures, the setting-up, working and evaluation on consultative committees, aspects of public order, police housing and many management projects.
8. And, of course, subsequently to evaluate them, another topic which will be taken up in this essay.
9. Nor is it enough in any organisation where change and new ideas or

new approaches are required, since thinking creatively and imaginatively is an essential ingredient in the long process of problem-solving and decision-making which, given good communication and consultation, leads to the effective implementation of change.

10. Dr Tudor Rickards and Mr Mark Brown. Dr Rickards is director of creativity and innovation programmes at the Manchester Business School. Mr Brown divides his time between research on 'mind-set' breaking, writing, and creativity training. He is director of 'Sound Thinking'.

11. In some of the creative thinking programmes, there are problems which most adults, however intelligent, find difficult but most reasonably intelligent children of early secondary school age (i.e. 11– 14 years) find incredibly easy. The reason is that that part of their young brains which is creative and imaginative is still alive, working and in practice, untrammelled by the worries of family or job or the constraints imposed by the organisation or society itself.

12. The business setting of this extract is especially revealing when, later in the article, the authors record in some detail the results of creative thinking and creativity training in industrial and commercial organisations on both sides of the Atlantic including the continent of Europe. They even cover Japan. They finish with examples taken from financial administration.

13. Another part of the vicious circle because, if one of the most well-known techniques appears to be unsuccessful through misunderstanding or misuse, there is little inclination to attempt creative training generally. Brainstorming does not mean simply 'swapping ideas', or exchanging views. That is merely a discussion, seminar or 'round-table' session, and a proper brainstorming session goes much further than that.

14. In sessions held in the educational sphere, for example, some 'instant winners' come from probationary teachers and even from teachers still under training. Even more important, in my view, is the benefit to the group, section, department or organisation of involving many people not only in the consultative process but in the problem defining and problem-solving stage. They feel part of the team and, in part at least, committed to the ideas put forward.

15. The magnitude of the task facing Sir Kenneth Newman in the Metropolitan Police is put into sharp relief when considering all items in this list, but at least, whatever the merits of the various new ideas and schemes which are proposed, the initial thinking has been completed. And even in a large Force the more people who can be involved both in the consultative and the thinking processes, the better the climate for the reception of change.

16. In the case of the police, that could include the more obvious channels of information and persuasion such as newspapers, radio and television (whether local and/or national in all three areas), public meetings such as consultative and other committees, open days etc. and also posters, handbills and even advertising, for the skills of advertising companies can be, and have been, usefully employed in the gentle art of persuasion, including work in the public sector. The aim should be to go further and try to educate the public to be realistic particapents and critics.
17. There is, particularly in the public sector, the difficulty of 'credibility'. If they are not thought to be practical or, at least, to possess some direct first-hand experience, they can produce whatever they like in the way of brilliant, new ideas and this flaw, real or imaginary, will prove fatal.
18. Winston Fletcher 'How to Manage Creativity' *Management Today* June 1983. There is, of course, the associated problem about which space prevents fuller exposition, of obtaining a career structure for those with special creative talent, since they cannot be left permanently in research or planning teams.
19. And it is not made any easier by the continuing need to monitor all stages of the proposed changes and ultimately to provide an overall evaluation, which may lead to modifications and amendments. This forms part of a recycling process outside the scope of this article, but one which only adds to the complexity.

Stress and Stress Management–
A Personal Approach
J. M. BRINDLEY

INTRODUCTION

There is a popularly held view that someone is only really under stress when he or she is close to 'cracking up'. In this view are undertones of the person being mentally and/or physically weak, not being able to 'take it' and perhaps lacking in moral fibre. Many police officers scoff at the subject of stress and would no sooner admit — even to themselves — that they are under stress than they would admit to being homosexual. This is hardly surprising given the fact that Police Forces are very 'macho' organisations: officers tend to judge others and themselves very much in terms of the stereotyped male characteristics of hard-headedness, toughness, vigour, pragmatism and potency. Yet the truth of the matter is that police officers, like everybody else, are often in some sense troubled by their work and by the way their work is organised and, like everybody else, they experience pressure, tension, frustration, anger, annoyance, anxiety, guilt and fear. These reactions are properly understood as symptoms of stress; they can and often do reduce our performance in our jobs and also affect the quality of our lives. One writer[1] puts it as follows:

> 'Stress has moved from the nether world of 'emotional problems' and 'personality conflicts' to the corporate balance sheet. The cause, directly or indirectly, of more than half the medical probems company doctors have to treat, stress is now seen as not only troublesome but expensive.'
> 'Stress can also lead to depression, general anxiety, low productivity, absenteeism and to breakdown in normal relations with friends, family and colleagues.'

Happily, the Police Service has come to recognise — albeit belatedly — the importance of the subject. The nature, effects and management of stress have been addressed at The Police Staff College, Bramshill since the mid 1970s; various research studies have been carried out on the British police[e.g. 2, 3, 4, 5] and in 1981, following a request from the Police Federation and the Superintendents' Association, the Association of Chief Police Officers instigated two working parties to look at occupational stress and physical stress and fitness. At the time of writing these working parties are at the reporting stage.

This paper is an attempt to provide the reader with an integrated exploration of the nature of stress, the ways in which stress can effect us and means by which we can best handle stress. The concepts, observations and suggestions offered have been drawn ecclectically from the literature on stress, the writings of authors in related fields, discussions with police officers and perhaps most tellingly, from personal experience.

THE NATURE AND CONSEQUENCES OF STRESS

The major initiative in the study of stress was made by Hans Selye in 1936 and since that time he has published extensively on the subject[6]. His study of our physiological reactions has led him to the understanding that anything which impels us to respond in some way i.e. anything which makes a demand of us causes within us, to a greater or lesser degree, stress. Anything and everything from making a cup of tea through facing a large pile of papers on our desks on Monday mornings to coping with the death of a loved one, can constitute a demand being made on us and as such, can cause us some level of stress. Thus Selye established that stress is an internal state of being; those aspects of our environments (and/or ourselves) giving rise to demand he calls STRESSORS:

STRESSORS ⟶ DEMAND ⟶ STRESS

| usually something external which we feel we must respond to; but might be self-imposed | the need to respond. | the impact made on our minds and bodies by the demand impingent on us. |

Following from the principle that all demand induces some level of stress, Selye stablished the notion that *we are all under some degree of stress all the time*. Indeed, even when we are asleep, our bodies and minds are meeting the demand to maintain equilibrium. As an FBI agent lecturing on the subject put it[7]:

'...the only time we are completely free from stress is when we are dead — and none of us want to be that comfortable.'

What then is stress? It is suggested here that it can be understood as the IMPACT made on our minds and bodies by demand impingent on us. The notion of impact is quite a useful one due to its connotations. Thus we know that demands producing certain levels of impact can *stimulate* us to give of our best: a degree of nervousness *spurs on* the athlete as it does a police officer to give a good account of himself in Court or in front of a promotion board. If the impact is considerable, we may feel *hurt*: being overlooked for promotion might be a major *blow* which sets us back for a while; seeing one of our children 'going wrong' gives us a lot of *pain*. If the impact is too great then we may *buckle* or *crack*. Some forms of impact may be of a long-term, abrasive quality: working in a noisy office or working under an overbearing boss may *wear us down*.

We will be fully aware of many of the stressors acting on us, consciously registering their demand and experiencing their impact e.g. we know when we are under severe time pressure and we experience the feelings that we associate with this such as excitement or frustration or anxiety. Often, however, we are not fully appreciative of the impact of demand either because of the insignificant level of the demand e.g. talking to a friend or because the focal point of the impact is the unconscious mind. Thus going on holiday, getting married, being promoted or even just driving a car are events which consciously we probably look forward to and enjoy but nonetheless can trouble us unconsciously. Such stressors usually constitute some kind of change of habit and/or some potential danger. A very good example of this is retirement; we might be happy to retire but due to not properly preparing for it, the changes in habits which retirement brings may constitute a sufficient trauma as to precipitate a heart attack or stroke within a year or so. Other sorts of demand can impact on the body itself. Illness, smoking, noise, pollution, injury etc. may all be consciously recognised but the major impact is initially registered on the physical systems of our body, upsetting equilibrium.

What, then, is the nature of impact and what are its symptoms? Perhaps at its most fundamental, impact is essentially physiological. In terms of our current state of evolution, we are physiologically equipped for a caveman existence: hunting our prey and fleeing from that which we fear. We are prepared for this 'fight or flight' behaviour by glandular and nervous system activity which stimulates powerful changes in our body: heart rate and breathing rate increase, there are elevated levels of sugar, fat and clotting agents in the blood which is redirected away from organs such as the stomach and intestines towards the muscles and brain. In other words, the body is 'hyped up and ready to go'. Of course, most of the situations which we find demanding today do not involve spearing bison or evading sabre toothed tigers, rather they tend to arise when we are sitting at a desk. Unhappily, the physiological stress response described above is activated by any kind of demand irrespective of whether or not it requires vigorous physical action on our part. Consequently the body is often 'hyped up' inappropriately and it operates rather like a badly tuned engine which runs inefficiently drawing an excessive amount of energy and that energy which is not used in performance serves only to damage the structure of the engine. In the same way, if our physiological 'fight or flight' response is not worked off or otherwise managed, in time it can deplete our energies making us more susceptible to colds and other minor illnesses. Over a longer period of time, the wear and tear may show itself in skin problems such as eczema, respiratory problems such as asthma, circulatory problems such as high blood pressure, digestive problems such as chronic indigestion etc. leading perhaps to cerebral haemorrhage, coronary heart disease, ulcers etc.

But the impact is not just physiological, there may be very significant psychological reactions involving *feelings* which can include nervousness, frustration, restlessness, irritability, dissatisfaction with job and relationships, boredom, hostility, low self-esteem, depression and despair. Our *thinking processes* may be similarly affected and may involve sensations of unreality, a tendency to confuse names, dates and times, indecision, refusing to accept the obvious, maintaining rigid views, ruminative anxiety-provoking thoughts, being susceptible to rumours and superstitions, and in the extreme — paranoia.

Some of the symptoms mentioned above may arise, at least in part, as attempts to cope with other symptoms. Thus we may smoke to aid concentration as our wandering mind keeps straying from the large quantity of work in front of us. We may drink to help us unwind or to forget; we may blame others and act aggressively towards them to avoid facing blame ourselves and to protect us from low self-esteem.

Sometimes a cyclic, spiralling process can occur if we do not manage stress properly: measures we consciously or unconsciously take to cope with demand themselves may produce an even higher level of stress which, in turn, may be coped with by even more unsatisfactory measures and so on. Consider the example of the man who finds he is not making as much progress at work as he wanted. Frustration and irritation build up and he starts taking it out on his wife; she feels resentful and the relationship deteriorates. He tries to escape arguments at home by spending his evenings in town and to make himself feel better he buys an expensive car. This causes financial problems which are not helped by his now heavy drinking. His bellicose behaviour to those who might have been his friends prevents him from receiving much needed support and guidance. His initial problem of lack of progress at work is now insignificant compared with his present problems as he struggles for survival trying to cover his alcoholism, his infidelity, his debts and his grossly inadequate attention to his job.

Another example of what we might call the 'stress maelstrom' is provided by a senior army officer[8] writing about his observations of stress amongst high ranking officers:

'In normal circumstances a man faced with some immediate challenging stress (demand) will evaluate the dangers and implications, consider his option of responses, and then act accordingly. This is all very well for an occasional short term stress, but if the stress is prolonged without any definite resolution he will become physically and mentally tired having had no opportunity of resting and recharging his psychological batteries. Tiredness induces a decline in the powers of concentration and analysis and inevitably his efficiency will undergo a qualitative descending spiral. Insomnia, discouragement and depression will result in more tiredness and the development of a vicious circle culminating in either complete exhaustion or overwhelming depression.'

If we make regular use of certain forms of coping then over the years changes may take place in our characters as these forms of coping become 'built in'. Thus some police officers who frequently deal with emotionally distressing events may experience a hardening of their emotions they may think that it relates only to their approach to their job but probably it is also identifiable at home and in other spheres of their lives. If we see our jobs as highly competitive we may find ourselves becoming less trusting and more suspicious — again, it is very difficult to limit such an outlook to our colleagues. In one interesting study[9], wives of police officers were asked to say how, if at all, they thought their husbands had changed since they had been in the police service. The study related to American police officers but look at the next table to see whether the results seem applicable to the British police.

According to the wives of American police officers, their husbands become:

1. More self confident.
2. More negative in their attitude about people.
3. More suspicious.
4. Less willing to socialise.
5. More pessimistic.
6. Less willing to talk about their feelings.
7. More rigid and authoritarian.
8. More ready to criticise wife and children.
9. Less willing to admit mistakes.
10. Less able to control their temper.

The paper by Robert Adlam in this volume gives further, detailed information on the subject of 'the police personality'.

We can see from this examination of the nature and consequences of impact that much of it is debilitating and leads to poor relationships, poor work performance and lack of enjoyment of life. This is not to say, however, that *all* stress is undesirable and to be avoided; clearly, if we accept that we are under some level of stress all the time then to say that all stress is unwelcome is to say that everything in our lives and every aspect of our living is unwelcome. This is manifestly not the case. Selye in addressing this issue has made the point that stress is not only a de facto characteristic of living but in many contexts it provides much of what we see living to be all about. Working exceptionally hard to achieve a goal, falling in love, being given new responsibilities, pushing our minds and bodies to the limits and even debauching ourselves: all these are likely to be highly stressful, however they may well constitute that which we find exciting, challenging, thrilling, satisfying and enjoyable about life and they may also constitute vehicles by which we can develop and mature as individuals.

Selye calls impact which is experienced positively, *eustress*. Eustress is motivating and invigorating and provides the richness of life. It is impact which gets us moving. If impact is too great, however, or if it touches a very sensitive area or is not seen to help us satisfy our needs or if it in any other way is negatively experienced, then that impact is *distress*. Distress produces the psychological and behavioural problems discussed earlier. We must remember, however, that both eustress and distress are both stress and as such they both generate wear and tear on the body.

Before we can progress any further it is necessary to develop a rather more refined understanding of what is involved in the experience of stress. It is an established principle in the study of any subject that understanding is helped by the setting up of a model. This allows us to picture how different factors of the object of study influence each other and it helps us to generate ideas about what initiatives have to be taken in order to achieve certain desired results. Thus economists set up models of the economy and are thereby able to make predictions about what would have to be done to bring inflation down etc. In the same way, a model of stress will help us in identifying means by which we might best manage stress.

The figure (page 51) portrays a model of stress developed by the author drawing ideas from a number of other writers[10, 11, 12]. It is a psychological model in that it attempts to say something about what goes on inside us — particularly, inside our minds. To fully explore the model is beyond the scope of the present chapter but current purposes will be served by a brief outline. The uppermost box in the model is labelled *actual demand*. As mentioned earlier, demand is what causes stress and really the whole model is an elaboration of this concept of demand and how it impacts on the mind and body. Actual Demand is an 'objective' statement of the demands acting on us. We can think of this, at least in theory, as comprising long-term, ongoing demand and short-term, specific demand. The former has to be understood in terms of the set of needs that seem to be fundamental to most human beings: physiological

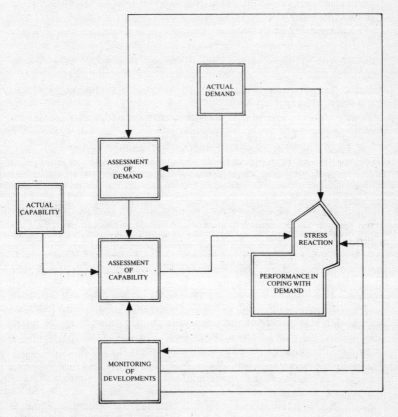

A psychological model of stress.

needs, safety needs, love and belongingness needs, esteem needs and needs to fulfil one's potential[13].

These needs together with others that probably arise primarily from our culture e.g. the need to be treated fairly, generate a continual stream of demand which we are constantly endeavouring to satisfy. The ways in which we do this will depend on our culture and our values, personalities and abilities but they may well include eating, drinking and sleeping regularly, living in a house, taking out insurance policies, making friends, joining clubs, getting married, trying to be very good at something, trying to live to certain standards, setting and achieving goals, etc. The initiatives we take and the responses we make in pursuing our particular means of satisfying our needs involve short-term, specific demands e.g. getting a particular report done in time, dealing with a difficult member of the public, attending a promotion board, etc.

Fundamental human needs.

PHYSIOLOGICAL NEEDS: availability of food, drink, shelter, warmth, sex.

SAFETY NEEDS: sense of security, trust in others, freedom from fear and anxiety.

LOVE AND BELONGINGNESS NEEDS: sense that others care, sense of fitting in and being accepted.

ESTEEM NEEDS: being respected by oneself and others.

SELF ACTUALISATION: fully realising one's identity and potential and living one's life accordingly.

The *stress reaction* is our pattern of symptoms of stress arising from the impact of the demands affecting us. Actual Demand can feed the Stress Reaction quite independently of how we think or feel about the stressors e.g. moving house, illness, injury, etc. Also, of course, we are usually aware of the situations we are involved with and we are appraising them in terms of how they affect us with respect to our needs. This gives rise to our *assessment of demand*. It is our 'sizing up' of our circumstances and it can — and usually does — constitute a quite different picture of the demand impingent on us from the picture in 'reality' i.e. Actual Demand. Examples of this abound: we work all through the night to produce a 30 page report for our boss only to be told in the morning, 'well thank you, but I only wanted a 2 page outline.'; we think that the level and extent of our communication with a loved one is satisfactory only to find that she/he feels neglected and taken for granted and in turn is starting to withdraw from us. Especially when the demand is seen as heavy and important then irrespective of our confidence in coping with it, Assessment of Demand may be expected to fuel the Stress Reaction.

Assessment of capability is our judgment of how well we will be able to cope with what we think we have to do. Beliefs about our skills, knowledge and potential and about our resources such as time, man-power, equipment, money, contacts etc. may all come into this consideration. Again, an important distinction can be drawn between what we perceive our capabilities to be and what an objective statement of them would be i.e. our actual capability. How often do we underestimate our potential response to a situation because we do not appreciate and make use of the help and support embodied in our friends, colleagues, boss, subordinates, etc.? How often do we, for some reason, feel low and find ourselves lacking in confidence in situations which, in the past, we have dealt with very successfully? Sometimes, of course, our Assessment of Capability with respect to our personal abilities is greater than our Actual Capability in this respect. This is sometimes seen when an officer newly appointed to a post for which he has little relevant experience, believes that because he has the rank and is a 'good policeman', he can handle the job without advice from other people.

Assessment of Capability may not match the level of demand we identify from our Assessment of Demand. There may be times when we think that the demands on us are greater than the resources we can bring to bear. When this is the case or even when we believe that we can meet the demand but we will be very stretched, the Stress Reaction may be expected to be fuelled — especially when coping is important to us. Furthermore, being stretched produces knock-on stressors: if we have to work twelve hours a day over a protracted period on a very demanding project, not only does the demand intrinsic to the project itself cause stress, so too does the frustration of our personal and social needs.

Performance in coping with demand may be taken as our effectiveness and efficiency in dealing with everything that comprises our living. The figure shows that it is linked with Stress Reaction; this reflects the fact that the nature of the impact that demand makes on us plays a very significant role in how well we perform. For example, we can feel so angry with a subordinate who has just made a mistake that in talking to the man we just succeed in alienating him; we can get so tired having been working all hours of the day that the mistakes we have been making mean that our last two hours work have been completely wasted; the challenge the boss gave us last week has really spurred us on to produce some very good work.

Naturally, all the time we are undertaking the monitoring of developments, continually reviewing what we need to do and how well we are doing. There is a constant feedback from this process to the Assessment of Demand and to the Assessment of Capability so that when things are going well, we may experience a sense of, 'it's not been so bad, after all' or, 'I must be getting better at this'. At the same time, any anxiety, doubt or worry that we experienced about the matter may well start to diminish. On the other hand, if things seem to be deteriorating, the Stress Reaction is likely to be fuelled and we may feel more anxious, frustrated etc. and start to pour more energies into our efforts to deal with the circumstances. Clearly a viscious circle between bad performance and distress needs to be avoided. Often there will be ego defensive processes cutting in to prevent us from consciously being too overwhelmed by certain elements of the Stress Reaction e.g. anxiety, guilt, self-doubt[14].

Some ego-defensive mechanisms.

DENIAL OF REALITY: Refusing to accept that which is so unpleasant that we can't face it.

FANTASY: Achieving successes in our imaginations to compensate for an unsatisfactory reality.

COMPENSATION: Masking our inadequacies by overemphasizing our strengths or overindulging in certain satisfactions because of frustrations in other areas.

PROJECTION: Blaming others when things go wrong or attributing to others undesirable traits found in ourselves.

RATIONALISATION: Endeavouring to make our actions appear sensible and correct so that we can maintain our self esteem and appear good to others.

REPRESSION: Pushing uncomfortable thoughts away from consciousness — keeping them out of our minds.

DISPLACEMENT: Releasing our feelings, generally of anger onto people or things less dangerous than those which caused our frustrations.

EMOTIONAL INSULATION: Withdrawing, refusing to take initiatives in order to prevent the possibility of failure or rejection.

REGRESSION: Resorting to more immature forms of thinking, feeling and acting and lowering our aspirations.

We can see from the above that many of the longer-term psychological aspects of the Stress Reaction are extensions of ego-defensive processes. Rationalisation, for example, leads to dogmatic thinking and a hypersensitivity to criticism; displacement of aggression from oneself i.e. self-blame onto others leads to irritability and to bad relationships; emotional insulation leads to opting out of work or from forming deep relationships, etc. Ego-defensive mechanisms, therefore, are part of the Stress Reaction but an operation of it which is a lesser evil to the individual than high levels of anxiety, severe depression or panic which might otherwise have been the manifestation of the Stress Reaction.

CAUSES OF STRESS

We have established that all demand produces stress but, clearly, we are particularly interested in demand that impacts on people sufficiently strongly to promote significantly high levels of stress. There are a number of features of circumstances and/or our perception of them which have been found to generate strong demand. These are: *CHANGE, UNCERTAINTY, IMPOTENCY and UNFAIRNESS*. Change has already been briefly mentioned: significant changes in our social, domestic, personal or work life involve adopting different behaviours and

54

maybe also different beliefs, attitudes and values. Change constitutes a challenge to our security needs: we are comfortable with what we know and have experienced — that which is different is, to some degree, threatening[15]. Being transferred to a new job — often a job about which he has little or no know knowledge — is a common experience for many police officers. He may well be dealing with unfamiliar things and procedures and people. It takes time to become clear about who and what is important and in what ways, and to find out what is expected and what the priorities are. Indeed, the first three months or so of a new job, whilst often exciting, can nonetheless be quite traumatic, especially if it entails moving house, reschooling the children, etc. Another form of change that police officers can find disturbing is a change of boss. The new incumbent may wish different procedures, standards and priorities to be introduced. Changes in personnel, especially at Superintendent and Chief Superintendent level can be quite frequent; junior officers may come, not unnaturally, to suspect that their bosses are making changes for their own personal benefit rather than for the good of the Force. This attitude may be particularly evident when policy and procedural changes are made without consultation, the lower ranking officers knowing that when the 'wheel comes off' they will get 'pain' for not making the change work. The Police Service as a whole has been undergoing tremendous changes over the last 15 years and perhaps the rate of change is still increasing as the Service struggles to respond to demands for greater accountability, better public relations, better response to serious crime and public disorder, better control over the use of firearms and sophisticated technology and greater overall efficiency and effectiveness. New training programmes, new policing schemes, new technology, 'policing by objectives', command and control systems, etc. all constitute significant demand on individual officers and on the Police Service as a whole.

Change often involves uncertainty, another major feature of high-demand circumstances. Uncertainty can relate both to not being clear about the nature of the situation we are in and also to not being sure about what to do in a situation. Being uncertain about the nature of the situation itself is a frustration of our security needs — we cannot feel comfortable if we do not know what is going on. How often do we hear people saying, 'it's the waiting that is the worst thing' — this is uncertainty. In relationships, uncertainty about whether someone loves us or not is often worse than knowing that they don't! Uncertainty is also likely to undermine our ability to operate effectively and hence to preclude satisfaction of our need to achieve and to feel positive about ourselves. In our jobs, sometimes we do not know what is expected of us, what we have to do to be judged proficient. This is a state called *role ambiguity*[16] and it has been associated with feelings of low job satisfaction, high absenteeism, etc. Typically in these circumstances what we do is to define the job ourselves. This can be a further source of problems if we later learn that our boss has got rather different ideas!

Uncertainty in terms of not knowing how to tackle a situation may arise even if the situation itself is well defined. Lack of training and/or experience is generally the cause of problems here. Unhappily, we are often faced with responsibilities for which we have had little preparation, indeed, the Police Service and the Social Services seem commonly to subject personnel to being 'thrown in the deep end'. The ability not to sink in these circumstances requires high levels of flexibility and learning skills.

Often uncertainty in responding can arise from being aware of a number of different options. Indeed, the more imaginative, creative and thoughtful we are and the more aware we are of grey areas and all the 'ifs, buts and howevers' about matters, the more uncertain we may feel about what to do for the best and the more indecisive we may be. Sometimes difficulties in responding can arise from uncertainty about priorities either with respect to responsibilities we have in our job or with respect to trying to satisfy conflicting demands made of us due to our holding many different roles in life, each comprising a set of expectations. When the expectations made of us due to our holding one role clash with those made of us due to our holding another, we experience *role conflict*[17]. Role conflict becomes a significant problem when we are uncertain which role should be given priority in a certain situation and how to manage the fact that we are putting to one side the expectations associated with the other role. These problems are not uncommon: we are in the role of subordinate to our boss and in the role of boss to our subordinates, often the expectations of our subordinates differ from those of our boss. We can feel conflicting loyalties with respect to the job and our families: we have both the role of employee and of husband/wife and we may often find difficulty in partitioning our time, attention and care.

Knowing what should be done but not being able to do it i.e. impotence, is feature of many circumstances that we find ourselves in and it is a factor in many of the aspects of the job that police officers report as being stressful. Impotence is severe frustration of our needs to achieve and for esteem. It can arise in many different ways, one of which is not having the resources to do what we see is important: inadequate or inefficient equipment, inadequate manpower and the poor utilisation of what manpower there is are frequent sources of frustration. So too is not having the level of authority required to do the job in the way we feel it should be done. Another powerful stressor is being rendered impotent to properly do the important things by being tied up with matters which we may see as petty e.g. paperwork, investigation of obviously trivial complaints. One officer comments on paperwork in the following terms[18]:

> 'With many crime reports it has become ludicrous, we spend literally hours writing about things rather than doing things. The reason we do it is because everyone is looking over his shoulder at the next in line boss, who in turn has to show that he is useful, by perhaps picking fault with the guy beneath him because he is conscious of the man above him and so on. In fact, you can liken the crime report to sitting an examination except that you have to get 100% every time. These are the things causing me stress because it is these people out there (meaning the public) that should be important, not chasing paper around in ever decreasing circles just so that we can keep the boys in cosy offices.'

Another feature of circumstances which can result in them being experienced as significantly stressful arises when things are seen as being unfair. It would appear that we have an expectation that people, circumstances and fate will treat us fairly. Yet the world is manifestly unfair and this often causes us frustration and bitterness. The socially deprived see others who they feel are unjustifiably better off than themselves and they resent it; we may fall victims to handicap or serious disease and we may find our minds and hearts being eaten away by thoughts of 'why me?'. Appraisal systems, promotions, postings, perks etc. are often thought of as being unfair and are a source of much stress. The media are seen by probably the majority of police officers to be unfairly biased against the Service; some officers experienced considerable frustration and annoyance watching television accounts of events they were involved with during the 1981 riots and found they had to guard against their morale being undermined. Hostility from certain sections of the public sometimes constitutes a stressor not only because of the physical threat that it can involve but also because of the consciously or unconsciously held notion of being resented by people whose wellbeing he, as a police officer, is trying to maintain. Some Courtroom decisions, too, are seen as unfairly lenient and can be interpreted as being indicative of a society that doesn't care. Frustration of the expectation of fairness is likely to lead in the long term to cynicism — the doubting of any goodness in human nature and understanding of life as a game in which the cunning and the strong win whilst the gullible and weak deserve to lose. Unhappily, cynicism would seem to be an institutionalised value within the Police Service.

There have been many studies of American and British police officers attempting to itemise all the aspects of police work which are experienced as stressful.[19,20,21,22]. Collectively they provide a mass of data which, in itself, may not be very useful although many of the stressors that have been identified by these surveys have been included in the above discussion. It is felt here that determining the features of circumstances which lead to these circumstances being experienced as stressful is a far more flexible and helpful approach. However, we might make two observations from the data generated by these surveys. Firstly, the stressors identified by police officers can be usefully classified using Cooper and Marshall's categorisation of sources of stress[23]. This categorisation has been applied in research carried out on stress in many different occupations. Secondly, implicit in the findings of many of the surveys and explicit in the report of the ACPO Working Party on psychological stress, is that officers identify sources of stress arising from the way in which the organisation is run far more readily than stressors inherent in doing the job itself. The Working Party pointed to management styles that were autocratic, uncaring, unconsultative and unduly critical. These styles are often facilitated and maintained by poor management systems involving unsatisfactory methods of selection, training and career development and which encourage unrealistic expectations of officers. Furthermore, a lack of management support was identified by which officers could be properly helped through the difficulties that they experienced. We might need to be a little cautious about aiming too much criticism at the organisation; police officers involved in surveys may find it more comfortable to say that the circumstances of doing the job (for which they may not feel responsible) are a source of more problems than actually doing the job (for which they may feel responsible). Nonetheless, it is probably the case that management- induced stressors are likely to be experienced negatively as distress as they may be seen as obstacles to effective performance; the stressors inherent in the work itself may be more likely to be experienced more positively as eustress i.e. challenge and excitement.

Cooper and Marshall's categorisation of sources of stress:

INTRINSIC TO THE JOB: The nature of the work itself, working conditions, having too much or too little to do, etc.

ROLE IN THE ORGANISATION: Role ambiguity and role conflict, having responsibility for people.

RELATIONSHIPS AT WORK: With boss, subordinates and colleagues.

CAREER DEVELOPMENT: Feelings of being under or over promoted, inconsiderately posted.

STRUCTURE AND CLIMATE: The way the organisation is run, its values, reward systems, etc.

HOME/WORK INTERFACE: Reconciling family and job demands, financial problems, etc.

THE MANAGEMENT OF STRESS

We have examined what stress is, what its effects are and what causes it, but what about handling it? If we care about improving the quality of our work and the quality of our life and if we care about improving the quality of work and of living for those for whom we have responsibility, and if we wish the organisation in which we work to operate in a way that allows this, we need to know about stress management. Stress management is to do with:

a. Avoiding or overcoming counter-productive levels of tension, confusion, frustration, anger, anxiety, guilt, etc., and consequent counter-productive behaviour. Thoughts, feelings and behaviours become counter-productive when they begin to reduce rather than increase performance.

b. Generating and maintaining more productive levels of interest, alertness, responsibility, involvement, challenge, commitment etc. and consequent productive behaviour. Thoughts, feelings and behaviours become more productive when they increase performance.

We can exercise our concern for stress management in each of three overlapping arena. The first of these is ourselves, we might call this the intra-personal arena; here we are concerned with developing an awareness of our own stress reaction patterns and the knowledge and skills by which we can maintain these within sensible, productive limits. Secondly, there is the inter-personal arena which involves an awareness of stress levels in others and the ability to render appropriate support. Thirdly, the organisational arena: the understanding of organisational structure, procedures and culture and the ability to identify and, if appropriate implement, means of strengthening the supportive framework of the organisation. Due to limitations of space, this chapter will address only the first of these: the intra-personal arena.

STRESS MANAGEMENT IN THE INTRAPERSONAL ARENA

In the final analysis, the responsibility for our personal experience of stress lies with us. The richness and value of our work, relationships and life is determined by each of us, individually for ourselves. The quality of our existence is dependent not on the pattern of events impacting on us but in our pattern of responding to those events. Here again, we meet the principle that stress lies inside the person. Being treated badly, illness, overwork, stretched financial resources, even the loss of a loved one — these experiences insofar as they make demand of us, are stressful but it is how we interpret and respond to the experiences that determines exactly how stressful they are.

Increasing Self-Awareness
In order to manage our own stress effectively we need to know as much as we can about ourselves. Knowing ourselves helps us to take control of our lives — it gives us the power that we need in order to accept the responsibility of responding positively to that which we find stressful and by so doing, enables us to develop in our jobs and to grow as individuals. There are many ways by which we can increase our understanding of who and what we are and some of these are explored below.

a. What is Important? Earlier, we discussed a set of needs that is perhaps common to everybody. Each of us have different ways in which we expect to be able to satisfy these needs. The following exercise can help us identify what is important for us.

1. Imagine yourself at the end of your life (hopefully, many years in the future). You are on your deathbed looking back over your life. What would you have liked to have experienced, achieved and become in order for you to be completely satisfied and contented. Generalisations such as, 'Oh well, I would want to have lived a happy life and taken every opportunity to better myself', are not sufficient. Be specific. Write your thoughts down.
2. Now ask yourself *why* you answered in the way you did; what essentially is important to you, what are your priorities?
3. Relate these importances back to the set of needs shown earlier.

This is a useful exercise for many reasons: it can help us become more aware of values that are central to what really makes us 'tick'; it helps us generate a framework by which we can keep day-to-day problems in perspective; it can provide guidelines for helping us make certain decisions and it can help reorientate ourselves at a time when perhaps we are so busy that we may be losing track of where we are going and why.

b. Stage of Life. The problems that we face, the concerns that we have and the drives that motivate us are likely to be affected by the stage of life we have reached. The life cycle has been studied by a number of psychologists e.g.[24], [25], [26] and a brief summary of their findings may be useful to provide a context for your observations from the above.

It would appear that when we are in the period between the late teens and the late twenties, marriage and children give rise to much of the stress —mostly eustress — and a good deal of demand arises from concern to establish a stable base with respect to job and home.

From the late twenties to the late forties, *generativity* is likely to be experienced as a very powerful drive: generativity with respect to children but also with respect to things, ideas and experiences. Unless we achieve this 'outpouring' of ourselves, there may be dangers in becoming too self-interested and self-indulgent. It is during these years too, particularly between about thirty and forty-five, that disenchantment with spouse and general dissatisfaction with marriage may take place. This is especially likely if the marriage was not based on real intimacy, openness and honesty. Money and possessions may take the place of other people in being valued.

Around forty-five years, the 'male menopause' is thought to take place and men may experience moodiness and irritability and perhaps will not always think too clearly as they undergo physical and emotional effects of glandular changes. Psychologically, we may be struggling to keep in touch with the strong and healthy young person we once were and may be unduly concerned with appearance and attractiveness to the opposite sex. All this at a time when we might be receiving very substantial responsibilities at work! Women's 'change of life' generally takes place around the late forties or early fifties. Depression and anxiety are not uncommon correlates to glandular changes and possibly weakened bonds with children.

On approaching the fifties, we are likely to find our friends and loved ones becoming more important to us again, material things being less valued. Health considerations can no longer be so easily repressed and we start to take such matters very much more seriously.

As we approach and then enter retirement, the major issue facing us is that of reconciling ourselves to the past and to the fact that time is now limited. Personal relations are perhaps especially important to us at this stage as they help us maintain a sense of significance and a sense of dignity.

c. Personality. What ways of looking at the world, of thinking, of feeling, of making judgements and of behaving are typical or characteristic of ourselves? If we can come near to answering this question, we will have a good idea about our personality. Personality is to do with what is essentially us, what it is that we take with us wherever we go: what seems to be always there.

Our personalities have a lot to do with how we experience situations. Consider, for example, an officer who has a strong sense of self-sufficiency and perhaps a feeling of being better than those around him. He is likely to have a real problem in ever going to anyone for help. Not only will he be disinclined to even contemplate such a behaviour but even if he did, he probably would not know *how* to ask. If he is put into a new post for which he has little relevant experience, he may well start

For each of the 10 items below, circle the number which you believe best represents your own behaviour.

1.	gives everything 100%	1	2	3	4	5	6	7	easy-going; can be casual about most things.
2.	speaks emphatically; may pound desk	1	2	3	4	5	6	7	mild and slow in speech
3.	never feels rushed — even under pressure	1	2	3	4	5	6	7	always in a hurry
4.	shows and talks about feelings readily	1	2	3	4	5	6	7	hides feelings
5.	takes things one at a time	1	2	3	4	5	6	7	does many things at once; thinks what he is about to do next.
6.	finds others talk too slowly — anticipates what they will say	1	2	3	4	5	6	7	good at listening sensitively to others
7.	not at all competitive	1	2	3	4	5	6	7	very highly competitive
8.	enjoys those peaceful times; can relax easily	1	2	3	4	5	6	7	always active; never happy doing nothing
9.	sees colleagues, subordinates, etc. as less motivated than self	1	2	3	4	5	6	7	sees others as equally or more motivated
10.	few interests unconnected with job	1	2	3	4	5	6	7	many interests unconnected with job

SCORING
1. Add together numbers circled for items 3, 4, 5, 7, 8 to give subtotal X.
2. Transpose numbers circled for items 1, 2, 6, 9, 10 according to the table below:

circled number	1	2	3	4	5	6	7
transposed number	7	6	5	4	3	2	1

thus if you circled '5' for item '1' you would transpose the '5' to '3' etc.
3. Add together the five transposed numbers to give subtotal Y.
4. Sum subtotal X and subtotal Y to find your score.

making mistakes. In this case he is not only his own worst enemy but he is likely to be a stressor on two legs for his subordinates!

To take another example, an officer who is imaginative and innovative and who dislikes routine is likely to find that his level of job-satisfaction depends a great deal on how much 'elbow-room' he is given by his boss. If the boss, because of his own personality, supervises him closely and tells him not only what to do but also how to do it, the imaginative officer's working life will be full of frustration. If the imaginative officer, as a boss himself, imposes his ideas for change onto his subordinates in an insensitive way, he will be likely to generate confusion, resentment and resistance.

The use of psychological questionnaires is one very good way to get to know ourselves a little better. The following exercise allows us to learn something about our general approach to life. The questionnaire on p. 62 has been developed from those used elsewhere [27, 28].

In this exercise, the higher your score is above 40, the more your behaviour may be described as 'Type A'; the lower your score is below 40, the more your behaviour can be thought of as 'Type B'[29]. Type A behaviour may be regarded as 'hurry sickness'; Type A people tend to live a time-pressured existence and are likely to be aggressive, self-driving, competitive and impatient. They may tend to feel guilty over idle time, and may have little capacity to relax, to quietly enjoy social relationships or to appreciate beauty. Their energies tend to be primarily focused on their work; they tend to be preoccupied by deadlines, suppress their fatigue and measure their success in quantity rather than quality of output.

Type As can be very productive and very successful but a price may have to be paid for this. At work they may find difficulty in delegating and may have more serious conflicts with subordinates and boss. They can be mistrustful of others and doubting of their competence. They are likely to take on far more than they should and tend to look for quick solutions to problems — they are unlikely to be very reflective. Whilst Type As tend to be committed to their families, home and personal relationships may suffer because of involvement in work. They may have little interest in hobbies, often miss holidays and bring work home at weekends. When holidays are taken, they are likely to be as packed and as hectic as the working life. Because of their busy, highly stressful way of life, it is not unusual to find type As who smoke — cigarettes rather than a pipe — drink too much, fail to exercise properly and eat badly.

Type B behaviour may be thought of as the inverse or absence of the pattern of behaviours characteristic of Type A people. Type Bs tend to be calm and relaxed in their approach to life, easy-going, less competitive, more in touch with their feelings and less likely to become impatient or to lose their temper.

Due to their approach to life, Type As are likely to maintain their physiological stress reaction at a much higher level than do people showing Type B behaviour. The long term effects of this have been clearly demonstrated in a number of well controlled studies: Type As have between 2 and 7 times the risk of heart disease compared with Type Bs. About 75% of British police officers of supervisory rank appear to typically display Type A behaviour[30], [31].

d. How Do You Respond to High Levels of Demand? Perhaps the most important understanding we need to have of ourselves is how we respond to high levels of demand: what is our particular pattern of Stress Reaction?

1. To identify your particular pattern of Stress Reaction think about what symptoms you typically show. Your spouse or close friend might be able to give you useful insights! Think about: a. physiological symptoms e.g. tension, headaches, nervous stomach, sweating, feeling hot or cold, chest pains or heart irregularities, nervous tics, etc.

   b. psychological symptoms involving feeling e.g. nervousness, excitement, frustration, anger, sulkiness, fear, inadequacy, etc.

   c. psychological symptoms involving thinking e.g. dogmatism, black-and-white thinking, inability to concentrate, getting muddled, forgetfulness, sense of unreality, going blank, concentration on irrelevancies, etc.

   d. behavioural symptoms e.g. smoking or eating or drinking too much, sleeping problems, snapping at people, pacing up and down, avoiding people, etc.

2. What are the kinds of pressures (stressors) that typically give rise to your pattern of Stress Reaction? Think about your work life, domestic life, social and personal life. Can these be understood in terms of the features of change, uncertainty, impotence and unfairness — or any other features which may be pertinent?

3. What sort of circumstances do you tend to avoid? What would you experience if you tried to tackle them?

4. Try to link your answers to the above with what you know about your importances and your personality.

Using the Model of Stress in Stress Management
We have now progressed some way down the path of intra-personal stress management: an understanding of the nature, causes and consequences of stress, not only in general terms but also applied to us as individuals, empowers us to have more control over our lives. A reader who has

worked through the exercises will at this stage be likely to have formulated many ideas on his own personal forms of stress management.

Whilst many notions about stress management are implicit in what has already been discussed, the model of stress allows us to explicitly identify strategies by which stress may be managed. Limiting our considerations to distress, we have seen that the problem with distress is that it involves and generates thoughts, feelings and behaviours that undermine our performance. The model suggests three approaches to reducing the harmful effects of distress:

a. reducing the extent to which the Stress Reaction is fuelled e.g. by Assessment of Demand.
b. dissipating the Stress Reaction before it can build up and undermine performance.
c. reducing the detrimental effect of the Stress Reaction on performance by increasing tolerance to the Stress Reaction.

Each of these approaches will be explored albeit briefly and certainly not comprehensively, but it is hoped the discussion will be sufficient to stimulate further and fuller thought.

Reducing the extent to which the Stress Reaction is Fuelled.
The model shows the Stress Reaction being fed by Actual Demand as in the case of significant life changes, illness, etc. To some extent we can minimise any distress and unconscious shock caused by many of these stressors by preparation. Retirement is a good example here — ensuring that we become *actively* involved in outside interests some two or more years *before* we retire; living in an area where we know a good many people and are in reasonable travelling distance of our loved ones (personal relationships become that much more important as we grow older), etc. — such considerations help us manage the difficult transition that retirement constitutes.

Assessment of Demand and Assessment of Capability can both fuel the Stress Reaction, particularly when we feel that the demand is in danger of overwhelming our capacity to respond. Very often the perceived magnitude of the demand is much greater than the Actual Demand warrants — we make mountains out of molehills. We may often benefit from remembering a piece of wisdom that is now some 2000 years old:[32]

'Men are disturbed not by things but the views they take of them.'

This is an encouragement to closely examine the understanding we have of the circumstances we are in.

A common source of considerable frustration is not receiving promotion when we think we are fit for it. Let's explore an example of this as an illustration of how our Assessment of Demand can be reappraised in intra-personal stress management.

65

Imagine one officer, Bill; he has twenty years service, ten in the rank of Inspector. For some years now he has been anticipating promotion to Chief Inspector, believing himself to be good at his job. With each successive disappointment following promotion boards he has become increasingly frustrated and has now reached the point where he tells people that he is 'not appreciated' and has 'had it up to here' with the job and he is generally angry, depressed and apathetic about his work. Bill obviously believes that he *must* get promotion. He sees this as absolutely necessary for his well-being: it is one of the major importances in his life — not to get promotion is a catastrophe. But the distress Bill experiences arises not from the fact of being overlooked but from his set of beliefs about what that means. If Bill can stand back and examine the roots of his concerns he might come to see that consciously or unconsciously, he has assumed that his needs for esteem and achievement will only be met through being promoted. There is, of course, nothing written in tablets of stone about promotion being the answer to these needs — it is just the way he sees it. Bill might also come around to a more rational appraisal of his circumstances along the lines, 'I have not obtained the advancement I have been looking for but I know from my past achievements that I am hard-working, good at my job and respected by many. Because I have not received promotion to Chief Inspector in the past does not mean that I will not do so in the future either in this Force or another. In the mean time I realise that anger and disinterest are self-defeating and I will apply myself diligently seeking satisfaction in the work I am doing'. Such an assessment of his present position takes the edge away from his frustration, allows him to obtain more fulfilment from his work and allows him to pursue his career interests in a more constructive fashion by bringing problems-solving techniques to bear. Also, in the event of his desires not being realised, this kind of assessment of his circumstances will make it easier for him to come to terms with the disappointment.

This example hopefully illustrates the importance of examining the way in which we Assess the Demand and detecting irrationalities in our thinking that might have led to a distorted understanding of our circumstances. These irrationalities often take the form of believing that a particular event can only be interpreted in one way and that there is only one possible reaction to that interpretation. If that interpretation and reaction involve the experience of much stress then the irrationality serves to lock the person into his own distress. In a television interview, the singer Janet Baker told of how she used to see giving a performance (Assessment of Demand) in terms of all the responsibility of satisfying a lot of people who had paid much and possibly travelled far, to hear her. The anguish she used to experience prior to making an appearance almost induced her to give up her career. A long discussion with a friend resulted in her changing her Assessment of Demand: she came to the view that she had a gift — a gift that it was right to share with others; to bring happiness and pleasure to her audiences could only be a source of joy and satisfaction.

Like Janet Baker, we can well make good use of other people in the process of examining our Assessment of Demand. We can encourage our family, friends, boss, etc. to share their views of the nature and size of the demand in a certain circumstance. Such discussions with our boss, for example, can help to reduce any uncertainty with respect to the responsibilities and priorities of our job.

Imagine a Community Relations Officer who, being very good at his job, receives more and more requests for his time. He believes that to do the job properly (Assessment of Demand), he has to respond positively to all approaches. Before long he is working all evenings and weekends, is experiencing family problems and is close to being overwhelmed by his work i.e. his ever expanding Assessment of Demand has outstripped his Assessment of Capability. Clearly, this man needs — either individually or, more likely, in discussion with his boss — to come to a more realistic and attainable understanding of what is entailed in him doing his job well.

Research that the author is engaged in at the time of writing, suggests that the relationship between boss and subordinate is one of the most significant factors — if not *the* most significant factor — in determining how positive the subordinate feels about the job he is doing. In a good relationship, the boss may be seen as, amongst other things, supportive, trustworthy, competent, able to enthuse and able to judge how much elbow room to give each subordinate. If the relationship is bad, the subordinate may see his boss as inconsistent, dogmatic, liking to take all the credit, lazy, etc. If we believe we have a bad boss then the Assessment of Demand with respect to the job is likely to be that much greater: we experience the boss as a frustrator of our needs for achievement, esteem and perhaps of the needs for security and belongingness, as well. We might think that the relationship, good or bad, is a static, almost predetermined affair, dependent on the compatibility of personalities. This, however, would be another example of irrational thinking: there is nothing static or predetermined about relationships. Relationships are dynamic, they are constantly changing in ways that are, of course, consequent to the activities of the parties involved. As such, they can be *managed*.

'Recent studies suggest that effective managers do take time and effort to manage not only relationships with their subordinates, but also with their bosses.'[33]

This means that we have to do something other than simply accept unquestioningly and perhaps cynically, the directives of our supervisors. Neither is ingratiating agreement with everything he says appropriate. A first step in managing our boss is to come to understand him — getting to know his typical approach to problems, his typical approach to people, his goals, what he expects of us, the problems facing him, etc.

> 'Knowing your boss's preferred style, his objectives, his expectations, and the pressures on him, enables you to decide how to act to make him more effective and of more value to you in doing your job . . . Joint work planning, continuous flows of information, informal sessions on key aspects of the work and objectives can produce situations in which the boss surfaces his expectations — and also enable *you* to communicate your own expectations to your boss, find out if they are realistic, and influence him to accept the areas which are important to you.'[34]

Such an approach is most likely to allow us to strike that most productive balance of accommodating the boss's style and objectives whilst still retaining our own autonomy of thought and identity in action: both necessary if we are to satisfy our esteem needs.

Assessment of Capability is our understanding of the resources we can bring to bear on a problem. Most of us, liking to think of ourselves as self-sufficient individualists, probably see this mostly in terms of our own knowledge, skills and the time that we can allocate. But there are other resources as well, of course, most importantly: other people. Bringing others into our problem solving is one of the most effective ways of increasing the potency of our response to a problem and may also serve to diminish the size of the Assessment of Demand. Jim is brought into his boss's office and asked to do a report at a time when he is already very stretched. Jim's natural response might be to inwardly think, 'My God, how am I to get that done?' whilst actually saying, 'Very well, sir.' and leaving the office so 'shell-shocked' that he does not even take the opportunity to fully determine what was required in the report. A different approach might be to bring the boss into his difficulties. Having found out what the report entails, Jim might say something along the lines of, 'I see this is an important piece of work; I'd like to do it but I'd like to do it well. At the moment, with the amount of work I've got on at the moment, I cannot do it justice unless I disregard some of my present responsibilities. How do you think we can sort this one out?' It takes a very uncaring, autocratic boss not to respond positively and constructively to such a statement, if it is genuine; unhappily, there are still some bosses who do act in uncaring and autocratic ways. Nonetheless, at least it lets the boss know that his subordinate is busy! The structure of the initiative is:

> WE have a problem, let's explore what WE can do

Subordinates, friends, family, etc. may be brought into our problem solving in the same way with the result that not only do we benefit from their views and suggestions but also we elicit from them a level of involvement with and commitment to whatever is decided that might not otherwise exist. The tactic is especially useful when there is a potential conflict of interests between us and the other party because it allows everybody involved to appreciate the concerns and constraints affecting the others and it helps to generate a degree of solidarity out of a potentially devisive situation.

Confidence is a major issue arising out of any consideration of Assessment of Capability. Lack of confidence can make us respond in a number of self-defeating ways including complete withdrawal, ineffectuality and destructive over-reaction. For example, a young P.C. is taunted by a group of youths on a street corner. He might, lacking confidence in dealing with this, walk away and try to avoid similar situations in the future. Or he might attempt to talk with them but, getting flustered, he could elicit even more of a derisory response. He could go up to them and precipitate unnecessary violence through using aggression to mask his insecurity.

A supervisory officer, lacking in confidence in his supervisory capacity, may withdraw from this responsibility either by trying to do everything himself or by letting his subordinates do their jobs however they please. He might dither and be inconsistent in the role or he might become strongly authoritarian: usually a form of defensive aggression.

Self-confidence comes from valuing ourselves as people, being aware that others value us, being aware of past successes and of what we have learned when things did not go so well. It comes from knowing that we have prepared as well as we could in the circumstances for whatever it is we are facing. And it comes from setting *our own* realistic expectations of what we can do; with the knowledge that should we not perform to other people's satisfaction, this is no discredit to us in our eyes, albeit another time we can do better.

J.R.R. Tolkien created a character, Wormtongue,[35] a highly eloquent and persuasive weasel of a creature with an engraciating, subservient manner. Wormtongue delighted in undermining his master's confidence and potential by continually referring to and rationalising his weaknesses. We all have our own Wormtongue. When he is active and we feel inclined to withdraw, a degree of externally directed determination can help us through. Bernard Manning understood this on advising an anxious young comic going on a large stage for the first time: 'Make them have it!'

Thus we can see that by examining how we assess either demand or capability, we can affect the extent to which these assessments fuel the Stress Reaction. Similar considerations apply to the Assessment of Performance. By ensuring that this assessment is as objective as possible and not based on pessimistic thinking (generated by Wormtongue) nor, indeed, based on wishful thinking or flattering comments by subordinates, we can maintain that grip on reality that is necessary for good performance.

Dissipating the Stress Reaction
Let us now turn to techniques by which we may dissipate the Stress Reaction before it can build up and undermine performance. There are many tried and trusted means of doing this — if only we think to use them! One of the most straightforward is a certain form of deep breathing.

Deep Yoga Breathing
1. The exercise may be carried out standing, sitting or lying down.
2. Exhale and then take a deep breath through the nose to the mental count of 8 as below:
   a. up to the count of 3, draw air into the lower parts of the lungs by pushing out the abdomen.
   b. during counts 4–6, draw air into the middle section of the lungs by expanding the chest.
   c. during counts 7 and 8, raise the collar bone and push back the shoulders slightly to completely fill the lungs with air.
3. Hold the breath for the count of 3.
4. Exhale to the count of 8 by drawing in the abdomen (1–3), contracting the ribs (4–6) and lowering the shoulders (7+8).
5. With a little practice, the three components of the inhalation and the exhalation becomes a single, fluid, wavelike motion.
6. Carry out this exercise three times and experience a significant beneficial calming effect.

Carrying out this easy, quick and unobtrusive exercise can be of substantial value in helping us to keep our 'nerves' and feelings under control and in clearing our minds prior to Courtroom appearances, interviews, speaking in public, talking to somebody with whom we are very angry, etc.

Most of us are aware that we need time to unwind at the end of a busy day. In one study [36], male British police officers reported that it takes them, on average, about three quarters of an hour to relax; their wives considered that it takes significantly longer. Some wives felt that it takes their husbands two hours or more.

True relaxation is the reduction of unnecessary tension in the muscles of the body. When our bodies are tense the muscles which make our skeleton move — some 620 of them — are contracted; relaxation involves enabling these muscles to assume a more restful state by allowing them to elongate.

Relaxation techniques — exercises in which the muscles are systematically relaxed — are becoming more widely discussed and utilised today and they may be seen by some as 'trendy' — a view guaranteed to make the vast majority of police officers highly sceptical. Nonetheless, their use has been found to substantially reduce problems of 'edginess', tension headaches and insomnia. The release of tension brought about through relaxation serves not only to defuse the physiological aspect of the Stress Reaction but also to reduce undue pressure on the heart. When we are tense, there is an increased resistance to the flow of blood. This occurs because hard, tense muscles hinder the expansion of the blood vessels as they accept the surge of blood generated by each heart beat. Used over a period of time, relaxation techniques can help prevent or reduce hypertension. It is not surprising therefore that many large companies train their executives in such procedures and that more and more, family doctors are successfully prescribing these techniques instead of tranquillisers to patients.

Proper relaxation is a skill of self-control. Like any other skill, it has to be practised to be learned and, of course, practice takes time. One authority[37] suggests that we need to spend 20 to 30 minutes a day on this practice if we are to build relaxation into our lives so that it becomes a natural part of our living. Many of us might find such a time commitment difficult:

> 'The high powered businessman may complain that he cannot find 20 minutes a day to relax. Such a life-style merely demonstrates the need for such a period. Even Churchill whilst Prime Minister during the Second World War always took time to relax[38].

Excellent detailed practical instruction on relaxation techniques is provided elsewhere (see reference 37) nonetheless, the procedure described below is simple and beneficial.

Relaxation Exercise.
1. Find somewhere quiet where you can sit or lie down comfortably.
2. Close your eyes, breathe slowly and deeply (naturally, not deep yoga breaths) and just let the body settle for a couple of minutes.
3. Now focus your mind on your right foot and leg; tense all the muscles really hard, screw the toes up and hold the tension for three seconds; immediately let the tension go so that all the muscles in the right leg and foot are completely relaxed. Note the difference in what the muscles feel like when they are tense and when they are relaxed. Carry out the tensing, holding and relaxing cycle three times.
4. Apply the same three-stage procedure three times for each of the left leg and foot, the right hand and arm, the left hand and arm, the buttocks and abdomen, the chest and shoulders, the neck and face. For each area of the body remember to focus the mind and to register the different sensations when the muscles are tense and when they are relaxed. Once a group of muscles has been 'processed' try not to move them again unless discomfort makes it necessary to do so.
5. Continue to take slow, deep breaths. With each outbreath imagine your whole body getting heavier and heavier and beginning to sink into the chair/bed.
6. Try to picture yourself now in surroundings which have very restful associations e.g. basking in the sun on a deserted beach; beside a

rippling stream. Do not force your concentration on this but just gently bring your mind back to the restful scene whenever it starts to wander.

7. After twenty minutes or so, take a number of very deep breaths, stretch, cover your eyes with your hands, open your eyes 'into' your hands, have another stretch and very slowly get up. Shake your head and limbs around loosely and notice how refreshed and at ease you are.

A more vigorous means of dissipating the physiological aspects of the Stress Reaction is, of course, to burn it off by physical activity. The best forms of exercise to help us unwind is exercise which is non-competitive and rhythmic. Running, jogging, swimming, dancing, digging the garden and working out on a punch bag are all excellent.

Deep yoga breathing, relaxation and exercise, in making us physically less tense, also reduce our mental tension: we cannot be mentally 'het up' if our bodies are relaxed. There are, however, some strategies which we can apply directly to our minds. Many of us are often prevented from obtaining much needed sleep by a restless mind which generates a torrential outpouring of thoughts. These thoughts appear to be accompanied by very slight movements of our eyes and of our throats and tongues as we visualise and silently talk through what we are thinking about. Having gone through stages 1–5 of relaxation in bed, last thing at night, try keeping eyes, throat and tongue as still as you can. Do not force this otherwise your face and neck will become tense and, of course, you do have to swallow from time to time! Nonetheless, this is a very helpful means of taking the 'wind out of the sails' of our minds.

Sometimes we may be plagued by recurring thoughts from the past — mistakes we have made, opportunities we have missed, the times when we made fools of ourselves and so on. We all experience these thoughts from time to time; they are the spectres of unresolved distress. The reason they come back to haunt us is because we have tried to repress unhappy experiences instead of acknowledging them and forgiving ourselves or others for what has been done. When such a memory comes flooding back, we immediately become tense and experience distress. Three yoga breaths followed by saying to ourselves that the mistake or misdeed is forgiven and then spending a little time looking at the experience and drawing lessons from it, comprises an effective remedy.

When something tragic happens such as becoming infirm or a major emotional or material loss, we may find bitterness welling up inside us and the question of 'why me?' pervading our minds as we dwell on the unfairness of our circumstance. In a most moving televised interview, a recently handicapped person described how such feelings had begun to overwhelm him until he came to ask himself, 'Why *not* me? What is so special about me that like many hundreds of thousands of others, I should not be handicapped?' The foundations of his distress undermined, he was able to rebuild his life.

A rather intriguing and perhaps somewhat amusing technique can be used to discourage specific unwelcome thoughts e.g. the 'why me?' question, distress from the past, thoughts about cigarettes if we are trying to give up smoking, thoughts about work when we are on holiday, etc. This simple and effective procedure involves keeping a large elastic band around one wrist. When the undesirable thought enters the mind, the elastic band is drawn back with the other hand and then let go. At the same time we tell ourselves that we are not going to entertain that thought. This form of 'punishment' builds up a conditioned aversion response to the thought and before long, the response operates without recourse to the elastic band.

Studies of people experiencing high levels of stress consistently show a reduction in the physiological stress reaction when there are others around to share the experience. Other people can provide tremendous emotional support when times are difficult — if we let them. Emotional support comes not from talking about the detailed nature of whatever we are concerned with but from being able to express how we feel about it: whether we are depressed, anxious, angry, or whether we are pleased, contented, elated, etc. Neither is emotional support necessarily given when our confidant responds to us with an objective, logical, clinical appraisal of our situation: there are times when we just need to be accommodated by somebody who accepts our perspective. On receiving a degree of care and sympathy, much of the edge of a distressing emotion can disappear naturally. Similarly, sharing our more joyful feelings with someone who is empathic can reinforce and enrich these feelings.

Friends, trusted colleagues, ministers, etc. are all potential sources of support as, indeed, we are sources of support for others, however, for those of us who are married, our spouses may be best placed to fulfil this role for us.

One study of police officers in an American force[39] found that officers who became very frustrated with their jobs and eventually lost interest, were less likely to talk with their spouses about the job and were more likely to get angry if their spouse attempted to raise the subject with them, than officers who remained well-motivated. Most male British police officers would appear to be rather unwilling to share their experience of work with their wives, often claiming that they want to protect the family from the unpleasant side of policing. Yet in a small British study[40] it was found that wives of police officers wanted to discuss the job significantly more than they did. Furthermore, they felt they could easily detect when their husbands were under strain and desired to provide more support than they were allowed to.

A further consideration is that if the spouse (or paramour) does not, or is not encouraged to, provide emotional support then the relationship may itself become a significant source of chronic stress. Lack of openness and

73

communication usually leads to misunderstandings which in turn can give rise to anxieties and mistrust. The spouse may feel excluded from what is often the most salient feature of the officer's life (i.e. the job) and may well have a sense of being secondary to it. This can lead to resentment.

Of course, between any two people who have known each other for maybe many years, patterns of communication will have evolved which are very difficult to change. A starting point in attempting to deepening the communication with someone who is close might be to show him or her the last few paragraphs and ask for comments!

Increasing Tolerance to the Stress Reaction
The third strategic approach to stress management at the intra-personal level involves increasing our tolerance to stress such that for any given strength of demand, the impact is less harmful i.e. less likely to give rise to high blood pressure, job-dissatisfaction, etc. Tolerance in this context can be understood as *mental and physical resilience* arising from our state of health. Health is defined by the World Health Organisation as:

> 'A state of complete physical, mental and social well-being, and not merely the absence of disease or infirmity.'

What is it that allows mental resilience — what is it that constitutes mental health? Whilst it may not be possible to give a definitive answer to this question, there are certain attributes which may well be components of the healthy mind. One such attribute is having confidence in ourselves and being true to ourselves so that we can face anybody without fear and without pretence.[40] Another is the capacity to tolerate differences between ourselves and others. Other attributes are: lack of the emotional dependency on 'crutches' such as alcohol, cigarettes and food, that leads to compulsive consumption; being able to express our emotions and share them with others without becoming emotionally dependent on them; the ability to forgive ourselves and others for things that have happened in the past; humility which allows us the willingness and ability to learn and grow from our experiences; the ability to be rational in our assessment of demand; being fully involved in, and sensitive to, what is happening now —rather than mentally dwelling in the past or the future.

Another attribute which is worthy of note is the ability not to be unduly concerned about things which are beyond our control. If our Assessment of Demand includes requirements for us to bring about the impossible, we are building substantial frustrations into our lives. A friend of the author encapsulated this point:

> 'There was nothing I could do about it, so it stopped being a problem.'

An ideal attitude to maintain whilst caught in a traffic-jam!

There may, of course, be times when it is not always easy to know whether or not a matter really is beyond our control; an old saying sums it up well:

'God give me the courage to change those things I can change, the serenity to accept those things I cannot change, and the wisdom to know the difference.'

The factors allowing us *physical resilience* have in recent years become the source of much popular interest and discussion. Maintaining our body weight within certain limits is very important[41]:

Height and desirable weight-range: applicable to adults of both sexes.

HEIGHT		WEIGHT RANGE				
ft	in	st	lb	to	st	lb
5	4	8	3	to	10	2
5	5	8	6	to	10	6
5	6	8	9	to	10	10
5	7	8	12	to	11	0
5	8	9	1	to	11	4
5	9	9	4	to	11	9
5	10	9	8	to	12	0
5	11	9	12	to	12	5
6	0	10	2	to	12	10
6	1	10	7	to	13	1
6	2	10	12	to	13	6
6	3	11	3	to	13	12
6	4	11	8	to	14	4

An overweight body is a body that puts undue pressure on the heart as the latter has to work to provide the fat with a supply of blood. In a muscular body, on the other hand, the activity of the muscles themselves as they contract and relax, helps the bloodflow.

Besides being guilty sometimes of eating too much, many of us also fail to ensure a proper balance within our diet. The typical Western diet is thought to contain more fat in the form of fatty meat, dairy produce, cakes, pastries, etc. than is good for us. High intake of animal fat, the solid 'saturated' fat, may well be associated with the build up of cholesterol in the blood and the clogging of the blood vessels with fatty deposits. Many of us would benefit from eating far less fatty material but increasing the proportion of roughage in our diets. Roughage or 'fibre'[42] to use the currently popular term, consists of certain plant substances which, in being indigestible, help the digestion by giving the system something to 'bite' on. Bran cereals, baked beans, peas, wholemeal bread, potatoes and dried fruit are all excellent sources of roughage.

Exercise is another important consideration in our pursuit of health:

'Your body was designed for vigorous daily activity. And it misses it... Exercise is necessary to stimulate the body's own natural maintenance and repair system. Your bones, joints and muscles — and especially your heart — are likely to stay younger if you keep them busy.'[43]

The forms of exercise that are most beneficial in this respect are the same as those that are best in helping us release tension i.e. rhythmic exercise such as jogging, rowing, cycling, swimming, etc. Such forms of exercise require large volumes of oxygen to be taken in by the body, hence they are known as 'aerobic exercises'. Aerobic exercise, undertaken for at least twenty minutes, three times a week, helps us keep fit; it assists tension release; and it serves a third function in that it readily burns up fat in our bodies. If we have been sedentary in our lifestyles for some period of time, we must be particularly concerned to approach exercise in a careful manner, going easy to start with and building up gradually. We must not expect too much too soon, it may take up to two months of planned exercise before the benefits become obvious.

STRESS MANAGEMENT AT THE INTER-PERSONAL AND ORGANISATIONAL LEVELS

The emphasis given in this chapter to stress management at the intra-personal level should not blind us to the need for stress management at both the inter-personal and organisational levels and it would be remiss not to discuss, albeit briefly and in the most general terms, what might be involved in the latter.

All three levels are, of course, inter-related. Thus in the case of Bill, the overlooked Inspector, we could have discussed the responsibility of his senior officers in recognising that Bill was becoming disturbed by repeated disappointments and in discussing with him, openly and honestly, how they saw his career. Equally, we might have examined the adequacy of a promotion system which fails to give feedback to unsuccessful candidates and, indeed, we could have discussed the organisational culture which perhaps encouraged bad management practices.

To be truly effective in managing stress at the inter-personal level, we need to entertain a certain view about the role of a manager. This is the view that the essence of a manager's responsibilities — whatever his level in the organisation — is to help those under him to do their jobs to the fulfilment of their potential. Giving help to others involves *empowering* them to do their jobs and to live their lives well. Giving power to people rarely means taking problems away from them or giving them solutions — rather it means reducing their *impotency* with respect to their responsibilities and concerns: most people want to be able to solve their own problems! To empower our subordinates we need to be able to communicate openly and freely with them thereby minimising their *uncertainty* about their jobs. We also need a sensitivity to others, skills of listening, and a willingness to resist the temptation to assume control of matters. In other words, we need the skills of counselling. The ACPO Working Party on Psychological Stress identified a substantial dearth of these skills in the Police Service.

Stress management at the organisational level means providing an organisational environment which best promotes good performance in personnel. This is, of course, primarily but not exclusively, the domain of upper and top management. Within the context of determining the role and aims of the organisation, organisational stress management involves monitoring the structure, culture and procedures of the organisation with a view to identifying those elements of the organisational environment that appear to unnecessarily frustrate and disenchant personnel. Research on causes of stress is particularly relevant here: as mentioned earlier, police officers report experiencing far more stress from the way the organisation is run than from the nature of the work itself. Organisational stress management also involves recognising present and future needs of personnel with respect to equipment, training, manpower, etc.

The requirement for senior officers to consider organisational stress management is perhaps at its most critical when they are introducing substantial change programmes into the organisation. The demands for greater effectiveness and efficiency have stimulated Police Forces throughout Great Britain to engage in much more systematic forms of operation such as 'Policing by Objectives'. These steps have been taken hastily and it is perhaps not surprising that many officers are finding this a difficult time. As one middle-ranking policeman put it:

> 'These changes subject all members in the service to pressure. Everybody is expected to respond in a constructive and sensitive way to the challenging new environment. Many feel a sense of confusion and uncertainty, possibly heightened by their own inability to rise up to meet the new demands. They adopt defensive positions and there is little doubt these men and women are currently suffering stress because they cannot, or will not adapt. Even those officers who welcome the new challenge and are endowed with the necessary skills, are not finding the transition easy and are going through a degree of suffering.'

The need to facilitate change programmes by communication, consultation, achieving a broad basis of commitment and by adequate preparatory training, cannot be overstated.

In short then, organisational stress management is to do with minimising levels of uncertainty, impotency, unfairness and unnecessary change in the organisation and involving personnel in, and preparing them for, change that is necessary.

OVERVIEW

The author firmly believes that we must be responsible for managing our own stress. The emphasis on intra-personal stress management in this chapter is a reflection of that belief.

The ideas found in the sections on stress management are really just the beginnings of ideas and should not be taken as the sum total of useful thought about the matter. They are offered as leads for the interested reader to pursue maybe by further reading, but more importantly by applying and elaborating the ideas within the context of his or her own concerns. Intra-personal stress management is not an exact science in which we might simply fit circumstances to a formula and wait for a satisfactory conclusion, it is, rather, a creative art. An understanding of who and what we are, our personalities, interests, etc. is an essential element in this art as is a continuing sensitivity to the level of activity of our own patterns of Stress Reaction. Together, these allow us to anticipate and/or diagnose our state of being in any circumstance. Possessing a repertoire of initiatives involving both how we think about matters and what we do with respect to them, we can exercise both preventative and remedial measures to facilitate maximum performance in all situations.

In the first part of this chapter much attention was given to developing a model of stress. This model is an attempt to provide a coherent theoretical framework for the subsequent examination of intra-personal stress management and also to provide a framework from which further ideas about stress management at all levels can be generated.

The study of stress is the study of human experience in meeting the demands of living; it is, in effect, the study of the quality of life. As such it encompasses the physical, mental and social dimensions of our lives, as we have already seen. There is, however, another dimension to man: the ethical/spiritual dimension[44]. Perhaps it is only when we have completely integrated all four dimensions that we will have stress management's equivalent to the Philosophers' Stone, in being able to transmute the base leaden weight of distress to the golden richness of eustress!

REFERENCES AND NOTES

1. Slobogin, K. 1977. Stress. New York Times Magazine. Nov. 20; 48–55.
2. Grimley, P. 1982. Stress and the Operational Detective Police Officer; unpublished dissertation; UMIST, Manchester.

3. Gudjonsson, G. H. and Adlam, K. R. C. 1983. Potential Stressors in Police Work. Police Review. 14. Oct. p. 1931.
4. Gudjonsson, G. H. and Adlam, K. R. C. 1984. Occupational Stressors among British Police Officers. Police Research Bulletin.
5. Robinson, P. 1981. Stress in the Police Service. Police Review. Nov. 20; Nov. 27; Dec. 4; Dec. 11.
6. Selye, H. 1974. *Stress Without Distress*. New York: Lippincott.
7. Reese, J. 1983. Lecture at The Police Staff College, Bramshill.
8. Pozner, H. 1972. Stress. In report of the seminar on Health and High Command held at the RUSI. Nov. 29.
9. Roberts, M. The Police Personality. Quoted in F.B.I. Academy Course Syllabus: Stress Management in Law Enforcement, 1983.
10. Selye, H. op. cit.
11. Cox, T. 1978. *Stress*. Macmillan.
12. Lazarus, R. S. 1966. *Psychological Stress and the Coping Process*. McGraw-Hill, New York.
13. Maslow, A. H. 1954. *Motivation and Personality*. Harper and Bros. New York.
14. Coleman, J. C. 1950. *Abnormal Psychology and Modern Life*. Chicago:Scott Foresman.
15. Toffler, A. 1970. *Future Shock*. New York:Random House.
16. Kahn, R. L. et al. *Organisational Stress*. New York. Wiley, 1964.
17. ibid.
18. Robinson, P. op. cit. p. 2257.
19. Kroes, W. H.; Margolis, B. L.; and Hurrell, J. J. 1974. Job Stress in Policemen. J. Police Sci. & Admin. 2(2): 145–155.
20. Stratton, J. G. 1978. Police Stress: An Overview. Police Chief, 45(4): 58.
21. Gudjonsson, G. H. and Adlam, K. R. C. op. cit.
22. Robinson, P. op. cit.
23. Cooper, C. L. and Marshall, J. 1978. *Understanding Executive Stress*. London: Macmillan.
24. Kimmel, D. C. 1974. *Adulthood and ageing*. Wiley.
25. Erikson E. H. 1964. *Insight and Responsibility*. London. Faber.
26. Gould, R. The Phases of Adult Life: A Study in Developmental Psychology. American J. of Psychiatry. vol. 129, no. 5, pp. 521–531. 1972.
27. Bortner, R. W. and Rosenman, R. H. 1967. The Measurement of Pattern A Behaviour. J. of Chronic Diseases, 20, pp. 525–533.
28. Cooper, C. L. 1981. *The Stress Check*. Prentice Hall.
29. Rosenman, R. H. and Friedman, M. 1974. Neurogenic Factors in Pathogenesis of Coronary Heart Disease. Medical Clinics of North America. 58, pp. 269–277.
30. Robinson, P. op. cit. p. 2364.

31. Brindley, J. M. Unpublished Study. The Police Staff College, Bramshill.
32. Epictetus. Quoted in Beech, H. R.; Burns, L. E.; & Sheffield, B. F. *A Behavioural Approach to the Management of Stress*. Wiley, 1982.
33. Uncredited paper: Getting the Best out of your Boss. School of Management, Cranfield Institute of Technology.
34. ibid.
35. Tolkien, J. R. R. *Lord of the Rings*. George Allen and Unwin. 1969.
36. Ingham, G. Unpublished Study. The Police Staff College Bramshill.
37. Beech, H. R. op. cit.
38. ibid.
39. Maslach, G. and Jackson, S. E. A scale measure to assess experienced burnout: The Maslach Burnout Inventory. Paper presented at the convention of the Western Psychological Association. San Francisco. April, 1978.
40. Storr, A. 1960, *The Integrity of the Personality*, Heinman.
41. Garrow, J. S. 1981. *Treat Obesity Seriously*. Edinburgh: Churchill Livingstone.
42. Eyton, A. *F-Plan Diet*. Penguin, 1982.
43. The Health Education Council. Looking After Yourself.
44. Toogood, T. Developing Managers' Survival Skills: A Holistic Health Education Approach. Journal of Management Development, 2,1. 1983.

The psychological characteristics of police officers: empirical findings and some comments upon their implications

R. ADLAM

'. . . and everybody's shouting, which side are you on?' B. Dylan.[1]

There has been a bourgeoning of sociological writing on the British police: Manning (1978) was even moved to refer to a first, a second and now a third generation of these writers and their writings. There is also a gradual accumulation of material exploring the characteristics of police management and the essence of the police organisation. Here the police officer is just as likely to have made some contribution as the student of management or the organisational theorist. Taken together both police officers and interested academics have fashioned a fairly sophisticated understanding of the police institution. There remains however a paucity of knowledge about the psychological characteristics of British police officers although Butler et al (1977) and (1980) have published informative and stimulating articles. One must add, too, that whilst there is a relative absence of orthodox psychological data on the police, sociologists have provided plenty of detail about the police consciousness and have not been backward in characterising police officers, either through some form of typology (Reiner, 1976) or through listing collections of traits which distinguish the police in some rather homogenous way (Manning, 1982).

The main purpose of this paper, albeit in a limited way, is to present new empirical evidence concerning the psychological characteristics of groups of police officers. This evidence will be considered against a background of research and opinion primarily concerned with the psychological attributes of police officers.

The study of the police personnel has achieved considerable sophistication in the United States of America — indeed by 1972, Balch was able to write a lengthy and seminal review article focusing almost exclusively on the 'charge' that police officers were authoritarian. Earlier researches were also commenting prolixly upon police stress (Levy, 1967), the police 'working personality' (Skolnick, 1966) and police cynicism (Niederhoffer, 1967). By contrast the systematic investigation of the psychological attributes of British police officers has only begun to develop during the last decade. However, British sociologists since Banton (1964) have made, inter alia, essentially psychological remarks about police officers. Those psychologists who have begun to study the police have — by and large — relied upon standardised psychological tests although there have been certain exceptions (e.g. Adlam, 1982). By contrast sociological researchers have relied on surveys, questionnaires, structured and semi-structured interviews and, of course, participant observation, as methods of study. Happily a review of the British literature reveals two things: first, the psychological work parallels the findings of the sociologists; second, (and perhaps surprisingly), there is an essential congruence between the British and American findings. In consequence one can be relatively confident that the picture characterising police officers is reliable, valid and coherent; in addition this coherence extends to additional areas such as the police culture and the police organisation.

As one sifts through the various American and British publications it becomes readily apparent that certain themes recur. Policemen *are* typified. What is more, they are not just typified by disinterested academics but also by police officers themselves (e.g. McKew, 1981). How then are police officers typified? A preliminary sketch could include the following: police officers are suspicious, distrustful, cynical, impersonal, conservative, reserved, assertive, practical, expedient, controlled, clannish... and so on. One learns too that the police occupation is like no other occupation and it is this very uniqueness that reaches down into the personality structure of the officer affecting him in both predictable and idiosyncratic ways. One also learns that policemen find themselves just lower than the angels (in theory) and just above the noble *or* ignoble savage (in a range of practical settings). They are isolated yet indispensable, ambivalent towards the public they police, especially sensitive to remarks made about them and replete with opinions, beliefs and notions — about themselves — and about the society they police. Through one's own experience with police officers one notices two particular elements about their social style: firstly they are fascinated by 'motive': They like to probe into the soul. Secondly they are loath to indicate their ignorance on most matters. They are practised at bluff.

The most salient review articles which stimulated the study to be reported here (and which are full of absorbing commentaries upon the police) are those by Balch (1972), Lefkovitz (1975), Fenster, Wiedemann and Locke (1977) and Hanewicz (1978). These will be commented upon briefly: Balch (1972) chose to examine the view that the typical police officer was essentially authoritarian. After meticulous consideration of the available data he concluded that this data was inconclusive. He emphasized his misgivings about the very idea of a 'police personality'. Balch believed that, in a sense, the American police officer was just like the average middle or lower class white citizen. In his account he stressed the exigencies of the police role and the imperatives of the police organisation: role demands, Balch held, would call out authoritative behaviours and a lack of compliance with these postures would result in an authoritarian response. Thus, for Balch, the police persona impressed as authoritarian: but the police personality was 'normal'.

Lefkovitz (1975) did propose a set of characteristics distinguishing police officers from the general citizenry. He indicated that officers might be characterised according to, 'Trait Syndrome I: Isolation and Secrecy, Defensiveness and Suspiciousness, Cynicism'. (This formulation parallels in part Skolnick's (1967) earlier summary of the policeman's working personality) and, 'Trait Syndrome II: Authoritarian, Status concerns and Violence'. (This latter syndrome is essentially perjorative yet Lefkovitz regards his characterisations as evaluatively neutral!) Furthermore, Lefkovitz indicates that officers — probably in response to their status concerns — are assertive. He mentions that police officers are conservative but adds that comparatively speaking there is no evidence that police officers are psychologically unhealthy.

Fenster, Wiedemann and Locke (1977) again referred to a host of studies characterising police officers in various ways. In part their concern was to counter the unfavourable evaluations that necessarily followed these earlier characterisations but they also sought to provide social scientific data on police officers. Using a battery of psychological tests on samples of New York patrolmen and New York citizens they concluded that police officers were, in general, more intelligent, more masculine, less neurotic and more extroverted than the civilian sample. They summarized their work by saying: 'it may fairly be said that differences appearing in the data presented tend to redound to the credit of police and to suggest that they may represent a *superior* sub-sample of the general population'.

Hanewicz (1978) sought less to distinguish police officers from other occupational groups but rather to indicate that police officers were likely to share certain psychological characteristics with individuals suited to related occupations. After a somewhat original review of the literature he presented evidence that a certain type was well represented among large samples of recruit and veteran patrolmen in both Michigan and Florida. This type was essentially practical, matter-of-fact, impersonal and orderly, preferring routine and rules to spontaneity, surprises and unstructured situations. Hanewicz was keen to stress that these characteristics were also likely to be found among personnel in occupations such as law, business, accountancy and the mechanically-orientated technologies. It was this last summation of characteristics which provided the main stimulus for the present research project. Banton's (1964) remarks about police officers seemed, in large part, to be echoed by Hanewicz; Banton had described British police officers as reserved, dignified, impersonal and detached. Similarly when police officers are inclined to stereotype themselves they tend to mention the following mélange of attributes: Police officers are suspicious and not easily duped. They are practical and expedient, sceptical about theory and jaundiced about new policing schemes. They are loyal to their peers and especially reliant upon their immediate colleagues in operational contexts. Police officers agree upon the nature of real police work; this is the front-line stuff — 'where the action is'. Finally, there is consensus about the appropriate police style. Thus, officers should be cool and authoritative, should batten-down emotions and should conform with police sub-cultural norms.

Hanewicz had used an elaborate test of personality the Myers-Briggs Type Indicator to provide empirical data for his conclusions. Would British officers reflect a similar concentration of the particular types described by Hanewicz? This question represented the crux of the present study.

PROCEDURE

Several separate research groups were contacted by the author ranging from samples of recruits during their first week of training to superintendents attending command courses at the Police Staff College, Bramshill. In addition, Kakabadze[2] provided data on two other groups. All respondents referred to in this study, were male. Furthermore, all subjects were given the opportunity to remain anonymous; this latter step was regarded as crucial because previous researchers have commented upon the particularly suspicious nature of police officers and their cunning abilities to lead researchers astray either for prudential or for antagonistic reasons. The research instrument used was the Myers-Briggs Type Indicator. This is described below:

The Myers-Briggs Type Indicator:

The Myers-Briggs Type Indicator, Form F, is a 166-item, forced-choice non-pathological, self-disclosure instrument designed to implement Jung's theory of type. According to Briggs-Myers rendition of Jungian theory, an individual's personality structure develops from four basic preferences, each providing two alternative choices. The Myers-Briggs Type Indicator provides indexes for each choice: they are:

Index	Alternative Preferences
E or I	Extroversion or Introversion
S or N	Sending or Intuition
T or F	Thinking or feeling
J or P	Judgment or Perception

Thus, individuals come to prefer to use and develop one of the alternative preference functions in each of the four pairs of preferences. The preferences may be conceptualised in the following way:

1. *Extroversion v Introversion*

   If the individual prefers the 'extroverted' mode, perception and judgment are directed upon the external environment. Psychological energy is outer-directed. If the individual prefers the 'introverted' mode, perception and judgment are directed towards the internal world of ideas, cogitations and so on. Psychological energy is inner-directed.

2. *Sensing v Intuition*

   If the individual prefers the 'sensing' mode the person prefers to work with known facts. Consciousness seeks the concrete and tangible. If the individual prefers the 'intuitive' mode consciousness is drawn towards hypothesis, conjecture, reflection, imaginings and the search for possibilities and probabilities.

3. *Thinking v Feeling*

   If the individual prefers 'thinking' reliance is placed on logical and analytical judgment. A certain impersonal aura characterises the person with the thinking preference. If the individual prefers 'feeling' judgments are based more on personal values rather than impersonal analysis and logic. A correlate of this preference is a certain warmth of personality and a touch of sentimentality.

4. *Judgment v Perception*

   If the individual prefers to use the 'judging' attitude, a planned, decided, orderly way of life is preferred to a flexible and more spontaneous one. If the individual prefers to use the 'perceptive' attitude a consciousness and life-style emerge where new ideas are pursued, new experiences are sought and new ways of doing things are entertained.

   Those who prefer judgment *like to reach decisions*. Those who prefer perception have a hunch that more information may be necessary before coming to a conclusion and/or making a decision. They may procrastinate.

   Hanewicz (1978, 158) writes: 'Thus with four basic preferences, each carrying two alternative choices, sixteen personality type categories are possible under this conceptual framework. Each combination of preferences provides an explanatory basis for behavioural traits peculiar to it . . .'

   These 16 possible combinations are described next:

The Myers-Briggs Type Indicator Preference Combinations
(The 16 types)

| | Sensing Types | | Intuitive Types | |
	With Thinking	With Feeling	With Thinking	With Feeling
Extroverts Judging	ESTJ	ESFJ	ENTJ	ENFJ
Extroverts Perceptive	ESTP	ESFP	ENTP	ENFP
Introverts Judging	ISTJ	ISFJ	INTJ	INFJ
Introverts Perceptive	ISTP	ISFP	INTP	INFP

In essence then, the Myers-Briggs Type Indicator developed by Briggs and Briggs-Myers builds upon Jung's theory of type and considers that behaviours, interests and attractions emerge from the particular combinations of the type characteristics.

The initial research sample: A group of 100 Inspectors and Chief Inspectors attending the Junior Command Course at Bramshill were tested in small groups varying in size between 9 and 14. Hanewicz had found a preponderance of the ESTJ and the ISTJ types in his American samples. The first part of this study sought to test the hypothesis that British police middle-managers would reflect a similar concentration of those types reported by Hanewicz.

The results were as follows:

The distribution of type combinations for 100 inspectors
and chief inspectors.

Types	Total number of Cases	Percentage
ISTJ	36	36%
ESTJ	25	25%
ISTP	3	3%
ESTP	2	2%
ISFJ	2	2%
ESFJ	6	6%
ISFP	1	1%
ESFP	2	2%
INFJ	2	2%
ENFJ	1	1%
JNFP	3	3%
ENFP	2	2%
INTJ	4	4%
ENTJ	5	5%
INTP	5	5%
ENTP	1	1%

The table indicates the particularly striking concentration of officers within one of two type combinations — the ISTJ and ESTJ types. Together these two types account for 61% of the sample.

The table also indicates the relative absence of the 'NF' combination among inspectors and chief inspectors. This combination occurred in only 8% of the total sample.

The original data published by Hanewicz (1978) feature in the next table which provides the first opportunity for comparison.

The distribution of type combinations among U.S. patrolmen
N = 1,282 (Source: W.B. Hanewicz 1978)

Types	Total number of Cases	Percentage
ISTJ	179	14.0%
ESTJ	265	20.7%
ISTP	108	8.4%
ESTP	98	7.6%
ISFJ	94	7.3%
ESFJ	117	9.1%
ISFP	70	5.5%
ESFP	60	4.7%
INFJ	12	0.9%
ENFJ	19	1.5%
INFP	40	3.1%
ENFP	52	4.1%
INTJ	29	2.3%
ENTJ	55	4.3%
INTP	31	2.4%
ENTP	53	4.1%

The data provided by Hanewicz compare with the British sample in particularly fascinating ways: firstly, although the American sample reveals that 34.7% fell into either the ISTJ or ESTJ type combinations, British officers appear to cluster ever more densely in these combinations. This was confirmed using the Z test of significance (comparing sample proportion with sample proportion). Thus at the 99% level of confidence one is able to conclude that the British sample contains significantly more ISTJ and ESTJ types than the American patrolmen.

Among the American patrolmen there was a similar absence of the 'NF' type combination. 8% of the British sample reflected this combination whilst 9.6% of the American sample reflected these types.

Before explaining the psychological characteristics of the ISTJ and ESTJ types a replication of the initial British finding was attempted. Here the main objective was to investigate the possibility that the original finding was an anomaly. In consequence, a further 100 inspectors and chief inspectors attending subsequent Junior Command Courses at Bramshill were sampled and tested in small groups under anonymous conditions. The next table describes the results.

The distribution of type combinations for 100 inspectors and chief inspectors

Types	Total Number of Cases	Percentage
ISTJ	39	39%
ESTJ	21	21%
ISTP	5	5%
ESTP	2	2%
ISFJ	1	1%
ESFJ	2	2%
ISFP	2	2%
ESFP	4	4%
INFJ	3	3%
ENFJ	0	0%
INFP	4	4%
ENFP	1	1%
INTJ	2	2%
ENTJ	6	6%
INTP	4	4%
ENTP	4	4%

The two samples of 100 inspectors and chief inspectors display a virtually indistinguishable pattern. Once again, the main features of the data are: 60% of the sample fall into either the ISTJ or ESTJ type combinations with a rather higher incidence of ISTJ types. The NF combination and the SF combination are conspicuously under-represented whilst the NT combination scarcely fares any better.

The next table combines the data for the two separate samples of inspectors and chief inspectors at Bramshill.

The distribution of type combinations for 200 inspectors
and chief inspectors

Types	Total Number of Cases	Percentage
ISTJ	75	37.4%
ESTJ	46	23.0%
ISTP	8	4.0%
ESTP	4	2.0%
ISFJ	3	1.5%
ESFJ	8	4.0%
ISFP	3	1.5%
ESFP	6	3.0%
INFJ	5	2.5%
ENFJ	1	0.5%
INFP	7	3.5%
ENFP	3	1.5%
INTJ	6	3.0%
ENTJ	11	5.5%
INTP	8	4.0%
ENTP	6	3.0%

Thus the study of 200 police inspectors and chief inspectors revealed that 121 fell into one of the two type combinations. Stated differently, 6 out of every 10 officers tested were either an ISTJ or an ESTJ type. This result indicates that British officers (albeit of more senior rank) differ significantly from the American patrolmen. The difference is one of accentuation; whilst Hanewicz (1978) was impressed with the fact that 1 in 3 patrolmen were either ISTJ or ESTJ, the samples described here emphasize these attributes at significantly higher concentrations.

(It should be noted at this juncture that one other sample of British police officers was compared with the American patrolmen described by Hanewicz: A sample of 63 experienced constables gathered from 9 separate forces was given the Myers-Briggs Type Indicator and the results differed once again, from the American patrolmen sample. Thus, a Z test (comparing sample proportion with sample proportion) revealed that at the 99% level of confidence the experienced constables were more concentrated among the ISTJ and ESTJ types than their American counterparts).

How might one describe the psychological and behavioural charac-teristics of the two dominant types found among the middle-management ranks of the British police service? Briggs-Myers (1962, Appendix A.

A.6) discusses the ISTJ or Introverted sensing type in the following way: 'This combination makes the super-dependable. He has a complete, realistic, practical respect for the facts. He likes everything put on a factual basis, clearly stated and not too unfamiliar or complex... He is the most thorough of all types, painstaking, systematic, hard-working and patient with detail and routine... He is an obvious choice for the responsibilities of maintenance... He will go to any amount of trouble if he can see the need of it but he does "hate to be saddled with a policy that doesn't make sense".' Hanewicz (1978 p.164) offers a more pithy description: 'Such persons are painstaking, thorough and useful in their attention to detail. They tend to be matter-of-fact rather than imaginative and can adapt easily to routine.' ISTJs are prone to use logic and analysis and are decisive.

It is important to recognise that ISTJs and ESTJs share many characteristics: Briggs-Meyers :1962, Appendix A, A-1) characterises the ESTJ or Extroverted thinking type as follows: 'He has a great respect for impersonal truth thought out plans and orderly efficiency. He is analytic, impersonal, objectively critical and not likely to be convinced by anything but reasoning. He organises facts, situations, and operations well in advance and makes a systematic effort to reach his carefully planned objectives on schedule... He enjoys being an executive and puts a great deal of himself into such a job. He likes to decide what ought to be done and to give the requisite orders. He abhors confusion and inefficiency... Being a judging type he may neglect perception. He needs to stop, look and listen to other people's points of view.' Hanewicz(1978 p.163) offers another succinct description: 'They (the ESTJs) are:

1) Analytical and impersonal
2) Good at organizing facts or anything close within reach
3) Decisive

and 4) Prone to value truth in the form of fact, formula and method.'

He concludes: ESTJs are more prone to matter-of factness and practicality, more receptive and retentive of factual detail, more tolerant of routine... and more realistic than other types.'

As long ago as 1964 Banton noted that police officers were reserved, dignified, impersonal and detached. The predominant type, reported in this research is the ISTJ type and this type meshes well with Banton's description. When one recalls the ways in which police officers typify themselves then the ISTJ and ESTJ types provide rather accurate confirmation of those typifications.

Briggs-Myers recognises the ability of ESTJs to be vigorous executives and the ISTJs to be dependable administrators. To some extent the fact that these two types are so predominant among the police officers sampled and especially among the middle-management strata of the service is appropriate and reassuring in the context of organisation efficiency and intra-personal harmony. However, both Briggs-Myers and Hanewicz note deficiencies about these individuals; Hanewicz for example, remarks (p.164): 'Lacking adequate development of the feeling (F) dimension to balance the thinking (T) preference, both ISTJs and ESTJs may experience difficulty in human relationships.' He then quotes Briggs-Myers (1980): 'They are much more prone to use the judging attitude when the perceptive attitude would be more appropriate'. Thus, ISTJs and ESTJs can make judgments too hastily.

The major problem with the study reported above (and that published by Hanewicz) centres upon the absence of any appropriate data for purposes of comparison. All that has been demonstrated is that a prevalence of the ISTJ and ESTJ type combination occurs among police officers. How though do police officers compare with others? Hanewicz did report differences between other groups[3] and the police but the present study proceeded to address a slightly different question: How do British police officers in the middle-management ranks compare with middle-managers in a variety of other occupations?

In order to build up an appropriate police sample, a further 104 superintendents attending command courses at Bramshill were tested in 4 separate groups. Test completion was again conducted under conditions guaranteeing the anonymity of the officers.

The results were:

The distribution of type combinations for 104 superintendents.

Type	Total Number of Cases	Percentage
ISTJ	40	38.5%
ESTJ	21	20.2%
JSTP	4	3.8%
ESTP	3	2.9%
ISFJ	7	6.7%
ESFJ	4	3.8%
ISFP	1	0.9%
ESFP	1	0.9%
INFJ	1	0.9%
ENFJ	0	0.0%
INFP	1	0.9%
ENFP	4	3.8%
INTJ	6	5.8%
ENTJ	8	7.7%
INTP	0	0.0%
ENTP	3	2.9%

Once again, the pattern observed among the two earlier samples of inspectors and chief inspectors repeats itself. Here, 58.65% of the superintendents fall into either the ISTJ or ESTJ type combination. Again, the ISTJ combination occurs with the highest frequency and again the NF combination is scarcely represented. No significant differences were found between this sample and the previous samples of inspectors and chief inspectors. We can now amalgamate the data found on 304 officers tested at the Police Staff College:

The distribution of type combinations for inspectors, chief inspectors, and superintendents N = 304.

Types	Number	Percentage
ISTJ	115	37.82%
ESTJ	67	22.04%
ISTP	12	3.95%
ESTP	7	2.30%
ISFJ	10	3.29%
ESFJ	12	3.95%
ISFP	4	1.32%
ESFP	7	2.30%
INFJ	6	1.97%
ENFJ	1	0.33%
INFP	8	2.63%
ENFP	7	2.30%
INTJ	12	3.95%
ENTJ	19	6.25%
INTP	8	2.63%
ENTP	9	2.96%

This represents the distribution of types found among a large sample of police officers occupying middle-management positions within the police service.

1. 59.86% are ISTJ or ESTJ
2. 76.98% are Sensing (Practical) types whilst
   23.02% are Intuitive (Theoretical) types
3. 81.91% are Thinking (Impersonal) types whilst
   18.09% are Feeling (Warm) types
4. 79.6% are Judging types whilst
   20.4% are Perceptive types
5. 57.56% are Introverted types whilst
   42.44% are Extroverted types

Kakabadze provided data on a sample of 374 middle-managers in industry, the professions and the semi-professions. He indicated that this sample could usefully be taken to represent a comparison group, for the police middle-management sample. (Unfortunately his data simply reported the number of individuals falling into each *separate* type category. How the categories combined together for each individual is unknown). The next table compares the police data with the non-police data in terms of numbers within each type category:

Police managers and non-police managers compared.

Police N = 304		*Non-Police* N = 374	
Introverts	Extroverts	Introverts	Extroverts
175 (58%)	129 (42%)	183 (49%)	191 (51%)
Sensing	Intuitive	Sensing	Intuitive
234 (77%)	70 (23%)	258% (69%)	116 (31%)
Thinking	Feeling	Thinking	Feeling
249 (82%)	55 (18%)	269 (72%)	105 (28%)
Judging	Perceptive	Judging	Perceptive
242 (80%)	62 (20%)	284 (76%)	90 (24%)

What emerges from an inspection of this table is that middle-managers in industry, the professions, the semi-professions and the police tend to be sensing (factual) thinking (impersonal) and judging (decisive) types. Non-police managers are inclined to be extroverted whereas police managers are more likely to be introverted. (Adlam (1978) using the E.P.I. had already found that police inspectors were somewhat introverted.)

One might say that to be sensing, thinking and judging is to be normal. The STJ type dominates in the police sample, may well dominate in Kakabadze's sample and certainly represents a relatively high proportion of high-school students sampled by Briggs-Myers. Nonetheless, the two samples were compared to see whether the police managers differed from their counterparts in other occupations. The Z test of significance was used. In each instance sample proportion was compared with sample proportion. The results are tabulated below:

Police sample and non-police sample compared using
the Z test of significance.

1. Police proportion of Introverts v Non-police proportion of Introverts
   $Z = 2.259$ Difference significant at 95% level of confidence.
2. Police proportion of Sensing types v Non-police proportion of Sensing Types
   $Z = 2.32$ Difference significant at 95% level of confidence.
3. Police proportion of thinking types v Non-police proportion of thinking types.
   $Z = 3.058$ Difference significant at 99% level of confidence.
4. Police proportion of Judging types v Non-police proportion of Judging types.
   $Z = 1.142$ Difference *not* significant.

Thus, significance testing revealed that the police middle-manager sample is more introverted, more sensing (factual) and more thinking (impersonal and detached) than the sample of middle-managers. The samples did not differ significantly on the judgment/perception dimension. Overall then one finds that in the context of their working environments police middle-managers impress as a group who like an established routine, are patient with details, are relatively unemotional and are best when they can plan their work and are left to follow that plan. The slight predominance of introverted types reminds one of the reserve which some have said to be so characteristic of many police officers.

DISCUSSION AND CONCLUSION

The first and second parts of this particular investigation into the psychological characteristics of police officers occupying the middle-management ranks in the police service had been accomplished. The results indicated that British police officers were more homogenous in type than American patrolmen; furthermore the data supported the idea of a 'typical' policeman because of the especially high concentration of STJ types. Even though these types are well represented among non-police middle-managers, statistically significant differences were found when the two groups were compared. The emerging differences featured higher levels of introverted, sensing and thinking types among the police sample. From the Myers-Briggs Type Indicator a composite picture may be developed where, in general, police officers could be described as a trifle reserved, factual in orientation and impersonal in cognitive style. In addition the proportion of judging types indicates their preference for reaching decisions and working in environments where control, order, stability and predictability are the norm[4].

The present data complements previous studies reporting the psychological characteristics of British police officers. Some of these reports will be mentioned to highlight the points of congruence: Gudjonsson and Adlam (1983) studied a group of 112 inspectors, chief inspectors and superintendents (as well as groups of more junior ranking officers) using two tests of personality. The first test (the E.P.Q.) measured, among other things, Introversion and Extroversion. Whilst the police samples were not significantly more introverted than the normative control group they tended towards introversion. The EPQ also revealed that the sample scored significantly lower on the psychoticism scale compared with the control group. Low scores on psychoticism are associated with rule-adherence and conformity, a finding which enhances the claims made by Briggs-Myers and Hanewicz about the psychological properties of the STJ types.

Gudjonsson and Adlam (1983) also used a relatively new psychological test, the I 5, on this same group of 112 police officers. The results of this part of the study become more significant when compared with the type data revealed by The Myers-Briggs Type Indicator. The I 5 measures venturesomeness, impulsivity and empathy. The police sample obtained low scores on all these scales. Low scores on empathy are consistent with the low incidence of the Feeling type. Persons who score high on venturesomeness and impulsivity are more likely to be out-going risk-takers, qualities not associated with the rather fastidious dependability of the ISTJ type or the relatively rule-bound ESTJ type.

Adlam (1982) published the results of an essentially phenomenological study of inspectors and chief inspectors attending the Police Staff College, Bramshill. Here, in a more idiographic sense, officers were asked to indicate how they perceived developments in their own personality during their careers in the police service. Themes and patterns were found to emerge: by and large, an emotional hardening was experienced. In addition officers found themselves conforming to the over-arching police culture with its distrust of intellectuals and its positive regard for commonsense and the practical man. These self-perceived developments in personality structure provide excellent corroborative data for the dominant characteristics described by the Myers-Briggs Type Indicator.

Furthermore, material from an unpublished study by Adlam (1980) endorses this overall impression of the general qualities displayed by police managers. Here the instrument used was the Rokeach Value Survey — an instrument with a long history of use among some American researchers. Two samples were obtained, one comprising 40 superintendents and the other 137 inspectors and chief inspectors. On the instrumental value scale (a scale including 18 values concerned with desired states to be sought and maintained in everyday life) both groups ranked 'Honesty' and being 'Responsible' highest. However, they placed 'Forgiving' and 'Helpful' towards the lower end of the hierarchy and the values 'Intellectual' and 'Imaginative' were found at the bottom of the scale. Once again this evidence is concordant with the scarcity of the feeling and intuitive types among the 304 middle-ranking police officers.

Finally it should be noted that other groups of police officers ranging from samples of recruits to sergeants on the Special Course at Bramshill up to Chief Constables and Deputy Chief Constables have been tested (the latter group by Kakabadze) using the Myers-Briggs Type Indicator. This data indicates that the STJ profile is developed through police experience although the sample of experienced constables already mentioned reported slightly lower levels of thinking. The experienced constables were interesting because they reported even *lower* levels of intuition than the inspectors, chief inspectors and superintendents. Whilst intuition is quite rare among police middle-managers it is almost unknown among the experienced constables. The Special Course sergeants did differ significantly from both the experienced constables and the middle-management police group. There tended to be less STJs among them (40%) and a much higher incidence of the NT type (38%). This finding warrants further comment: The NT combination often enables an individual to excel at dispassionate rational analysis and multi-criteria decision making. Thus, the Special Course sergeants may well provide some of those additional qualities that appear to be too under-represented in the middle-managerial ranks of the police service.

The present study confirms and extends an impression of police officers held by police and academics alike. Thus police officers have been characterised as impersonal, matter-of-fact, emotionally hard, decisive and somewhat reserved. Original data presented in this article provides strong, empirical support for these notions. That these notions date back to 1964 provides fitting testimony to Banton's excellent insightfulness. Furthermore, current research projects provide strongly corroborative data for the general findings highlighted by the Myers-Briggs Type Indicator.

At one level, the data augurs well for the police organisation. ISTJs and ESTJs impress as reliable administrators and dependable executives. On the other hand one is left with the inescapable impression that the very preponderance of this types ossifies that same police organisation. Current ideas in management training argue that managers should be developed to cope with change and uncertainty rather than permanence and fixity. Officers who are relatively unusual types — especially in the context of the police occupation — have problems. They are likely to report a range of frustrations, specific stressors and other dis-satisfactions with their life in the police service. Many of their frustrations seem to relate to the sense of suffocation and constraint they feel within their working environment. For some, specialisation may provide the answer but whilst the general police culture still holds to a conception of 'real police work' which necessarily denigrates certain specialist roles the specialist may well find that his work is not especially valued by his colleagues. Worse still, his own personal attributes may be the subject of some vilification. These assaults on the self are hard to bear, and difficult to counter in the general organisational milieu.

It is interesting to note that data supplied by Kakabadse on the type characteristics of the most senior police personnel suggest something of a reversal of the pattern found among the experienced constables, inspectors, chief inspectors and superintendents. Although Kakabadse's sample was small (N = 35) his chief constables and deputy chief constables revealed more extroverted than introverted types, more intuitive than sensing types, an equal number of thinking and feeling types and finally more perceptive than judging types. Thus, were one to typify the most senior officers one would be more likely to comment on their out-goingness, their concern with hypothesis, idea and theory and their preference for making decisions after careful appreciation of the multiple sources of information at their disposal. It is not clear whether this set of attributes is developed in role or whether chief officers and their deputies are selected because of their personality structure. Jung's original theory of type does not offer much assistance on this matter although one is inclined to believe that personality is not especially susceptible to change and the STJ individual is less likely to reach the very highest positions in the service.

Lastly, a note of caution should be sounded in relation to the whole enterprise of aggregating individuals into psychological types. As long ago as 1948, Kluckhohn and Murray made the remark: 'Every man is in certain respects a) like all other men, b) like some other men and c) like no other man'. This article has, of course, concentrated upon the similarities among men within a certain occupation. Policemen also *share* countless attributes with all other men. They impress, too, as singular men. In the context of the study of personality it does no harm to recall Niehzsche's maxim: 'What we do in dreams we also do when we are awake: we invent and fabricate the person with whom we associate — and immediately forget we have done so.' The Myers-Briggs Type Indicator may well 'invent' and 'fabricate' the person but co-incidentally those inventions and fabrications are consonant with earlier typifications of police officers.

Marcel Proust had much to say about experiencing others and noted the existence of 'successive personalities'. One often notices this with policemen — but, once again, there is pattern in these 'successive personalities' and behind the personae one senses those common attributes described above.

REFERENCES AND NOTES

Adlam K. R. C. (1978), Extroversion and Neuroticism Among Police Inspectors. Unpublished paper.

Adlam K. R. C. (1980), Police Values. Unpublished paper.

Adlam K. R. C. (1982), The Police Personality: Psychological Consequence of Being a Police Officer. J. of Pol. Sci. and Admin. Vol. 10 No. 3 344–350.

Balch R. W. (1972), The Police Personality: Fact or Fiction? J. Crim. L., C. and P. S. 63(1): 106–119.

Banton M. (1964), *The Policeman in the Community*, Tavistock Publications.

Briggs-Myers I. (1962), The Myers-Briggs Type Indicator. Manual. Consulting Psychologists Press California.

Briggs-Myers I. (1980), Consequences of Psychological Type. Unpublished research.

Butler A. J. P. and Cochrane R. (1977), An examination of Some Elements of the Personality of Police Officers and Their Implications. J. Police Sci. and Admin. 5(4): 441–450.

Cochrane R. and Butler A. J. P. (1980), The Values of Police Officers, Recruits and Civilians in England. J. Police Sci. and Admin. 8(2): 205–212.

Fenster C. A. and Wiedemann C. F and Locke B. (1977), Police Personality — Social Science Folklore and Psychological Measurement in Sales B. D. (Ed.). Psychology in the Legal Process, Spectrum Publications, New York.

Gudjonsson G. and Adlam K. R. C. (1983), Personality patterns of British Police Officers. J. Person. Individ. Diff. 4(5) 507–512.

Hanewicz W. B. (1978), Police Personality: a Jungian perspective J. Crime and Delinquency 24, 152–172.

Kluckhohn and Murray (1948), Personality Formation: The Determinants in Hollander E. P., and Hunt R. G. (Eds.) (1972) Classic Contribution to *Social Psychology*, Oxford University Press.

Lefkovitz J. (1975), Psychological Attributes of Policemen: a Review of Research and Opinion. J. Social Issues 31, 3–26.

Levy R. J. (1967), Predicting Police Failures. J. Crim. Law. Crimin. Police Sci. 58, 265–276.

Manning P. K. (1978), Police and Crime: Crime and Police. Sociologische Gibs July 1978 pp. 487–501.

Manning P. K. (1982), Organizational Work: Structuration of Environments. Brit. J. of Soc. 23(1) 118–134.

McKew (1981), A Police Personality: Fact or Myth? Bramshill Journal 1(3) 23–30.

Niederhoffer A. (1967), *Behind the Shield*, Doubleday and Co., New York.

Nietzsche F. (1973), *Beyond Good and Evil*, Penguin Classics.

Reiner R. (1978), *The Blue-Coated Worker*, Cambridge University Press.

Skolnick J. (1966), *Justice Without Trial*, John Wiley and Son Inc.

Notes:
1. The line is from the song 'Desolation Row' featured on 'Highway 61, Revisited'.
2. Professor A. Kakabadse provided a wealth of very useful data on the Myers-Briggs Type Indicator. This research proved to be very valuable.
3. Those other groups reported by Hanewicz may have been slightly inappropriate for purposes of comparison.

4. There is a certain irony here when one considers the Policy Study Institutes' findings on police management.
   See, Police and People in London
   Policy Studies Institute, especially Vol IV;
   The Police in Action by David J. Smith and Jeremy Gray.

Developments and problems in police-community relations

D. W. POPE

As 1983 closes the police, and many members of the public, are actively engaged in discussion and debate of the relationship between police forces and the communities whom they serve. It is an area of fundamental concern at a time when both police and citizens perceive a distancing to have developed between them; in essence it is a fear that a system of law enforcement has gradually evolved in which the element of public consent has been diluted as the police themselves have increasingly professionalised their occupation.

In examining the developments in, and the problems arising from, police community relations activities, it is as well that we begin by defining the so-called 'preventive' or 'pro-active' aspects of the policing task of which community relations is the vital constituent. They have been very adequately discussed, and persuasively argued, by John Alderson[1]; as then Chief Constable of Devon and Cornwall it was his view that:

> 'Of all the strategies of policing it is the preventive one which is superior. It is superior in the ethical sense, since by preventing crime it saves people from their follies and the moral obloquy which confrontation with the criminal justice system brings' (p. 38).

He then goes on to outline the 'primary prevention' or 'pro-active policing' task which he sees as 'any lawful form of human activity which results in a diminution of conduct forbidden by the criminal law' (p. 39).

Those police activities which are primarily geared toward crime prevention, or best lend themselves to being adapted to it, are delineated in the papers of the Ditchley Conference of 1977[2] on 'Preventive Policing':

1. A visible police presence — but especially that of uniformed beat patrol.
2. Crime prevention in its narrowest sense — such as advice upon security of premises.
3. Road safety and accident prevention.
4. Juvenile liaison.
5. Schools liaison.
6. Public relations.
7. Community relations.

All of these contrast markedly with the 'reactive' or 'fire-brigade' type of policing where police respond to events.

In trying to account for the present emphasis upon preventive policing and community relations, it is my intention to concentrate upon the last two decades because it is here, in my submission, that we locate the critical point where — for the first time since a modern police force was established — the police-public relationship was diagnosed as in need of a fundamental reappraisal. From that diagnosis has emerged the preventive policing and community relations movement.

Further elaboration is needed, however, of the concept of 'community relations'. It is not merely the placing of more men back on the beat, nor the devising of Neighbourhood Watch Schemes; rather it is the revitalising of the whole tradition of policing by consent by increasing the level of trust of the community in its police, by fostering a deeper understanding by the police of community problems and community needs.

To achieve these ends police seek to liaise and work with other agencies, consult their public, and stimulate the self-policing capacities of communities themselves. In so doing police provide initiatives and leadership, draw interested parties together, and tailor their policing to neighbourhood needs. Far more is entailed, in other words, than what some doubting policemen would have us believe when they label these developments as 're-inventing the wheel'.

With these definitions in mind one turns to a society which was still seen in the years immediately following the Second World War as enjoying a very mild form of policing that had been built upon a long-established law enforcement system characterised by:

1. roots deeply buried in the community;
2. which stemmed from an early structure of law almost wholly oriented towards peace-keeping and public tranquillity;
3. in turn giving rise to the peculiarly local institution of the office of Constable, an office interwoven with the normal obligations of citizenship.

Thus, when a structured system of policing finally emerged with paid law enforcement officers, it was strongly argued in terms of the need to police by the consent and co-operation of the public.

With this mild policing, which was local in nature and given popular support, went a reputation for justice and fairness which had gained an international reputation for the British police service. The community relations and preventive policing dimension of its duties were primarily discharged by the urban foot patrol officer and the village bobby.

'Popular support' does not mean, incidentally, general popularity. As Schaffer[3] has pointed out, for example, the police may never be popular; they remind us of our weaknesses, foolishness and irrationality, they see us at times we might best wish to forget, present an authority which is restrictive upon our perceived freedom, and bring a cynicism to their view of human nature. At one stage she writes, 'It is inevitable that a police service should not be particularly popular' (p. 14).

Whatever the standing of the police in the eyes of the public we see, in the amalgamations of 1968 and 1974, the creation of 47 police forces in which, by the latter year, there had begun to emerge — certainly in those forces containing the bulk of New Commonwealth settlement — the institutionalising of the community relations function into full-time H.Q. departments or a system of part-time divisional and sub-divisional responsibility.

If we look at:

The Metropolitan Police
Greater Manchester
Leicestershire
Merseyside
Nottinghamshire
South Yorkshire
West Yorkshire
West Midlands
Thames Valley

then all had force H.Q. departments with the equivalent of Force Community Relations Officers (the title varied between forces). The immigrant liaison work in the Thames Valley was subsumed, at that time, within the 'Press and Public Relations Department'[4]. Bedfordshire had a part-time C.R.O. who was also Head of Planning and Inspection; Derbyshire's C.R.O. was full-time but part of the Inspection and Development Department. These details are worth mentioning since the whole community relations movement was new, by no means nationally thought out, and varied between forces. This was a period of experimentation in structures and functions; forces were feeling their way and concerned with such things as whether or not to have a full-time C.R.O., the level at which to pitch the rank, the staffing requirements and the job tasks.

BUT WHAT BROUGHT THE MOVEMENT ABOUT?

I have already pointed, albeit briefly, to the relevant antecedents in the historical development of our policing system that argue and buttress the 'community consciousness' of our police. The service nature of policing is strongly evident[5] and it is hardly surprising that that should be so when one considers that, from their inception, forces had specific welfare functions (aspects of Poor-Law administration for example) and voluntarily took upon themselves welfare interests within their communities (such as the Boot-and-Shoe and Soup Funds which could be seen in industrial borough forces in the earlier part of this century).

One should also be mindful of the police concern for young people as a further instance of involvement in the community.[6] As early as 1905 we see, in the Glasgow City Police, a formal 'Warning' (i.e. cautioning) system operating for juveniles; parents were invited to a 'Superintendent's Court'. It was in Scotland, too, that David Gray, Chief Constable of Greenock, established a Juvenile Liaison Scheme — though the first specialist provision for young people had come in the Liverpool City Police in 1949.

In the context of the English forces which I have specified it is, however, difficult to pick out the exact appointment of officers to community relations posts. Amalgamations make this a complex research task, as indeed does the poor record keeping, by some forces, of community-related initiatives.

However a major development that marked, in my view, the genesis of a structured system of police community relations, came in Scotland in the 1960s. The launching of a community project in the Weir Street — Ladyburn area of Greenock by David Gray[7] was stimulated by what he saw as the hopelessness of police efforts to combat the anti-social behaviour of youth in a deprived environment. The police were initiators of a scheme which incorporated liaison with statutory and voluntary services. The point to be made is that this attack on crime is what one might call *social crime prevention* and it contrasts sharply with conventional ideas about *physical crime prevention*. It is also significant that problems which arose then are problems which still fester in police community relations work — how far police should engage in work of this kind, whether it is a proper policing role, and the animosity it can generate within police organisations by those who see it as a 'soft option' in dealing with offenders.

Even as late as 1974 we see, in a Report of a Strathclyde Working Unit[8], a reference (p. 12) to:

'...considerable disapproval, open and otherwise, by some police officers toward community relations... The chief opposition comes from those officers who believe that a 'hard line' or uncompromising approach is the way to settle all problems... nuts and bolts crime prevention is acceptable, all other preventative measures with young people in the community or in schools is a waste of time and not, in any case, really a matter for the police'.

Yet the Scottish experience is valuable because:

1. It was the pioneering of community relations in the form of a project (by David Gray) which set a pattern for forces in England and Wales to follow.

2. The absence of colour ethnic minorities does give substance to the view that the police community relatiòns movement was not solely a product of an immigrant presence.

Similar developments, often drawing upon the Scottish initiatives, were going on in forces which had New Commonwealth settlers, and in those forces we can argue a general progression along these lines:

(a) The Asian and Afro-caribbean ethnic presence was helping to give much greater visibility to the problems of inner-city areas.
(b) In particular, forces found difficulties of communication and of understanding sub-cultural practices.
(c) Thus the initial response was to appoint staff to a liaison function normally as part of their wider policing duty. Such officers were called Community Relations or Community Liaison Officers.

Even before the Notting Hill incidents of 1958 such appointments could be distinguished in the Metropolitan Police and the disturbances stimulated further staff recruitment to the liaison task. Local Liaison Committees were in evidence by the 1960s on which police would be represented by their Community Relations Officers. In 1967 we had the setting up of A7, the Community Relations Department of the force; it was no accident one feels, that this was the year before the creation of the Community Relations Commission.

In provincial forces the same moves were afoot. By the mid-60s Bradford City Police were using liaison officers, including Asian members of the public. Full-time Community Relations Officers had been appointed in Birmingham City, Manchester City and Salford City by 1967 and as amalgamations took place so some Headquarters Departments appeared with a wide-ranging responsibility for community relations and headed by a Force Community Relations Officer (as in 1974 in the West Midlands Constabulary).

There were many factors at work in this policing development in which one could include:

(i) Police initiatives and experiments within forces themselves.
(ii) Home Office and Inspectorate leadership; the Home Office Memorandum on 'Police and Coloured Communities' of July 1967 was a good example of this, as was the setting up of a Senior Officers' Race Relations Course in conjunction with the Extra-Mural Department of the University of Manchester (1966).
(iii) Changes in law; the Children and Young Persons' Act of 1969 had, for instance, wide implications for the role of police in relation to juveniles and in relation to other social agencies.

(iv) The Church; the Church Assembly Board was quite active in promoting public thinking about community relations in the late '60s and early '70s[9].

The cumulative effect of these, and many other diverse pressures, was a growing degree of interest in the policing of ethnic settlement. Thus:

1971: Working Party on 'Police Training in Race Relations'.
1972: (1) Report of the Working Party on Race Relations and Immigration.
       (2) Report of the Select Committee on Race Relations and Immigration: 'Police Immigrant Relations'.
1973: Home Office 'Observations on the Working Party Report'.

The amalgamations of 1974 provided the opportunity for the restructuring of existing Police Community Relations Departments and the establishing of new. In that same year the first national meeting of Force Community Relations Officers was held at Hendon and a regional structure was set up to allow such officers to meet more regularly and at a more parochial level. It is worth adding that a further national meeting in 1976 appears to have been the end of such an initiative although the regional structure has continued to function in a sporadic manner.

By the mid-'70s there was a much wider recognition of the magnitude of the problems facing the inner city and most forces with ethnic communities had a community relations structure of some kind with a variety of tasks[10] such as:

(a) *West Midlands*: To generally co-ordinate the work of other departments in the context of public relations; to develop internal training and awareness of community relations matters; to supply lecturers, deal with visitors, liaise with High Commissioners and assume an overall responsibility for community relations within the force.

(b) *Leicestershire*: To train all members of the force in all aspects of police community relations; to examine the methods of dealing with juvenile offenders and to establish a centralised system of regulating the prosecuting of offenders; to establish a dialogue with local immigrants, especially their leaders; to arrange talks to them by police officers and vice-versa; to conduct or make similar arrangements to deal with problems; to be a clearing house to exchange information and eliminate mistrust and differences; to inaugurate and supervise an extensive police schools relationship scheme.

Looking across the U.K. forces at that time one notes a tremendous emphasis upon establishing a dialogue with the Community (especially immigrants in the Metropolitan forces), upon the need for the public to co-operate in the policing task, and upon police contacts with youth. What was not quite so apparent was a national climate in which the return of men to the beat was regarded as critical — although, in the forces of ethnic settlement, there was a marked concern for deploying foot patrols of a 'home beat' type and systems were experimented with which Force Community Relations Officers saw as essential to those specific areas.

A most important point to be made at this stage is the rejection by Force Community Relations Officers that their work was wholly brought about, and wholly geared to, ethnic minorities; the Scottish experience certainly rebuts this thesis in the case of Scotland. Later developments in Devon and Cornwall could be used to rebut the thesis when applied to English and Welsh forces; in the Royal Ulster Constabulary, similarly, for Northern Ireland. What my own research suggested[11] was that senior officers in community relations work saw the movement as inevitable — ethnic minorities had simply accelerated its coming about.

Even more important was the consistent argument advanced at that time[12] that community relations work stemmed from traditional police concerns for public consent to, and acceptance of, the policing endeavour. Thus the underpinning philosophy appeared to be that the whole nature of British policing was 'of and for the people', that there was a tradition of service to the community which was a characteristic of our policing system, and a rightful emphasis upon the prevention of crime at which community relations was essentially aimed.

One should also add the belief that community relations developments were reflecting a police apprehension of the many and speedy changes taking place in society. Policemen felt that what they were now attempting to do in the inner city was itself making visible their own cognizance of social change, it was spelling out far more clearly their service objectives, even indicating a new emphasis in policing and a new role for police as a greater awareness was growing of community needs.

There were problems to be seen in the newly arising community relations structures and procedures. Not least of these were:

(1) *FUNCTIONAL*: It is difficult to delineate a particular rationale at work in the allocation of functions to community relations departments. Many, for example, included work with juveniles and schools liaison: others did not. As the later '70s witnessed, however, there did grow up a tendency to embrace preventive policing functions in their more general sense in addition to those of community relations.

(2) *STRUCTURAL*: The kinds of questions involved in this context were to do with whether to have a Headquarters Department, whether to appoint full-time officers, the rank level at which to pitch the Force Community Relations Officer, and the relationship with operational staff.

(3) *STATUS RELATED*: Many officers did not perceive community relations as a central police activity — it smacked of 'going soft', of indulging the criminal. At ground level this also took the form of the many satirical allusions to home beat officers as 'hobby-bobbies', 'chocolate bobbies', and 'immunity constables'.

(4) *SPECIALISM RELATED*: Since specialisms were growing in the police service, a real fear of senior officers was that community relations would come to be viewed as an area of particular expertise practised by particular officers. This carried the marked danger of encapsulating an activity which was central to the work of each and every officer to the detriment of the police public relationship.

Concentrating upon the internal perceptions and apprehensions of police officers must not, of course, lead us to ignore the external climate of the latter part of the decade. Crime had continued to grow at an alarming rate, the issues of inner city decline and multiple deprivation were increasingly occupying government attention and a major threat to public tranquillity emerged in the wake of economic recession and industrial unrest. The 'Flying Picket', the public demonstration and mass gathering, the scuffles between demonstrator and counter-demonstrator and demonstrator and police, all became the stuff of media reportage as indeed did the cry from some quarters for new public order legislation.

At the same time the quality of the police immigrant relationship was held to be markedly deteriorating in certain inner city areas and it was no coincidence that substantial numbers of West Indians were now entering the adolescent age banding. British birth had made them far more sophisticated in their awareness of racism and the pernicious effects that the practice of discrimination held for their life-chances. The attitudes of young blacks to policing, and their involvements in certain types of crime, led them to be a focal concern in parts of many force areas.

Policing was therefore being carried on under a public and media spotlight. The national debate, fragmented though it sometimes appeared, was essentially one about police accountability, inter-twined with which was the demand for greater consultation with the community. From the police perspective this inevitably led to a perception of local and national politicians as trying to gain control over police operations. In terms of police command, the outcome was a politicizing of virtually every aspect of street operations in areas of ethnic minority settlement, with factions of both right and left wing seeking every opportunity to exploit situations to their own particular advantage.

Concurrently, under-manning and under-establishment, together with rising public demands and the so-called 'Crime Explosion', had made beat patrol officers a very scarce police resource in most U.K. forces. In trying to maintain standards of service the emphasis in police organisations was placed upon a drive towards a greater professionalism which manifested itself in the application of science and technology to policing, in the growth of new and specialised police departments, and in the development of innovative patrol strategies.

Unfortunately, however, the price to be paid for this new thrust was the driving of a wedge between the police and the public; unobtrusive though it may first have been, the growing realisation of the latter years of the decade was that this occurrence was changing a traditional style of policing with adverse consequences for police and citizenry. In this way emerged a police response that came to be labelled as 'fire brigade' policing — the stress lay upon reacting to events and measurement of performance by response time, upon law enforcement rather than service to the community.

Growing public demands for a uniformed beat patrol presence can be identified throughout the '70s, as also can be seen a growing willingness of chief officers to deploy men in such a way and to restructure their priorities to make it possible. Most importantly there was a growing realisation that the law enforcement function of policing had been overly resourced at the expense of crime prevention — an aspect of policing which suffered both from difficulty of measurement and a comparative unattractiveness in not being seen as directly crime related.

The recognition of the vital nature of this 'proactive' policing activity came with the Ditchley Conference of 1977[13] which delineated the preventive policing aspects of normal police duty and gave due weight to the preventive function of uniformed police patrol. Interestingly, too, the conference provided an ideal opportunity for John Alderson[14] to adumbrate his ideas on community policing from which later came the setting up of a community policing system in Devon and Cornwall, and the most coherent statement by any chief officer of a belief in the primary policing bond as being the quality of its relationship with the community[15].

It is just to place John Alderson as one of the most influential forces in the whole debate about preventive policing and community relations, but due regard must also be given to Sir Robert Mark as the man who began to familiarise the British public with the articulate expression of police apprehensions concerning changes in society and societal value systems and of the many ill-founded criticisms made of police performance[16]. Together both Chief Constables broke with the tradition of the silent service. I am aware of the narrowness of my perspective in concentrating upon policemen and police organisations. A tremendous debt is owed to John Brown of the Cranfield Institute for his pioneering work in community relations.

That the police should wish to speak out is hardly to be wondered at when media reporting of criticisms of police had given the impression of a service which was corrupt ('Countryman'), which was brutal, which engaged in persistent malpractice and discriminated markedly against coloured ethnic minorities (harassment, planting of evidence, abuse of 'Sus'[17]). The police felt themselves to be a beseiged minority and 'at the storm centre around which many of the tensions of modern society are working themselves out'[18].

In truth, media reporting of police had not done justice to the efforts that some forces were making to improve their police-public relationship. The canvassing of forces which had been undertaken for the Ditchley Conference by the Home Office, for example, showed 29 forces to have community relations structures and another 12 which were giving consideration to similar systems; the Metropolitan Police had 40 full-time staff in A7, including 21 full-time Community Liaison Officers on divisional deployment, and Cleveland Constabulary appeared to have the largest commitment of provisional forces with 47 full-time staff.

The Association of Chief Police Officers and the Home Office had instituted a 4 week training course at Derby for newly appointed Community Relations Officers, projects were being undertaken to improve the quality of communal life (as in West Midlands), the help of communities was being enlisted in developing facilities (as in Devon and Cornwall) and specific areas were being given priority in the return to the beat of resident patrol officers (as in West Yorkshire).

Nevertheless, so successful had the critics of police been in determining the popular climate in which the whole policing debate was carried on that each initiative by police brought forward stern comment about the real nature of their intent. For example:

1. E. P. Thomson[19] saw the police as becoming too successful in persuading government and public that their problems were those of law and order. Police, he felt, were manufacturing public opinion.
2. Keith McDonald[20] doubted the part police should play in bringing about a more organised and integrated way of life and questioned their training for such tasks.
3. Left wing activists and organisations in general condemned community relations as a thinly disguised attempt by police to gain better flows of local intelligence.

The popular climate, in other words, was that which was more recently described (although more in relation to sociological research) as 'adversarial'[21].

Yet what was gradually emerging in the police appreciation of the difficulties facing the service was a philosophy to which Sir Robert Mark and John Alderson had been major contributors, and of a different order to that which had previously been obtained; it was a belief that the police alone could not contain crime, that people and communities had to help in the task and that 'self-policing' was the healthy feature to be nurtured amongst all social groups.

If necessary the police would provide leadership in bringing statutory and voluntary agencies, individuals and informal groups, together to tackle local problems but with the hope that, at a later stage, their presence could be considerably reduced. The 'service' element of policing was thus to be given due prominence and resources made available to meet local demands. One should add that inner city areas which had been designated as in need of government aid were better placed to exploit police initiatives since various sources of funding already existed to promote community projects.

An interesting and successful example of police involvement in such a scheme was the Lozells Project in the West Midlands Police. It was designed to:

(i) reduce crime and vandalism,
(ii) develop closer links with the community,
(iii) encourage people living in the area to participate with local agencies in solving the community's problems.

The area itself had been identified by the Force Community Relations Officer, Superintendent Alan Leivesley, as a suitable multi-cultural district for the experiment[22].

Of especial note is that the Birmingham Inner City Partnership provided an initial sum of £30,000 for the period 1979–82 which was subsequently raised to £50,000 per annum for a further 3 years. The general supervision of the project was placed in the hands of an Inter-Departmental Group of senior officers (including the Deputy Chief Constable, Chief Education Officer, Senior Representatives of the Planning Department of the West Midlands County Council) meeting quarterly to receive reports from, and to give overall guidance to, the Project Team (which was again interdepartmental in composition).

From the project has emerged a community centre (the Wallace Lawler Centre) with a full-time warden, and a variety of schemes of distinct benefit to the community: adventure playground, community workshop, family centre, recreational group playhouse, school camps, and 5-a-side soccer tournaments. Innumerable grants were made, especially for the purchase of equipment, and police advice and help given, together with that from other agencies, to help activities get on their feet.

The involvement of government in inner city partnership schemes undoubtedly helped to create a receptive climate for police endeavours, as did the promptings of the Home Office in urging police and other agencies to liaise in the complex task of preventing juvenile delinquency. The Home Office Circulars of 1978, 1980 and 1982[23], for example, touched

113

upon schools liaison, leisure and sporting activities, and youth work — and incidentally brought police into closer contact with Education, Probation and Social Services Departments.

Thus the '80s opened with a better defined and more generally agreed police stance towards the nature of their part in community relations, a recognition of the need to advance in collaboration with the community and various agencies, and a continued move toward establishing community relations departments in forces. There was also a marked feeling amongst many senior officers that the police service was making far more effort to deal with prejudice and discrimination than any other public occupation serving the public[24].

The public debate about policing, however, remained acrimonious in nature, an acrimony that was a reflection of the disquiet caused by incidents such as the Bristol Riot, the fears of potential new powers for the police which might emerge from the deliberations of the Royal Commission on Criminal Procedure, the clamour for the repeal of the 'Sus' law, and the repeated claim by Asians that the police did not properly protect them from racial attacks.

Against this background of increasing sensitivity by the coloured community to its disadvantaged position, a sensitivity heightened by the publication in 1981 of a White Paper on British Nationality Law[25] and the emotional reaction to the perceived indifference to the death of 13 young blacks in a fire in Deptford[26], erupted the Summer Riots of 1981. Brixton, Moss Side and Toxteth featured particularly in these but the important outcome, irrespective of place, was the setting up of the Scarman Enquiry and the eventual publication of the Scarman Report[27].

The report did not indict the police in the way many police critics had anticipated but it did delineate 'a complex political, economic, and social situation which is not special to Brixton'[28] and a combination of factors which, together, produced 'conditions which create a predisposition toward racial violence'[29]. Scarman diagnosed the police dilemma to be, 'how to cope with a rising level of crime and particularly street robbery (in the coloquial phrase, mugging) while retaining the confidence of all sections of the community, especially the ethnic minority groups'[30].

Lord Scarman's recommendations have been analysed[13] in terms of those 'within', where co-operation of other agencies is not required, and those 'without', where co-operation is essential. In the former the emphasis was upon recruitment and training, in the latter upon consultation and liaison. More pertinently the Report received a generally enthusiastic response from the police with the proposed disciplinary offence of racially prejudiced or discriminatory behaviour the outstanding bone of contention.

Consultation between police and public was quickly taken in hand with a pioneering committee established in Brixton in early 1982 and the issue of a Home Office Circular in July of the same year[32] in which the purpose and pattern of consultation was explained and suggestions made as to the potential representation. Other forces are now active in setting up similar committees.

One also sees the commencement of Lay Visitors Pilot Schemes in 1983 which the Home Office is monitoring and upon which it has issued guidelines to all forces. Such schemes allow periodic visits to police stations by an independent panel of citizens; the purpose is to increase public confidence in the police by more open access to police premises.

Of greater significance in 1983 has been, however, two reports by Working Parties of the Police Training Council:

1. In February came the Report on 'Community and Race Relations Training for the Police'[33]. Very substantial recommendations were made for the training of all police personnel up to, and including, Assistant Chief Constable. The idea was mooted of a 'Training and Support Centre' which would bring a multi-professional dimension to bear upon training needs and the actual training of trainers. The Home Office acted very quickly in response to the Report and a 'Centre for Community and Race Relations Studies' has been set up within the Department of Government at Brunel University.
2. In July followed the Report on 'Police Probationer Training'[34] which lengthens initial training to 14 weeks, makes structural changes to the training schedule, but above all else tries to enshrine in the two years of probationer training a professional performance in actually dealing with people.

Even the most casual observer of the policing scene can therefore observe a great deal of activity in the sphere of police community relations. Within forces themselves community relations departments continue to be established or existing ones to be overhauled, and community relations staff have normally been crucially involved in consultation arrangements, in tension measurement and in training developments.

It is possible to envisage every force giving a central direction to preventive policing and community relations activities to discharge such vital functions as:

1. maintaining the force performance amongst its public;
2. alerting the force to any fall-off in performance and to ways in which improvements could take place;
3. developing programmes and processes to remedy inadequacies in performance;
4. contributing to the training of officers at all levels of the organisation's hierarchy and developing training resources.

The nearest we get to this at present would appear to be the A7

(Community Relations) Department of the Metropolitan Police; the size of the force leads, however, to a bureaucratic structure which can make for remoteness from the operational officer. Nevertheless there has been considerable experimentation in training and in operational practice due to A7 initiatives.

At this point it is worth entering a caveat about community relations departments in the sense that their existence or non-existence is by no means an indication of the degree of involvement of any force in actual community relations endeavours. In the Police and Constabulary Almanac of 1983[35], for example, there are a number of constabularies for whom no force community relations officer is designated.

On the other hand forces may have indexed, separately, Press and Public Relations, Juvenile Bureau, Crime Prevention, and/or Road Safety Officers. All of these, and others, will be working in different ways at the task of community relations, as indeed will all branches involved in operational police duties — from Special Support Units to uniformed beat patrol.

Consequently it is very difficult for any researcher to know, on a broad basis, how active the police service is in this sphere. All the indications seem to suggest that the level of activity is high and that preventive policing and community relations are the major response, in strategic terms, to the problems of recent years — and in this context every officer is a community relations officer since police argue strongly that this function is the essential characteristic of all policing.

Perhaps the best guide to the pattern of policing which will characterize the remainder of the '80s is the Metropolitan Police under the leadership of Sir Kenneth Newman. Even before taking up the Commissionership Sir Kenneth, as an Inspector of Constabulary and Commandant of the Police Staff College (Bramshill), had shown himself as a convinced supporter of proactive policing measures; when Chief Constable of the Royal Ulster Constabulary much imaginative and successful work had been carried out to improve police-public relations.

Sir Kenneth defined his Metropolitan problems and priorities[36] in such a way that an emphatically defined major thrust of his strategy was clearly indicated as crime prevention which 'will have two main facets, the rationalisation and redeployment of manpower and the utilisation of consultative committees as a vehicle for directing the overall strategy'. To this statement he later added:

'the assumption that the police alone cannot make an impact on crime, and that the major resources for crime reduction lie in the community itself, and in other public and voluntary agencies' (p. 5).

From this premise he went on to better define the kinds of links which the police might establish with their communities, the nature of consultation and the securing of co-operation from other agencies.

The most interesting development under his leadership has been the use of citizens in forms of Neighbourhood Watch, a system of using members of the community which was pioneered in America[37] and has had very fruitful results. Avon and Somerset is also working along these lines as indeed are one or two other forces. Such experiments remain, at present, those which most directly involve the public in the fight against crime.

One suspects, despite these activities, that the present climate is such that the critics of policing in Britain are still unlikely to be satisfied. In particular the Police Bill, now suspended by the General Election, has stimulated a flurry of critical comment in proposing to give police more substantial powers over the citizen; the practice and procedure of investigating complaints against the police continues to provoke apprehension as well — so that the general reporting of police matters persists in being one that, against the canvas of a 'law and order' government, constantly argues for greater accountability of the service[38].

On the other hand the British Crime Survey[39] reported that, on average, the public were highly satisfied with the police and rarely complained about police misconduct. More strikingly the survey revealed the tremendous fears held by the public of becoming a victim of some criminal act, fears which were grossly exaggerated when measured against statistical evidence.

Preventive policing and community relations may be no panacea for public disquiet about crime but there are indications[40] that physical and social crime prevention measures do decrease public fears and make people feel safer in going about their business. There is a role for police to play in fighting crime which the citizenry demands, and it does involve increasing the visible police presence in the community; if the outcome is more to increase the tolerance of crime by the public rather than reduce crime itself, then this is what police must settle for.

Yet a major question remains which is two-dimensional in nature and touches at the very heart of the police community relationship:

(1) To what extent should the community shape police behaviour? Whilst the emphasis upon law enforcement has been held to have led to the undue application of legalistic and universalistic powers, a movement in the opposite direction could lead to the inequitable application of police powers, especially the use of discretion. Police could become what James Q. Wilson and George L. Kelling call, 'the agents of neighbourhood bigotry'[41].

The nature of the communities which make up our urban environments is diverse; to distinguish the point at which recognition of local wishes becomes an indulgence, is a markedly difficult skill to acquire. So, too, is the devising of a policy and strategy which retains sensitivity to the community, to individuals and groups within it, yet preserves equality before the law and the fairness and objectivity which supposedly pervade our criminal justice system.

117

Yet these skills requirements are the concomitants of increased consultation with, and greater accountability to, the public — and all political parties have emphasised the desirability of moving in that direction (even allowing for the somewhat paradoxical threat of the Conservative Government to abolish the G.L.C.). From a police perspective the outcome is what is seen as a politicizing of law enforcement.

(2) To what extent should police shape individual and community behaviour? Whilst proactive policing might be seen by many police and even more lay observers as the path for law enforcement to follow in the '80s, there is a danger that the police definition of community needs is occupationally biased and not in tune with the reality of public wishes.

It could be argued, for example, that response policing is by far the most democratic and reassuring of policing styles. Here the public trigger police activities, it is the judgments of citizens themselves which lead to calls for police service and the police are not given the same scope to decide what policing styles in communities should, or should not be initiated.

In this context the increasing emphasis upon inter-agency co-operation in dealing with crime prevention, pointed-up sharply in the 'Report of the Proceedings of a Seminar' held at the Police Staff College in the latter part of 1982[42], simply adds to the apprehension already stated — that the needs of people, especially in the inner-city, may not be quite the same as those perceived and defined by the 'social control' occupations (in which I include police and welfare organisations).

In their totality the complex of issues which have been touched upon in this examination of developments in preventive policing and community relations would seem to demand from police the judgment of Solomon, more especially so when one considers the internal pressures which tend to produce a sub-culture permeated by a value system leaning towards law enforcement and crime fighting rather than beat patrol and community involvement[43].

The internal challenge to police managers is to show that all aspects of preventive policing are legitimate operational activities, as much part of the 'sharp end' of policing as 'fingering collars' and locking up criminals — and this has to go hand-in-hand with the upgrading of the status of the uniformed branch in general where research has shown that the organisational ideology of foot patrol is not matched by actual practice[44].

Community Relations, in particular, has to be critically appraised and not euphorically accepted as the answer to the ills reflected in the Summer Riots of 1981. Community Relations can promise too much and take police into areas which are not their proper province; those same promises, if not realised, become the fuel for future criticism — those same police involvements in the community come to be seen as threatening and intrusive.

118

Even as one tries to draw one's thoughts together, however, events occur — or threaten to occur — which are bound to affect police community relations. The White Paper on an 'Independent Prosecution Service'[45] promises a centrally funded prosecution service; that on 'Police Complaints and Discipline'[46] proposes new procedures for investigating complaints against police. The revised 'Police and Criminal Evidence Bill' embraces such improved safeguards as further steps toward strengthening confidence in the police.

But it is not difficult to guess that the talking point at the close of 1983, and for some years to come, will be the Policy Studies Institute report of its investigation into the nature of the relationship between the Metropolitan Police and its public[47]. Despite the many comments made which are favourable to the force, the need for a thoroughgoing and systematic review of training is overwhelmingly made apparent, as indeed is the requirement for the setting of the highest standards of professional conduct.

In describing police relations with young people it is said, of young whites, that there is a 'dangerous' lack of confidence; but for young, black West Indians the preferred descriptive terms is 'disastrous'. To this one also adds the pervasive use of racist language and the abuses, infrequent though some may be, of numerous police powers.

Against this kind of background the police will inevitably be scrutinised and criticised now and for a long time to come — and so it should be. In the final analysis their response can only be measured in the actual performance and discharge of their law enforcement role; deeds will be more instructive than words, practices more indicative of police attitudes than philosophies. Only if a congruence can be achieved between the most forward looking policing policies and their operational outcomes will public confidence in the police be substantially restored.

REFERENCES

1. Alderson, J.   Policing Freedom (MacDonald and Evans, 1979).
2. Ditchley Foundation. Preventive Policing: Papers from the Ditchley Conference, (H.M.S.O., 1977).
3. Schaffer, E.   Community Policing (Croom Helm, 1980).
4. Pope, D. W. Community Relations: The Police Response (Runnymede Trust, 1976).
5. See, for example
   a) Punch, M.   The Secret Social Service (in Holdaway, S. (ed.), 'The British Police', Arnold, 1979).
   b) Punch, M. and Naylor, T.   Police: A Social Service (New Society, 24.1.73, pp. 358–361).
6. Schaffer, E. Op. cit., pp. 25–30.

7. Schaffer, E. Op. cit., p. 69.
8. Strathclyde Police. Regional Working Unit Report (Strathclyde Police, 1974).
9. Church Board for Social Responsibility. Police: A Social Study (Church Assembly Board, 1974).
10. Pope, D. W. Op. cit., pp. 12–15.
11. Pope, D. W. Ibid (pp. 6 & 7).
12. Pope, D. W. Ibid (pp. 5 & 6).
13. Ditchley Foundation. Conference on Preventive Policing: Report (Home Office, 1977).
14. Alderson, J. From Resources to Ideas: A Paper Presented to the Ditchley Conference, 1977 (Home Office, 1977).
15. Alderson, J. Op. cit. (1979).
16. Mark, Sir Robert. i) Policing a Perplexed Society (Allen & Unwin, 1977).
    ii) In the Office of Constable (Collins, 1978).
17. Pope, D. W. Preventive Policing in the Community (in Pope D. W. & Weiner N. L. *Modern Policing*, Croom Helm, 1981).
18. Critchley, T. A. A History of Police in England and Wales: 900–1900 (Constable, 1967).
19. Thomson, E. P. Law and Order and The Police (New Society, 15.11.79).
20. McDonald, K. A Police State in Britain (New Society, 8.1.76).
21. Waddington, P. J. Are the Police Fair? (Social Affairs Unit, 1983).
22. West Midlands Police. Lozells Project Report (W. Midlands Police, Undated (1980?)).
23. Home Office.
    i) Juveniles: Co-Operation between the Police and Other Agencies (Home Office Circular 211/1978).
    ii) (Home Office Circular 83/1980).
    iii) (Home Office Circular 49/1982).
24. Police Officer Magazine. Editorial (No. 2, Jan. 1982).
25. Home Office.
British Nationality Law: Outline of Proposed Legislation (Cmnd. 7987, H.M.S.O. 1980).
26. Runnymede Trust, Bulletin No. 130 (April, 1981).
27. Lord Scarman. Brixton Disorders, 10–12 April, 1981: Report of an Enquiry (Cmnd. 8427, H.M.S.O. 1981).
28. Ibid, (3.110).
29. Ibid, (2.38).
30. Ibid, (4.11).
31. Pope, D. W. Police and Coloured Ethnic Minorities: A Policing Dilemma (Unpublished Paper, Police Staff College, 1983).

32. Home Office. Local Consultation Arrangements between the Community and the Police (Home Office Circular No. 54/1982).
33. Police Training Council. Community and Race Relations Training for the Police (Working Party Report, Home Office, February, 1983).
34. Police Training Council. Police Probationer Training (Working Party Report, July, 1983).
35. Police and Constabulary Almanac. Police and Constabulary Almanac, Official Register for 1983 (Hazell & Co. 1983).
36. Newman, Sir Kenneth. Summary of the Report of the Commissioner of Police of the Metropolis to The Home Secretary (Metropolitan Police, 1983).
37. i) Olsen, R. L. Neighbourhood Crime Prevention: One Step toward a Crime Free Community (Police Chief, February, 1983).
    ii) Hale, D. and Leonik, R. Planning Community Initiated Crime Prevention (Journal of Police Sc. & Admin. Vol. 10. No. 1, 1982).
38. See, for example:
    i) Brogden, M. The Police, Autonomy and Consent (Academic Press, 1982).
    ii) Cowell, P. (et al). Policing the Riots (Junction Books, 1982).
    iii) Hewitt, P. The Abuse of Power (Robertson, 1982), A Fair Cop (N.C.C.L., 1982).
    iv) Kettle, M. and Hodges, L. Uprising: The Police, the People and the Riots in Britain (Pan, 1982).
    v) Regan, D. Are the Police under Control? (Social Affairs Unit, 1983).
39. Mayhew, P. and Hugh, M. The British Crime Survey (Home Office Res. Study No. 76, 1983).
40. Wilson, J. Q. and Kelling, G. L. Broken Windows (Atlantic Monthly, March 1982).
41. Ibid. (p. 35).
42. Home Office. Crime Prevention: A Co-ordinated Approach (Home Office, November, 1982).
43. Holdaway, S. Inside the British Police: A Force at Work (Blackwell, 1983).
44. Jones, M.
    i) Organisational Aspects of Police Behaviour (Gower Press, 1980).
    ii) Policing in a Riotous City (with J. Winkler, Journal of Law and Society, Vol. 9 No. 1, Summer 1982).
45. Home Office, (Law Officers' Dept.). An Independent Prosecution Service for England and Wales (Cmnd. 9074 H.M.S.O. 1983).
46. Home Office. Police Complaints and Discipline Procedures (Cmnd. 9072 H.M.S.O. 1983).

47. Policy Studies Institute. Police and People in London (P.S.I., November 1983).
    Vol. 1 Smith D. J.   A Survey of Londoners.
    Vol. 2 Small S.   A Group of Young Blacks.
    Vol. 3 Smith D. J.   A Survey of Police Officers.
    Vol. 4 Smith D. J. and Gray J.   The Police in Action.

Race relations and the police in Britain
N. GREENHILL

INTRODUCTION

The Argument

My object in this paper is to assess whether policing in Britain is an institution *serving* the population of Asian and Afro-Caribbean origin, in much the same way that it serves the indigenous population, or whether, on the contrary, it operates *against* them, in a racially discriminatory fashion. I do not propose to entertain the notion that the police service discriminates, as an institution, against elements of the indigenous majority, notably the 'working classes', in the interests of a 'ruling class'. Nevertheless, my argument will take the dialectical form of thesis and antithesis, with a brief concluding synthesis. As this argument will be as much evaluative as descriptive, the thesis takes the form of an indictment and the antithesis that of a rebuttal (something between a defence and a refutation). I make no apology for this value-laden approach. Analysis of complex social issues such as those of race relations, criminal justice and police work, inevitably involves questions of value and ideology as well as of empirical knowledge ('facts'). The reader is left to judge the ideological and evaluative assumptions as well as to appraise the accuracy of the 'facts' and logic of the argument.

It should be stressed that neither the indictment nor the rebuttal represents, in substance, my own opinion; rather they are intended to be fair summaries of what may perhaps be termed 'schools of thought'. My own opinion is expressed in the concluding section, in which I try to achieve a critical synthesis of the arguments previously cited.

The topic is a large and important one, meriting much fuller treatment than is possible here. I only hope that my approach has some merit in it.

THESIS AND ANTITHESIS IN OUTLINE

In its simplest form the thesis indicts Britain as a racialist society (I shall use the term 'racialism' to refer to adversely and unfairly discriminatory *conduct*, and confine 'racism' to contexts where prejudiced *opinions* are concerned. This essay seeks to establish whether or not the police service is racially biased in conduct, not whether police officers' opinions are racially prejudiced. Even public officials are entitled to their opinions provided their conduct is correct.) and argues that the police service not only reflects the national situation but plays a vital role in it[1]. National racism and racialism take several forms, according to this view. Individual

123

prejudice, based upon race, colour or ethnic minority is widespread. 'Institutional racialism', i.e. systematic organisational bias, pervades employment, education, housing, criminal justice, etc. Government race relations policy has been chiefly concerned to restrict coloured immigration, to contain racial minorities in enclaves, 'coloured quarters' or ghettoes, and with balancing racialism against anti-racialism, rather than effectively countering racialism.

As regards the police service, individual and organisational bias are normal, so the indictment runs; and steps ostensibly designed to counter racialism are spurious. The actual role of police is to assist in governments' racialist policies of control and containment. But just as the neutralisation of anti-racialist political pressures requires governments to institute measures giving the outward show of anti-racialism, so the police service finds it expedient to appoint Community Liaison Officers, to set up specialist departments and to engage in race relations training for public relations purposes which are essentially political. If these measures are found to have concealed potential for more effective control and containment of the minorities they purport to serve, that is a valuable operational bonus.

So runs the thesis. It is far less easy to reduce the antithesis to a few sentences, but essentially the rebuttal of the indictment takes the line that the reasoning of the thesis is fallacious; the conclusions drawn do not follow from the arguments advanced and evidence adduced in support.

THESIS PART I — BRITAIN: A RACIALIST SOCIETY

'Common Knowledge'
Whilst it cannot be denied that minority allegations of majority shortcomings may legitimately be received with that degree of reservation which is due to those who have a vested interest in their complaints, it is surprising how often fair minded members of the majority are persuaded of the truth of the accounts of racism and racial discrimination which they hear from those on the receiving end. This is doubtless because most people have direct experience of the racially prejudiced opinions, if not of the racially discriminatory behaviour of their fellows. According to this view, the widespread existence of racial bias is common knowledge, only its disapproval is uncommon.

Research Evidence
It is in this context that research into prejudice and discrimination has been received and evaluated. Those unconcerned about racial bias have ignored the research evidence. Those already concerned have accepted the research as scientific substantiation of their own perceptions. Thus the researches of Rose et al, P.E.P. and the Commission for Racial Equality[2]

have been deemed definitive by such unpartisan authorities as the authors of the White Paper on Racial Discrimination of 1975, the Parliamentary Select Committee Report on Racial Disadvantage of July 1981 and Lord Scarman's Report on the Brixton Disorders, of November 1981[3].

Institutional Racialism
It is probably true to say that most people view racial bias in terms of individual opinion and conduct. There is also a strong tendency to moralise and to be overly concerned with people's intentions rather than with the outcome of their actions. Thus Lord Scarman considers the term 'institutional racialism' in the context of the attitudes and policies of the senior management of the police service, and finding them free of any deliberate intent to discriminate adversely, declares that institutional racialism doesn't exist. This is, however, an idiosyncratic definition of the term, which is generally used to mean 'indirect' racial discrimination, as in the 1976 Race Relations Act[4]. Institutional racialism occurs where the normal procedures of an institution or organisation happen to operate to the relative disadvantage of a racial minority. Where such procedures cannot be justified by the essential functional requirements of the institution, they contravene the Act. Successful cases have been brought in the context of Asian dress, lack of English language, etc. In the British legal context, where only individual actions may be brought (in contrast to the system in the U.S.A. where 'class actions' may be brought by groups of people suffering collective grievances) it is difficult to take legal proceedings against many examples of institutional discrimination. This does not signify that their existence is any less real. Lord Scarman appears to acknowledge that racial bias of this kind is to be found outside the police service, but he seems to ignore the possibility of its existence in the police service too.

Again, the work of P.E.P. and others[5] has provided much evidence of the operation and prevalence of institutional racialism in several spheres of society, and there are several accounts of its nature and importance in the official literature of social problems and social policy[6].

Ineffectual Race Relations Policy
The combination of individual and institutional bias in relation to race, colour and ethnicity is ample justification for calling Britain a racialist society, but government policy has the potential for significantly moderating or exacerbating the position according to its tendency and degree of application. In the U.S.A., for example, where individual and institutional racialism are no less severe than in this country, the radical and energetic anti-racialist policies of the Federal Government have gone some way towards rendering American society less racialist[7].

In this country, race relations policy may be analysed in terms of three major components: immigration and nationality policy; community relations policy; and inner city/urban aid policy.

(i) *Immigration and Nationality Policy*
This may be traced back through the recent British Nationality Act (1981) via the Immigration Act of 1971, the Commonwealth Immigrants Acts of 1968 and 1962, and the British Nationality Act of 1948 to the Aliens Acts of 1919, 1914 and 1905. The common thread in this legislation has been the determination to keep out 'undesirables' and to ensure that those admitted for political and economic reasons (to meet the need for cheap labour) should not be granted more than a minimum of legal rights. Immigration policy has been a euphemism for 'coloured immigration policy' and has been unashamedly racialist, as well as sexist[8]. The British government has already lost cases brought before the European Commission of Human Rights, its treatment of Ugandan Asians under the terms of the 1968 Commonwealth Immigrants Act having been found contrary to the European Convention of Human Rights. Such authorities as Lord Scarman and Anthony Lester, Q.C., have declared the revised Immigration Rules (1980) to be similarly wanting[9] and further cases are currently in process. The transparent racialism of immigration policy throws light on the more obscure policies in the following areas.

(ii) *Community Relations Policy*
The Race Relations Acts of 1965, 1968 and 1976, and the Race Relations Board, Community Relations Commission and their successor, the Commission for Racial Equality, which were set up to administer the provisions of the legislation, were ostensibly concerned with the protection of minority rights in a climate of public opinion rendered more hostile by the anti-coloured immigration legislation referred to above. The effectiveness of these measures in the terms indicated has, however, been minimal. True, the more overt forms of racialism, such as offensive public notices and refusals of admission to places of public resort, which were common in the late 1950s and early 1960s, largely disappeared following the 1965 Race Relations Act, but the 1968 Act was far less effective in countering discrimination in employment and housing, with the result that, well before the disastrous general rise in unemployment in the late '70s, it was apparent that minorities of Asian and Afro-Caribbean origin were continuing to face widespread discrimination. The 1975 White Paper, 'Racial Discrimination', conveyed a clear picture of the situation and outlined a four-fold plan to tackle the four perceived dimensions of the problem, *viz.* lack of job opportunity, urban decay, language handicap and racial discrimination. However, despite the enhanced powers given to the Commission for Racial Equality and the energetic work of the Manpower Services Commission, the employment position of the ethnic minorities

continued to deteriorate disproportionately. This was acknowledged by Lord Scarman in his Report on the Brixton Disorders, endorsing the assessment of the Parliamentary Select Committee in its report on 'Racial Disadvantage' of July 1981: 'Asians and West Indians continue to be at a substantial disadvantage in employment long after their arrival in Britain and their children may also suffer substantial disadvantage in this respect, and '...I do urge the necessity for speedy action if we are to avoid the perpetuation in this country of an economically dispossessed black population.' (Paragraphs 6.26 and 6.27).

The Select Committee report identified lack of government commitment to policies directed against racial disadvantage: 'In some cases any action now would be too late, and past inaction has increased the difficulty of action now.'; 'Government must provide the direction so that the symptoms of racial disadvantage can be assuaged and its causes combated at source by a range of bodies and individuals.' (Paragraph 34). 'There does not seem to be more than the most perfunctory consultation between the Home Office and other departments concerned.' (Paragraph 36). 'From the evidence which is available, there is no effective co-ordination at Ministerial level...' (Paragraph 37). Lord Scarman also stressed the vital importance of positive governmental action and the consequences of its absence, actual or perceived: 'Unless a clear lead is given by Government... there can be no hope of an effective response... the black community in Britain are still hoping for such a lead, although they are cynical about what they see as the previous lack of response from all governments...' (Paragraph 6.31). 'What is required is a clear determination to enforce the existing law... It would be disastrous, however, if there were to be any wider doubt than at present exists among the ethnic minorities about the will of Government, employers, trade union leaders and others in positions of authority to see this through'... (paragraph 6.25).

(iii) *Inner City Policy*
The half-heartedness and ineffectuality of government race relations policy is also evident in the context of its third branch, inner city or urban aid policy. The funds made available under section 11 of the Local Government Act, 1966, and the Urban Aid Programmes of the Home Office and Department of the Environment have had some small local impact, but this has been swamped by major national economic, educational, transport and environmental policies. Thus the 'ghettoisation' of Asian and black minorities, initially produced by the exigencies of emigration and prolonged by individual and institutional discrimination in housing, education and employment, have been perpetuated by government neglect, tokenism and actual fuelling of institutionally discriminatory processes[10]. In an important Social Science

Research Council study of inner city problems and policies[11] the distinguished geographer Peter Hall concludes that 'There is a very real prospect of the development within a predominantly affluent and also enlightened society of a substantial minority of poor, frustrated, alienated and dysfunctional groups who could present a source of grave social malaise'. Powerful trends in this direction could be reversed 'only if there were some quite fundamental transformation of the basis of the inner city economy... not merely economic or technological but social and cultural in character.'

In both community relations and inner city policy, therefore, a failure of political will is discernible. At the various stages in the legislative history since 1965, the 'activist' liberal lobby has appeared briefly to be in the ascendant, successfully pressing for a strengthening or existing measures and looking towards the American example for guidance[12]. The 'passivist' view has, however, manifestly continued to dominate. This is the view that race relations are largely a function of factors beyond the capacity of legislation and government policy effectively to influence for good. On the contrary, according to this view, over-enthusiastic intervention is counter-productive, promoting minority over-reliance on measures operating to the disadvantage of the majority ('reverse discrimination') and stimulating 'white backlash': the best policy is to rely on the passage of time to resolve matters[13].

Sincere belief in the 'passivist' view in those in positions of institutional power and influence would go far to explain the ineffectuality of official race relations policy. Some, however, have discerned a deeper deception: they see in the importation of cheap Commonwealth labour in the 1950's when indigenous labour supplies were short, the key to subsequent race relations policy[14]. All the legislation and work of organisations such as the C.R.E. is seen as serving to maintain this racial 'under-class' by placing intitutional buffers between its members and the political means to their advancement[15]. It is in this light that the 1981 disorders are seen as acts of political rebellion, however futile[16]. In sum, then, in terms of its declared objectives, national race relations policy is ineffectual, whether by inadvertence, negligence or deliberate design, and contributes towards the persistence of endemic racialism in society at large.

It is evident from the foregoing argument that the indictment of society for racial bias may be supported by substantial evidence. What of the case against the police service?

THESIS PART II:
THE POLICE SERVICE REFLECTS SOCIETY

Circumstantial Evidence
A prima facie case against the police service can readily be assembled from a combination of factors of common knowledge and others which,

though allegations rather than facts, are so frequently attested as to be virtually unassailable. For example, on the subject of police harassment of black youths Lord Scarman commented that 'the weight of criticism and complaint against the police is so considerable that it alone must give grave cause for concern' (Brixton Report, paragraph 4.65); and on the subject of complaints against police officers he says, 'I conclude that any system for considering complaints against the police, which is subject to the range and weight of criticism I have heard of the present system in this Inquiry, must be unsatisfactory and ineffective' (paragraph 4.68).

Of the items of common knowledge, the following may be mentioned. Police recruit from the general population with no serious attempt as yet to screen out those with racial prejudice. Police protection of National Front demonstrations and marches is in marked contrast to their characteristic attitudes and response to ethnic minorities. Here one may mention not merely the racially abusive language, which is normal amongst officers working in areas of ethnic minority concentration, but also the oppressive attention given to young blacks, known appropriately enough as 'harassment', the use of excessive force in effecting arrests, and the habitual disregard of Judges' Rules in station interrrogations. The publication of the so-called 'mugging' statistics by the Metropolitan Police in March 1982 gave further clear evidence of the hostility towards the black population present in the nation's largest force. As regards the Asian population, the Home Office's own 'Racial Attacks' report[17] endorsed, albeit belatedly, the oft-repeated complaints that the police typically neglect to provide Asian victims of racial attacks with that degree of preventive and detective commitment which is their right. The ethnic minority press and such journals as 'Race and Class' regularly document cases of alleged police mistreatment of blacks and Asians, which are all of a piece with such notorious cases as those of Oluwale in Leeds in 1969 and of David and Lucille White in London in 1982, which have been exposed in the courts.

Research evidence
Research evidence in this area is scarce. The study by Coleman and Gorman[18], for all its limitations of scale and generalisability, gave evidence of the severity of racist opinions of at least some probationer constables. A. J. P. Butler's study[19] identifies police stereotypes of Asians and blacks and demonstrates that experience in policing ethnic minorities serves only slightly to modify the pre-experience stereotypes of Asians, whilst that of blacks merely becomes more negative. Daniel James, in Holdaway's 'The British Police'[20], finds that blacks suffer from the unprofessional methods (what he calls the 'practical professionalism') of police officers, though he tempers his findings with the conclusion that whites suffer equally in this regard! On the other hand, Tuck and Southgate[21], in

their Home Office Research and Planning Unit study of police/West Indian relations in Moss Side, Manchester, report that though 'The great majority of contacts with the police were described as friendly... West Indians were more likely (than whites) to describe contacts with the police as 'unfriendly' and to be dissatisfied with the way police treated them...' Nevertheless (at the risk of misrepresentation through selective quotations) Tuck and Southgate do say that the picture of police/West Indian relations on Moss Side is not one of 'massive police discrimination'; that their survey data 'cannot be said to show substantial differences in white and West Indian criminal victimisation or contact with the police'; that there is 'relative lack of clear evidence for West Indian complaints about excessive police attention' and finally, echoing James's point, 'A basic hostility was observed among a minority of all ages — but particularly among the young' *and amongst the West Indians and whites equally*.

But the most substantial research evidence of the nature of police relations with ethnic minorities is the Policy Studies Institute's Report, 'Police and People in London', which appeared piecemeal in November and December, 1983, as this article was nearing completion.[22] The sections specifically on police relations with Asians and Afro-Caribbeans (Volume 2 and Chapter 4 of Volume 4) are part of a four-volume study going way beyond the concerns of this essay. Nevertheless, what the P.S.I. report has to say about police and race relations, albeit in the context of one force only, is extremely important, though not so much for its revelations as for its extensive and authoritative documentation, rendered all the more devastating by its care to err on the side of understatement. The researchers write of their immediate impression, borne out by their subsequent research, that 'racialist language and racial prejudice were prominent and pervasive, and that many individual officers and also whole groups were preoccupied with ethnic differences.' (page 109). Particularly was this so in areas of ethnic minority concentration. 'Police hostility towards people of West Indian origin is connected with belief that they are rootless, alienated, poor, unable to cope and deviant in various ways.' (p. 111) A rhetoric of racial abuse of black people is encouraged by the norms of working groups, is expected, and is moreover condoned and sometimes even encouraged by senior officers. 'Someone who is basically sympathetic towards black people can come to adopt racialist language in order to conform to the expectations of the group, which are set by a minority of active racialists.' (p. 115) Incidents of gross mistreatment of black people which the researchers witnessed are vividly described and whilst instances of direct racism are the exception rather than the rule — or as the authors put it, 'police officers rarely behave badly in such a way as to make it obvious that a person's ethnic group is the reason for their bad behaviour' — it is the routineness of unprofessional conduct based upon racial ignorance and hostility which makes the strongest impression when one reads the report. As stated, the reseachers are careful not to overstate their case and go out of their way to draw a distinction between racially prejudiced attitudes, which are often of the worst kind, and racially discriminatory behaviour, which in their view is surprisingly rare. They comment on the frequently relaxed and friendly working contacts between police and black or brown people, and in a typically cautious statement remark that they are 'fairly confident that there is no widespread tendency for black or Asian people to be given greatly inferior treatment by the police.' (p. 335) (Elsewhere they draw attention to a reluctance to act energetically on matters involving Asians, but generally they see police racialism towards Asians as relatively mild.) The authors find it possible to maintain that police officers' actions normally belie their racist opinions, despite acknowledging that 'police officers tend to make a crude equation between crime and black people, to assume suspects are black and to justify stopping people in these terms.' (p. 128) In the face of the evidence of this report, given added authenticity by its having been commissioned by the Metropolitan Police itself, it should prove impossible to dismiss allegations of aggrieved Afro-Caribbeans as unwarranted slurs on the good name of a fair-minded and unprejudiced force.

Institutional racialism
Let us now turn briefly to the question of institutional racialism in the police service. Examples of the normal procedures of policing operating to the relative disadvantage of racial minorities include the numerically heavy policing of many areas of Afro-Carribean concentration, which increases the chances of law-abiding blacks coming into conflict with police officers. The police practice of seeing blackness combined with youth as a sign of potential criminality increases this tendency. Asians suffer from a comparable tendency to be looked upon as potential illegal immigrants. The correlation between ethnic minority and manual working class membership, associated with the disproportionate focus of police attention upon the crimes of the manual working classes, rather than upon those of the middle and upper classes, also produces institutional discrimination against members of ethnic minorities. It is clear that the police service as a whole, like other major British institutions and organisations, is supremely unaware of these indirectly discriminatory processes. Ignorance is a substantial obstacle to tackling the problems of institutional racialism, and it is, moreover, the kind of ignorance which is highly resistant to educative processes, as it rests upon deeply held beliefs and deeply ingrained habits and practices.

Police race relations policy
As with national race relations policy, the police response may be interpreted as at best a combination of well-intentioned tokenism, half-hearted

gestures and concessions to liberalism, and at worst as a disguised method of containment or control (though presented as a serious attempt to grapple with the problems of legitimate ethnic minority needs and rights).

Community relations departments have been classic 'buffer' mechanisms for insulating routine police work from otherwise importunate, though legitimate, demands of ethnic minorities. As the Chairman of the Association of Chief Police Officers acknowledged in his oral evidence to the Parliamentary Select Committee on Home Affairs in December 1981,[23] it has been police experience that in the community relations field the setting up of specialist departments has caused this area of police responsibility to be regarded by other officers as having subordinate priority. Ironically, just as the C.R.E.'s buffer function has frequently not been appreciated by those whose interests it has protected, i.e. the white majority, so police community relations specialists have suffered low status in the eyes of their colleagues doing 'real police work'. This has led to the community relations specialists seeking to justify their existence in terms of the 'crime intelligence' information which their work enables them to supply to the C.I.D. The community relations department thus adds a more traditional control function to its otherwise somewhat innovative 'buffer' function.

Training
Absence of community and race relations training has been indicative of the low priority given to ethnic minority relations. (Bramshill may be at least partly exonerated from this charge as race relations have featured prominently in the College Syllabus for many years, though to what effect is a moot point.) However, in view of the relative impotence of all formal police training when measured against the pervasive influence of the police sub-culture, even the highly ambitious plans of the recent Police Training Council Working Party report on police training in community and race relations seems unlikely to achieve much positive impact.

Recruiting
The emphasis given to recruiting ethnic minority officers has been disingenuous, in view of the extreme unlikelihood of finding many who are both interested and eligible, the latter generally having no wish to be part of an institution which is seen as oppressive by the majority of those whose respect they value.

Response to the Scarman Report
Finally, the response of the police service to the Scarman Report gives ample evidence of the true nature of police policy in this area. Though sharply criticised by Lord Scarman in ways which few officers found just it was felt to be politically expedient to adopt a public stance of general acceptance of the Report. Action on its recommendations has, however,

been highly selective. Advice on weaponry and disorder management was rapidly acted upon; that concerning the disciplining and dismissal of racially biased officers as quickly rejected. Consultative committees, though ostensibly a progressive development, are in reality something of a diversion; talking to ethnic minorities may be important, but it is in the context of day-to-day police encounters that such interchange is vital. The Bristol experience, prior to the 1980 conflagration, of anodyne consultative relations coinciding with inflammatory operational relations provides the clearest comment on the dangers of this tendency. The symbolic police response to Scarman was the notorious retaliatory raid on premises in Railton Road whilst the Inquiry was in progress, which ultimately led to compensation being awarded to innocent victims. For a moment, it seemed the facade was lowered and we were given a brief glimpse of reality.

As with the case against society, it appears that those who would indict the police service for being fundamentally biassed against those of Afro-caribbean and Asian ethnic origin can support their case by reference to very substantial evidence and authoritative opinion. But their is much to be said on the other side. I now turn to what I have called 'the rebuttal'.

ANTITHESIS

Introduction: British racialism and the logic of the case for the police service.

Since the indictment runs that (a) society at large is racialist and (b) the police service reflects that racialism, a successful case for the police has to demonstrate the fallacy of either (a) or (b) but not necessarily both. I take the view that whilst the case against society at large, as outlined above, is less than water-tight, it is a lot less leaky than the case against the police. Space being at a premium, I shall therefore attempt somewhat lamely to correct the stark picture of national and governmental racialism presented above merely by again quoting Lord Scarman. In 'Minority Rights in a Plural Society'[24] he says, 'The coincidence of (coloured) immigration with the awakened ambitions of women created in one decade a problem which neither the law nor our institutions were ready to meet'. The 'naturally tolerant British' sought a typically pragmatic, empirical solutions, that of detailed legislation; bureaucratic but 'based more upon the promotion of understanding and reconciliation than upon the heavy hand of the law'. He contrasts this approach unfavourably with the U.S. approach via the Constitution and Bill of Rights and concludes that in a plural society such as we now have, 'we are in danger of losing our sense of direction'. In concluding his report on the Brixton disorders he echoes this: 'It would be unfair to criticise Government for lack of effort', he says, 'the real

133

question is whether the effort... has been properly directed'. It has to be said that, at least on the governmental front, nothing has occurred since Lord Scarman made this considered assessment to indicate that a new sense of direction has been discovered. For better or worse, we are feeling our way on the old course.

If it is by no means easy to rebut the indictment against society and government, however, a much stronger case may be advanced for the police service, whilst recognising that the very defects of society and government are obstacles in the way of police achieving the appropriate standards.

The circumstantial evidence

The weakness of the circumstantial evidence is essentially that it consists in the highly selective accumulation of points which are individually insubstantial but which are somehow deemed to be significant when added together. An inferential leap of unwarranted magnitude is made from such factors as the social class origins, educational standards and mode of speech of police officers; the recruit selection methods employed; police response to marches and demonstrations; handling of street encounters; handling of prisoners, etc. Furthermore, the multiplication of allegations does not, in itself, substantiate a charge. In particular it must be said that allegations of racial bias in police officers which stem from members of the ethnic minorities themselves, however sincerely and passionately made must not, as such, be accorded greater evidential value than they warrant. Such allegations are the statements of plaintiffs with an interest, and very often with a case to be answered. But plaintiffs can no more be judge and jury in their own cause than can defendants.

The research evidence

The studies of Colman and Gorman, Butler and James, referred to above, provide some evidence of the nature of police officers' opinions about ethnic minorities. The first of these is scarcely more than a pilot study and its conclusions have no general validity. Butler's study demonstrates the poverty of many officers' thinking on the subject of race and ethnicity but says little about their actual behaviour (which he rightly sees as being the matter of real importance). James finds evidence of improper police behaviour, from which members of ethnic minorities may suffer, but maintains that race and ethnicity are quite incidental to this.

The Policy Studies Institute research provides much additional evidence of police officers' thinking and attitudes, but goes beyond this in giving a very full account of the ways in which police officers speak on the subject. Speech is, in a sense, intermediate between, on the one hand, thoughts, feelings and opinions and, on the other, actions. In some contexts speech partakes more of the former, in others of the latter. Thus free speech may be defended as merely an externalisation of thought, the freedom of which is paramount. On the other hand, where speech is closely associated with other actions, it is in practice unrealistic to deny that it is in itself a potent activity. It is undoubtedly the case that many police officers see their racialist speech in the former light and are generally unaware that it may have real practical significance. The P.S.I. researchers give convincing evidence that racist speech often gives offence, whether to members of ethnic minorities, to coloured officers or indeed to white researchers, but their findings go some way to supporting the police view that in other respects speech and behaviour are quite distinct. Racialist language, according to this view, is common currency, the language 'as it is spoke', to be taken no more seriously than the rather coarse or colourful language which is a normal part of the macho style. Disapproval of such expressions as 'nigger', 'spade' and 'spook' is seen in the same light as tut-tutting about four-letter words — this is vigorous Anglo-Saxon speech, no more, no less; in the tradition of Nelson and other great leaders of men; ridiculous to suppose that it is a sign of unprofessionalism, much less of illegality!

To appear to defend coarse and abusive language may well seem at best disingenuous, especially to those of respectable or 'genteel' social background: but it is mistaken to apply unconsidered standards of taste to the social mores of others, and thereby to be more censorious than is objectively warranted — an error akin to ethnocentrism.

One can go further than this, for this 'Anglo-Saxon' speech is essentially the emotionally tinged language of familiarity among peers and close colleagues, and also, in appropriate circumstances, with members of the public. (This language of familiarity and emotion is what Professor Basil Bernstein has called the 'unelaborated code', the normal mode of manual working class communication, subordinated to the formal or 'elaborated code' amongst the non-manual classes.) The use of familiarity as a means of communication with the public in certain situations is vital. Formal correctness and politeness have their place, of course, but as a method of influence or control they are often ineffective. It is a corollary of this that public resistance to police control involves resistance to both informal and formal techniques; to the familiar 'four-lettered' approach as well as to the polite 'Sir' or 'Madam'. This begs the questions of whether police officers typically know when to use the formal and when the familiar approach. The P.S.I. study cites instances where it seems likely that the wrong choice was made, but its authors are clearly completely unaware that what they see as at best vulgar abusiveness may, in many cases, be a legitimate technique (though contrary to the wildly impracticable Judges' Rules[25]).

Lest I be accused of seeking to defend the indefensible, let me say that, whilst it may well be necessary for constables to receive early training in the command of controlled and professional language, errors in the sphere of modes of speech should not be taken to signify racialist attitudes and, more importantly, patterns of behaviour in the absence of corroborative evidence.

Beyond criticism of police speech, there is little in the P.S.I. report which is critical of police conduct in the context of race relations. The disproportionately high degree of negative contact with people of West Indian origin (i.e. as offenders or suspects) is commented upon, especially as regards young West Indian males. 17% of arrests are of black people, who represent no more than 6% of the London population. But as 24% of offenders identified by victims are identified as black, this figure is not surprising. On the 'positive'side, 'where people of West Indian origin are the victims of crime, they are just as likely as white people to report the matter to the police, which is a very important behavioural indication of a level of confidence that would not be suspected from the answers to attitudinal questions' (p. 332) — further evidence of the vital importance of assessing behaviour directly and not inferring it from the indirect evidence of 'attitudes' and speech. The report even says that 'there is evidence that, in fact, the police tend to make more efforts on behalf of West Indian than on behalf of white victims' (p. 333). The motive here may be one of expediency, i.e. pre-empting complaint, but it is the behaviour which is important, not the motive. In general, the P.S.I. findings are entirely consistent with those of Tuck and Southgate in Moss Side, referred to above. There is nothing seriously wrong with police practice.

Institutional racialism

By definition, institutionalised practices are deep-rooted, taken for granted and potentially inequitable in their operation. The police service in this respect is an institution like any other. However, once one begins to examine the areas of alleged institutional racialism in the police service, it is evident that the situation is far from being one of simple and readily correctable bias. Taking the four examples previously cited: the numerically heavy policing of ethnic minority areas is justified on the grounds of both reported victimisation and crime rates. This is essentially a 'no-win' situation, inasmuch as it is as easy for police to be reproached for under-policing as for over-policing. The tendency for police to see young blacks as potential criminals is an operational rather than a racial bias, produced by the nature of local reported crime patterns. As Mawby[26] and others have shown, police operations are typically reactive i.e. initiated by public demand and public information, rather than 'pro-active' initiatives of their own.

The notion that police typically view Asians as illegal immigrants is far from being the truth in any practical sense. The extent of police activity on this area, with the possible exceptions of the London Metropolitan and Kent forces, is minimal. Moreover, police information in this area stems from members of the Asian communities more often than is generally acknowledged. Again, the police response is to a significant degree reactive rather than pro-active.

The bias towards manual working class and hence ethnic minority criminality, which is undoubtedly a feature of British policing, is again bound up with public demand stemming from within those sections of society. This is because most reported crime is intra-class rather than inter-class and because people in conditions of relative poverty have traditionally depended upon the police not only for law enforcement but for a range of other services. In Britain, to view the police as 'working-class oppressors' is naive.

Police race relations policy
Police relations with ethnic minorities have been in the public eye for more than a decade. The Parliamentary Select Committee on Race Relations and Immigration chose to study police/immigrant relations in 1971 and reported in August 1972. It is pertinent to quote their opening and closing remarks. 'The police are immediate, visible representatives of society...' and 'If the best examples of leadership in police and immigrant relations prevailed throughout forces in the U.K., many of the difficulties we have dwelt upon would, within a reasonable space of time, diminish. In some places they would wither away'. In between, whilst criticising particular short-comings, the Committee commended police efforts towards establishing good working relations with ethnic minorities and called for an expansion of activity. Since the Home Officer circular to chief constables of July 1967[27] recommending the practice of appointing Community Liaison Officers — the first of a series of promptings on police/community relations — the police service has indeed become increasingly active in this area. From 1975 there have been a number of drives to recruit ethnic minority officers, though with greater success in the Special Constabulary than in the regular force itself. Liaison with schools and social services has grown, together with involvement in Inner City Partnerships and Programmes. In 1980, some potentially racially inflammatory marches were banned upon police recommendation. Clearly the disturbances of 1980 and 1981 cannot be deemed to demonstrate the success of police policies over the preceding decade, but neither the Scarman Report nor the Hytner Report[28] on the Moss Side disturbances placed primary responsibility for the disorders upon failings in police policy, and both went out of their way to commend both individual officers and the force as a whole for achieving standards which are generally worthy of praise and often of the highest admiration.

Nevertheless, the riots and investigations that followed served both to induce a re-examination of policy and a redoubling of effort. The limitations of community relations departments and specialists have been more clearly recognised, together with the vital importance of achieving the right standards in all departments. The woeful inadequacy of relevant training is now more widely appreciated. In the Metropolitan Police, 'human awareness training' — now 'policing skills training' — street duties training and local familiarization are given considerable emphasis; at Bramshill intensive courses on police/ethnic minority relations, focusing on the responsibilities of sub-divisional command, have been introduced; and the Police Training Council Working Party Report on Community and Race Relations Training promises a very significant investment in this aspect of training in all forces and ranks up to assistant chief constable. Local consultative committees are steadily becoming established. In many areas it is true that there is little spontaneous community recognition of the need for such a formal consultative system. In Lambeth, however, where the Consultative Group meets twice monthly, enormous strides have been made and a fruitful exchange of information and views has already been achieved in a way which until recently would have been unthinkable. The police response has already demonstrated that if consultative committees prove ineffectual, it will not be the fault of the police!

The development of Lay Visitor to Police Station schemes is also under way and promises to pose considerable problems for the purveyors of stories about police ill-treatment of prisoners.

These are the most positive developments. As yet, most officers are opposed to the idea of a specific disciplinary offence of racially prejudiced behaviour. However, the practical difficulty of framing a suitable code which would make it possible to bring successful cases against offenders makes this omission relatively unimportant. The position is similar to that of the law against incitement to racial hatred, the presence of which on the statute books is largely symbolic, few cases being brought and fewer still succeeding.

The investment of £50,000 in the development of a recruit selection test to identify racist attitudes is also worthy of note, though it will not deal directly with the more fundamental question of attitudes acquired after entry.

Finally it should be stressed that the fact that police forces have also taken swift steps to improve their capacity to suppress potential incidents of serious public disorder in no way contradicts the various developments referred to. Public disorder in serious contravention of the law serves the interests neither of society as a whole nor of the ethnic minorities. The notion that rioting is the 'voice of the oppressed' is at best sentimental rubbish. To say that it is an indicator of inadequacies in the network of social control agencies is an over-simplification, but it is nearer the mark. It is one important duty of the police service to prevent rioting by all legal means; preferably, of course, by non-violent means, but if necessary with the use of minimum force. Minimum force may well mean force swiftly and deftly applied. Provided police are adequately accountable for their actions, this is as it should be. (Developments in the area of accountability are clearly highly relevant to the present issue. They are also progressing satisfactorily.).

In sum, whilst it would be foolish to deny that the major characteristics of society at large are reflected, both for good and ill, in the police service, the degree of correspondence between society and police varies enormously as between different characteristics. In terms of those characteristics which matter most, i.e. the actual treatment of members of ethnic minorities and the degree of commitment to practical policies which are supportive of the ethnic minorities, the police service contrasts favourably with other relevant social agencies. In a society which is clearly experiencing great difficulty in adapting to ethnic pluralism, the police service does not exemplify failure to adapt; on the contrary, it demonstrates the possibilities of successful evolutionary adaptation more than any other major social institution.

TOWARDS A SYNTHESIS

The nature of synthesis is to combine the principal elements of thesis and antithesis and to transcend rather than reject them. In presenting the two opposing arguments the exercise has been largely one of comprehending two points of view and summarising them as fairly and effectively as possible in a short space. The task of synthesis is of a different order, for it involves a process of creative assimilation, evaluation and reconstruction. It may well be that this bold aim will prove to be over-ambitious. Neither thesis nor antithesis does justice to the opposing arguments, however, and an adequate synthesis is badly needed.

On the social front, it was argued that society has been racialist, is racialist and will continue to be racialist. This thesis was countered with the argument that although there have, indeed, been severely racialist attributes in British society, that society is in a state of flux, with anti-racialist and racialist factors co-existing uneasily; a new sense of direction in our institutional leaders, learning from the American experience, can ensure that anti-racialism will get the upper hand. As regards the police service, the thesis was that police reflect and support the racialist structure of society and will continue to do so. The antithesis argued that the police service is in the vanguard of institutional change towards an ethnically plural yet just society. In this sense the police service leads society rather than reflects it.

The difference between the opposing arguments thus centres on the relationship between racialist and anti-racialist factors, especially in the context of social change. The thesis argues that so-called 'anti-racialist' factors, whether in society or in the police service, are devious means towards the perpetuation of racialism; the antithesis that, in given circumstances, the genuinely anti-racialist factors can become dominant, and that the experience of the police service over the last fifteen years or so gives evidence of the feasibility of such a development.

A possible synthesis runs as follows: society is indeed in a state of flux, with racialist and anti-racialist tendencies co-existing, but despite the obvious evidence of friction and instability, there is a genuine equilibrium which prevents and will continue to prevent one or the other tendency from becoming dominant. In particular, the 'new sense of direction' and the 'American example' are extremely unlikely to take hold. Equally, the scenario hinted at by Lord Scarman if vacillatory government policies persist is also unlikely, despite the vehement expressions of some members of ethnic minorities. What we have, then, is a typically British compromise — ineffectual yet strangely viable!

The police service does indeed reflect society rather than lead it. But it does not reflect a racialist society with spurious elements of anti-racialism; rather it is part of that rickety mechanism curiously and uneasily, yet successfully, balancing racialism and anti-racialism. It is by no means intended to suggest that half the police are racialists and the other half are not. Such a reduction to individual labelling and enumeration would be a crude misrepresentation of what I believe to be the case. The police service, like society at large, cannot be reduced to the sum of the individuals comprising it. A social organisation or institution like the police consists of patterns of group behaviour — rules, procedures, processes, etc. — as well as of numbers of individuals. It is my contention that the police service, like society, is Janus-faced (like Shiva, the Hindu god of both creation and destruction, and indeed like many other pivotal features of societies and cultures the world over). Such brief allusions to paradox and contradiction can, however, easily degenerate into mysticism and, where 'British compromise' is dredged up, into vulgar nationalism. An adequate synthesis must avoid these traps. The merit of the view that both society and the police service contain contradictory characteristics which are held in some kind of balance lies partly in its accuracy, relative to other views, and partly in the fact that it discourages the blanket discrediting of evidence and arguments which do not fit neatly into either the 'racialist' or the 'anti-racialist' theory, according to one's preference. My answer to the question posed at the beginning of this essay is, therefore, that it is misleading to say that the police service serves the population of Asian and Afro-caribbean origin as it serves the indigenous population: but it is equally unsatisfactory to say that it operates against them in a racially discriminatory fashion. The truth is more complex than either of these tempting over-simplifications. Whether I have in any way helped to clarify the complexity, I leave the reader to judge.

REFERENCES AND NOTES

1. The recent report of the Police Training Council Working Party, 'Community and Race Relations Training for the Police' (Feb. 1983), goes some way to acknowledging this. In paragraph 1.10 it says, 'It is a fact that racial prejudice and discrimination whether conscious or unconscious are widespread in this country. The police, as part of our society, reflect its mores and habits of thought....'.

2. E. J. B. Rose et al., 'Colour and Citizenship: a Report on British Race Relations'. (Institute of Race Relations and Oxford University Press, 1969).
   D. J. Smith, *Racial Disadvantage in Britain* (Penguin Books Ltd., 1977).
   J. Hubback and S. Carter, 'Half a Chance? A Report on Job Discrimination against Young Blacks'. (Commission for Racial Equality, 1980).

3. Government White Paper 'Racial Discrimination' (Cmnd. 6234, H.M.S.O., 1975).
   5th Report of the Home Affairs Committee, 'Racial Disadvantage' (H.M.S.O., 1981).
   The Rt. Hon. The Lord Scarman, O.B.E., 'The Brixton Disorders, 10–12 April, 1981' (Cmnd. 8427, H.M.S.O., 1981).

4. See, for example, L. Lustgarten, *Legal Control of Racial Discrimination*, (MacMillan Press Ltd., 1980).

5. D. J. Smith, 'Racial Disadvantage in Employment', (Political and Economic Planning, 1974).
   J. Rex, 'Urban Segregation and Inner City Policy in Gt. Britain', in C. Peach et al., *Ethnic Segregation in Cities*, (Croom Helm, 1981).
   S. Tomlinson, *Educational Subnormality: a Study in Decision-making*, (Routledge and Kegan Paul, 1981).

6. Community Relations Commission, 'Urban Deprivation, Racial Inequality and Social Policy: a Report', (H.M.S.O., 1977).
   C. Cross, 'Ethnic Minorities in the Inner City', (Commission for Racial Equality, 1978).
   5th Report of the Home Affairs Committee (Op. cit.).

7. See, for example, T. F. Pettigrew, *The Sociology of Race Relations: Reflection and Reform*, (The Free Press, 1980).

8. See L. Grant and I. Martin, 'Immigration Law and Practice', (Cobden Trust, 1983).

9. 1st Report from the Home Affairs Committee, 'Proposed New Immigration Rules and the European Convention on Human Rights', (H.M.S.O. 1980).

10. J. Rex, Op. cit. See also J. Rex and S. Tomlinson, *Colonial Immigrants in a British City'*, (Routledge, 1979).

11. P. Hall (Ed.), 'Prospects' in, 'The Inner City in Context', Final Report of the S.S.R.C. Working Party, (Heinemann Educational, 1981).
12. See, for example, J. Bowers and S. Franks, 'Race and Affirmative Action', (Fabian Society Tract No. 471, 1980).
13. This view is seldom articulated at length, but see D. L. Kirp, 'Doing Good by Doing Little: Race and Schooling in Britain', (University of California Press, 1979).
14. See J. Lea, 'The Contradictions of the Sixties Race Relations Legislation' in National Deviancy Conference (Ed.), *Permissiveness and Social Control*, (MacMillan Press Ltd., 1980).
15. See I. Katznelson, *Black Men, White Cities: Race, Politics and Migration in the U.S., 1900–30 and Britain, 1948–68*, (Oxford University Press, 1973).
16. See R. Moore, *Racism and Black Resistance in Britain*, (Pluto Press, 1975).
    A. Sivanandan, 'From Resistance to Rebellion: Asian and Afro-Caribbean Struggles in Britain', (Race and Class, Autumn 1981–Winter 1982).
17. 'Racial Attacks — Report of a Home Office Study', (Home Office, 1981).
18. A. M. Colman and L. P. Gorman, 'Conservatism, Dogmatism and Authoritarianism in British Police Officers', (Sociology, Vol. 16, No. 1, Feb. 1982).
19. A. J. P. Butler, 'An Examination of the Influence of Training and Experience on the Attitudes and Perceptions of Police Constables', (typescript, 1982).
20. D. James, 'Police-Black Relations: The Professional Solution', in S. Holdaway (Ed.), *The British Police*, (Edward Arnold, 1979).
21. M. Tuck and P. Southgate, 'Ethnic Minorities, Crime and Policing: a Survay of the Experience of West Indians and Whites'. (Home Office Research Study No. 70, H.M.S.O., 1981).
22. D. J. Smith et al., 'Police and People in London', (Policy Studies Institute, 1983).
23. 2nd Report from the Home Affairs Committee, 'Racial Attacks', (H.M.S.O., 1982).
24. Lord Scarman, 'Minority Rights in a Plural Society', (New Community, Vol. 6, No. 3, Summer 1978).
25. The argument advanced here is a development of the view that the meaning and acceptability of such expressions as 'coon', 'nigger' and 'black bastard' depends upon such considerations as the context in which they are uttered, their manner of expression, geographical location etc. As the Chairman of the Police Federation has himself defended their use along these lines, this

'contextual view' may perhaps be termed 'Curtis's theory of police language'.
26. R. Mawby, 'Policing the City', (Saxon House, 1979).
    D. Steer, 'Uncovering Crime, the Police Role', (H.M.S.O., 1980).
27. 'The Police and Coloured Communities', (Home Office Circular to Chief Constables, July 1967).
28. Report of the Moss Side Enquiry Panel to the Leader of the Greater Manchester Council, (Sept. 1981).

Reactions to Terrorism and Riots

J. R. THACKRAH

The police in the United Kingdom have largely been concerned, historically, at least, with only spasmodic outbreaks of terrorism, associated with the problems of Ireland and the British connection. Nevertheless, the United Kingdom, like all liberal Western states, is now open to the growth of international terrorism. The vulnerability of liberal states is magnified by their liberalism, including freedom of movement. The ease now by which people can move from country to country by air, by sea or by land has rendered police counter-measures particularly difficult.

One of the greatest problems facing the police in the 1970s has been to maintain public order in the face of political demonstrations, student demonstrations, mass picketing in industrial disputes, terrorist activities and bombings, racial tension and soccer hooliganism. Up to the present time, the police have managed to strike a balance between the preservation of law and order and the prevention of crime with the preservation of freedom of speech and the right to demonstrate. This is not a matter for the police alone, and the freedom of peaceful demonstration is one under the law. The ample scope of punitive, preventive and repressive powers implies that considerable restraint must be shown by the police and magistrates if the spokesman of unpopular or eccentric causes are to be allowed to voice their opinions.

The ending of the siege of the Iranian Embassy in London in May, 1980, gave the British people experience at close quarters of the dilemma of all civilised countries in countering the assault of international terrorism, how to set up and use specialised forces without falling into the terrorist trap of destroying the rule of law, and how to fight one monster without creating another. The Home Secretary had at his disposal the SAS, police units highly trained in the art of counter terrorism and teams of expert negotiators.

As events in Princes Gate proved, the sharp edge of Britain's security armed forces, the SAS and Royal Marines, are only called into action when a situation has got out of hand, and when military muscle is considered essential. British law clearly states the joint army/police role in Military Aid to the Civil Power (MACP)[1]. While the military are undertaking such a role they remain under the control of the civil authorities, and they enjoy no extra privileges. As soon as the emergency is over, and the level of violence has fallen sufficiently for the police to take over force of circumstance, the army and police have to work continually in harmony in Northern Ireland.

The police have considerable resources for dealing with terrorism and they operate a number of specialised units. The first to be formed was C13, the Anti-Terrorist Squad, in January 1971, when the Angry Brigade anarchist group exploded two bombs at the home of the Secretary of State for Employment, Robert Carr. It became the nucleus of the Bomb Squad which was formed in July 1971 following more explosions — it was based at New Scotland Yard and attached to the Serious Crimes Squad. It numbered about 150 men, although this varied according to the level of terrorist activities and it could call on the services of experts from a number of different fields. Members of the squad were drawn from the Special Branch, C.I.D., uniformed officers and provincial forces. This latter assistance helped to strengthen the squad, and meant officers could take back the knowledge they acquired to their own forces. In 1976, the Bomb Squad was reorganised into C13, the Anti-Terrorist Squad, and was given a wider field to cover and greater powers with which to do it.

D11, the 'Blue Berets', which is the Yard's firearms department, is the squad formed for emergencies by bringing together specialists led by the Yard's own weapons instructors. The personnel in the police who develop their own surveillance and monitoring devices and communications techniques are the Technical Support Branch, C7, in reality an adjunct of the Anti-Terrorist Squad.

The Special Patrol Group provides support — and was formed in 1965 as a mobile reserve to assist divisional police units in the Metropolitan area where and whenever needed, and was conceived as a highly mobile police support unit, to deal with serious disturbance and crime. The units have a high turnover — annually around 20% which means not only a continuous supply of fresh 'blood' but, more importantly perhaps, the regular return of policemen trained and experienced in anti-terrorist operations to their own divisions[3]. Demands for its disbandment grew after Blair Peach died during the Southall riot of 1979[4]. Countering the accusation that the Group is used against left-wingers in demonstrations, the Yard argues that the SPG is used on all marches, trade disputes and festivals where serious public disorder is anticipated and therefore it is bound to be drawn into any violence that occurs.

A11, the Diplomatic Protection Group is involved with the Anti-Terrorist Squad in the fight against terrorism; it is composed of highly-trained marksmen who provide immediate protection for the hundred plus foreign missions and embassies situated in London. Related groups are the Special Branch Protection Squad providing bodyguards for Ministers and important visitors; and the Royalty Protection Group which looks after the Royal Family. All these groups have now been re-organised into the Royalty and Diplomatic Protection Branch.

Any viable anti-terrorist group requires good intelligence and an organisation to enable them to forestall attacks, arrest terrorists or react quickly if an incident does take place. The Anti-Terrorist Squad relies heavily on the Special Branch for information. It was established to combat the Fenian bombing campaign of the 1880s. The Branch is responsible to the Commissioner, who determines operational matters with the help of the Assistant Commissioner, Deputy Assistant Commissioner and the operational head of the Special Branch. It conducts surveillance of persons regarded as a potential threat to the State, provides VIP bodyguards, deals with aliens and assists other State security services. The Branch's most successful anti-terrorist role has been the infiltration of IRA cells in London and the provinces.[5] Persons are recruited from the uniformed branch after three or four years' service, very close vetting of family background and an extremely rigorous interview board. Special Branch monitors the activities of the enemies of the State and as such must be regarded as both an offensive and defensive weapon.

It was significant that many of these organisations were created or perfected in the 1970s, after the police began seriously to evaluate the terrorist threat probably for the first time in 1968, the year of protest. That evaluation was part of a wider and extremely thorough examination of the whole force, and the Metropolitan Police in particular. Under the then Metropolitan Commissioner, Sir John Waldron, every effort was made to improve police management and planning in an attempt to cover for the manpower shortage. In 1968, special emphasis was placed on developing selective policing through the use of task forces. Management services were streamlined, and at the same time the police view on the growing public order problem was that the strategy would be one which adhered firmly to traditional methods. With hindsight, and particularly in the light of police successes in counter terrorism such as that at Balcombe Street, this decision to preserve the traditional police response was one of the most important taken in recent times. On 6th December, 1975, London's Balcombe Street siege, which vindicated police policy, started with shots being fired at Scott's Restaurant in Mayfair, resulting in the police springing a trap laid with 'Q' cars coupled with saturation patrolling. A running gunfight cornered four Provisional IRA men in a flat. Police refused to entertain a deal to free two hostages by letting the gunmen fly to Ireland and in less than a week the four surrendered. Similar patient tactics had previously secured the surrender of a criminal gang who held the staff of a London restaurant, the Spaghetti House — again without injury to hostages. Both these events indicated police strategy.

In the early '70s the Prime Minister, Edward Heath, gave a Cabinet Office Committee, chaired by Earl Jellicoe, the brief to review the internal security situation. Special emphasis was to be placed on enhancing police-military co-ordination. The police, however, only very grudgingly acknowledged the need for military assistance against the tougher varieties of terrorism. Previously blurred lines of police-military co-ordination were clarified — and clear schemes of military intervention in crisis were set down. Military Aid to the Civil Power (MACP) was where military assistance was to be given to combat armed terrorism if it was felt that the police were in need of such. To fulfil this provision a variety of specialist military units are now on permanent alert and call to the police — such as the Special Air Service. Military Aid to the Civil Community (MACC) would be where the army could be called in for disaster relief rescues, etc. Lastly, and in the environment of industrial disputes, is a contentious mode of intervention, Military Aid to Civil Ministries (MACM). This is to apply during industrial disputes of great longevity, so that troops, transport and equipment could be provided, to maintain essential services at, say, the docks and power stations.

Over the past decade there has been considerable debate about the utility of and the need for a 'third force' or para-military police specially trained in anti-terrorist techniques. The threat to public order is a serious one. Public order is a matter of constant concern; for it is difficult to maintain the balance between freedom and restriction — preserving the rights of ordinary citizens as well as the right to demonstrate.

Many views can indeed be marshalled in favour of the third force. Such units are specially trained in riot control; serve as 'shock troops'; saturate crisis areas and are, in effect, trained and hardened lightly-armed infantry.

A crucial argument in favour of a third force is that they relieve the police proper of their most sensitive and stressful function whilst at the same time reducing the need to call out the Army in aid of the civil power.

The UK police have been consistently opposed to a third force because it is felt that it would irreparably damage the special relationship that exists between people and police. Sir Robert Mark, the co-author of the Hunt Report on 'Policing in Northern Ireland' (Cmd 535 1969), stressed, along with Lord Hunt and Sir James Robertson, that policing in a free society depends on a real measure of public approval and consent[6]. This has never been obtained by military or para-military means.

While for many observers the third force mode of policing is regarded as the most effective police response to terrorism, the British stance continues to keep the distinction between soldier and policeman clear. Certainly an army is trained, organised and exists to kill although this can never be its only function. The police exist to enforce the rule of law and maintain order. Any army may kill in the execution of its normal functions — but the function of the police is fulfilled by apprehending and bringing to account. An armed policeman is not a soldier — a soldier is not an armed policeman.

The British police continue to enjoy a degree of public support unmatched anywhere in the world. Nearly a decade ago this view was upheld by the public inquiry, headed by Lord Scarman, into the disorders in Red Lion Square, London, in June 1974, in which 46 policemen and 12 members of the public were injured and a student killed[7]. The inquiry stressed that British police methods were designed to limit the degree of force that could be used in a public order situation; the aim was to prevent and forestall trouble and to minimise disorder when it occurs. The police had nothing to rely on but their own physical strength deployed in a disciplined way. In view of developments later in Southall and Brixton, etc., it is interesting to note that Lord Scarman judged it to be wrong to give the Special Patrol Group a more prominent role; if the police were to maintain public co-operation and confidence it was important that the major part in controlling and managing demonstrations should continue to be played by ordinary divisional policemen. The mounted police were considered of great importance. The point was made that without these men London might have seen a police force equipped with special riot equipment, possibly being deployed in para-military formations. Two years later riots in Notting Hill illustrated clearly the need for protection for police officers. The police had to improvise personal defence with such things as plastic refuse bin lids when proper equipment such as riot shields might have been provided to minimise injuries. As it transpired, 325 police officers were injured compared with 131 civilians.

With a vast majority respecting and trusting the police a third force would do little or nothing to improve this relationship. It is a relationship which underpins the balance of the public peace and governability and one which any sustained terrorist attack would have to end in order to break down the rule of law. Indeed without the fullest public co-operation, special preventive measures against terrorism are bound to fail. Take, for example, the matter of storage of detonators and explosive substances. It would be useless for a government to bring in a new Act to impose severe penalties for failing to keep explosives stores fully secure if the actual workers and managers involved in their industrial use still failed to observe the minimal rules of security.[8] Police are generally called in only when there is an explosive or weapons theft, i.e. when it is probably too late. Truly preventive action against terrorism demands the fullest co-operation of every member of the public.

The ideologically committed revolutionary naturally looks to the ranks of the underdog and the discontented for his mass support. The revolutionary seeks to heighten this awareness to channel instincts and experiences towards a deliberate purpose, in organised political activity which results in a sharpening of the conflicts between aggrieved minorities and authority. In Brixton, for example, there was a high level of left-wing activity before the troubles of April 1981 and this increased thereafter. At least half a dozen revolutionary groups, black and white, had premises in Brixton, or launched subsidiary groups and projects geared to the conditions of the area.

The problem of revolutionary theory and practice is a long standing one for the revolutionary Left. Black mistrust is derived from everyday experience, the Left's attitude arises from ideological necessity and from certain specific events. The Red Lion Square demonstration of 1974, the Grunwick dispute in 1977, the Lewisham riot in the same year and Southall in 1979 are inscribed in left-wing mythology like so many battle honours. It has been these set-piece confrontations which have played such a large part in moulding left-wing views of the police. Parallel to this is the radical Left's belief that modern computer and surveillance techniques are being used to stifle dissent[9]. For the revolutionary Left, violence in general has a beneficial effect, polarising opinions and sharpening rather than reducing tensions.

Deprivation, massive unemployment, inner city squalor, educational under-achievement, frustration in the young caused by enforced idleness and the lack of any visible brighter economic prospects in the future: all these and many more have been put forward as contributory factors and as deficiencies in the social system which need urgent attention. Yet these have been sentiments for change over the past decade let alone over the last two years. Social justice demands an immediate examination of the problems with a view to taking remedial steps although it is doubtful in the eyes of many persons whether any short-term measures will achieve more than cosmetic improvement.

In the 1981 riots unprovoked attacks with firebombs resulted in the police needing to take a fresh look at their capability to cope with lawlessness on such a scale[10]. Questions of protective equipment, arms and methods received urgent consideration, yet it was realised that the whole philosophy of policing by consent would be jeopardised if riot squads were formed on Continental lines and offensive postures were formally adopted[11].

What had provoked these measures? Though many forecasts of riots had been made in the 1970s, no one had expected that it would really start in Bristol. In the space of four hours on 2nd April, 1980, the work of a generation was undone. Twenty-seven police officers and 11 civilians were injured and 27 police cars destroyed or damaged beyond repair. The police faced a crowd of 2,000, many blacks under 17 years old. For most of these four hours police were withdrawn, to allow reinforcements from neighbouring forces, to arrive at the scene. This action meant that the police were conceding defeat and that the crowd was free to loot to its heart's content for the next few hours: at least £500,000 of damage was done to 21 buildings which were set on fire or looted.

The reasons for the causes of the riots polarised between those blaming high unemployment and discrimination against blacks in the job market, and others blaming a heavy-handed police operation. These views were also highlighted as causes of the far more widespread troubles in the spring and summer of 1981. The disorders in Brixton in April 1981 had as their immediate background operation *Swamp '81*, a police operation to try to deal with street crime. The Metropolitan District had witnessed major racial disturbances and incitement on two previous cases. During the 1979 election campaign, the National Front's insistence on putting up candidates in black areas led to problems — the worst violence being in Southall with its large Asian population. Three hundred Asian men were arrested and an anti-racist teacher, Blair Peach, was killed. No police officer was prosecuted, and black community trust in the courts and police was eroded. A year later in April 1980 the National Front marched through Lewisham and a massive police presence of 4,000, at a cost of £500,000, managed to reduce the amount of violence.

This cost was minimal when compared with the Liverpool Toxteth riots in 1981 — easily the worst experienced on mainland Britain. 461 officers were injured, 227 hospitalised and for the first time C.S. gas was used when the police were forced to abandon whole areas[12]. Many forces sent reinforcements to Toxteth in the form of 69 specialised teams each made up of an Inspector, 3 Sergeants and 30 Constables. Like many riots it was sparked off by a relatively minor and commonplace incident. A young person pleaded guilty to three charges of assaulting police officers causing them actual bodily harm. He had intervened to prevent the arrest of a black motorcyclist whom the police had been chasing, apparently for traffic offences. The person was allegedly spurred to interfere under the impression that the police were wrongfully seizing a relative of his. The incident caused the police to call for reinforcements and drew a large and angry crowd. The riots which followed resulted in an estimated £6 million of damage being done to property in Toxteth alone[13].

The initial Toxteth fight was against the police. It was alleged the police were behaving as uniformed street gangs; and that such policing methods were leading to the systematic criminalisation of Toxteth. The police complained of press vilification, and action by politicians and community leaders. Yet the core of the argument was about the accountability and control of regular police operations in the area. It seemed clear at the time and since that the abandonment of random 'stopping and searching' was essential if the police were not to alienate the majority of law-abiding blacks. They had to convince blacks that crimes against their persons and property were considered in the same way as those perpetrated against whites[14].

It is to these groups, whether black or white, that the police are seen as unreliable, unhelpful and not respected. Beyond the riots the problem of police-black relations resolves itself into the wider issues of the British society generally and the consequences of the economic recession. Good policing cannot solve these problems, but as we have seen in recent years 'bad' policing in the sense of inexperience in dealing with rioters, can immeasurably inflame them.

While Scarman commended the police handling of the Brixton riots he did condemn some existing police practices and assumptions. His rejection of the need for a new Riot Act was a rebuttal of current police thinking. The police are, however, pleased that Scarman has reversed the view he expressed in his earlier report on Red Lion Square, and backed statutory advance notice of marches and less stringent criteria for imposing bans. On the other hand his call for amendment to the *Public Order Act* — to allow the banning of individual marches threatening public order because they stir up racial hatred — was bad news for racists and a relief from blanket bans that were imposed. The police and society are now perhaps more aware that some of the rioters had a deep sense of outrage not only towards justice in economic and social opportunities, but also justice in the police.

The relative absence of racial analysis of the riots contrasts with the fashionable black conspiracy theories which are short on facts and long on fantasy[15]. At a time when the country was coming to grips with social problems of unprecedented perplexity, its attention was perforce distracted, and its political energy diverted, by the strains and stresses inseparable from the formation of a new multiracial society[16]. Maintaining law and order in these trying circumstances helps to drain the patience and sour the temper of the police — and sadly, to erode the once universal image of the friendly British bobby on the beat. Although the police, as a force, come in for ostentatious commendation from Scarman, the occasional evidence of police ineptitude, of prejudice, or arrogance, along with proposals for economic assistance in various forms, and for new procedures so as to avoid past errors or indiscretions — are all tantamount to an attempted vindication of the use of group violence as an effective political weapon.

To an even greater extent than terrorism, riots are more politically productive in Britain since they depend for their success on the social, political and economic conditions in which they take place. Nearly everyone is against the terrorist in Britain, and that is why the police have enjoyed such remarkable success in dealing with terrorism. The practical effect of terrorist activity, compared with riots, is negligible. Whilst terrorism presents problems and calls for vigilance, courage and technical skill, it cannot, in present conditions, be regarded as a major police anxiety.

The immediate greater problems are the threat to public order arising from hooliganism, political demonstrations, industrial disputes and racial tension, and, secondly, the danger of subversion of the operational independence and thus the impartiality of the police, especially by those who regard unlawful violence as a politically permissible tactic[17].

The most effective counter to violence in political demonstrations and industrial disputes is not the use of oppressive force or recourse to the uncertain and lengthy process of the criminal law, but the instinctive revulsion of the vast majority of all classes of people for the extremist minority who abuse the tolerance of the law in so unacceptable a way. It has taken the police a long time to accept that swift, clean co-ordinated arrests are the key to dismantling explosive situations[18] and to the isolation of political extemists so reviled by vast numbers of the populace. For their part the police are determined that never again will they be caught unprepared, untrained and unequipped for a major challenge to the rule of law on British streets. Contrary to many myths, the police too do not wish to see water cannons and tear gas used on the streets.

If the public are to help the police to avoid the violence of public protest some steps towards a programme of public education would be useful. Primarily, leaders of public opinion should speak out without equivocation and condemn the resort to violence for political or sectarian purposes. The police should not be expected to provide force as a substitute for the solution of social problems, and current tentative hints of the 'politicisation' of the police and criminal justice should continue to be firmly put down[19]. Force should come from an army aiding the civil power (i.e. assisting the police). This role can be vague and ambiguous since soldiers are by definition called upon to perform tasks not normally dealt with by the police, e.g. an ambush, a sniper or defusion of bombs, and so may be less inhibited in the methods used.

The public has also to be aware that despite numerous police forces being ranged on the anti-terrorist side to react to acts of terrorism, they are absolutely useless without a good intelligence organisation which enables them to forestall attacks, arrest terrorists or react quickly to an incident. The most appropriate body for the tasks of intelligence — gathering, collation, analysis and co-ordination — is the Special Branch. Police intelligence has to work against the Left trying to link the question of policing to what it sees as the underlying causes of the recent rioting; that repression is the government's inevitable response to the situation supposedly brought about by its own economic policies, mass unemployment and inner city squalor. Thus much of the far Left's comments on the disorders have been incorporated into its general attack on capitalism and monetarism[20].

Certain aspects of the riots showed how, if the police are to meet the ever more complex public demands and to be primary peacekeepers, consideration must be given to preparing officers for the task. In this context perhaps the American concept of 'crisis policing' should be studied. Officers are trained to infiltrate, mediate and to divert potentially

153

anti-social behaviour. In Britain the extension of Divisional Police Support Units is preferable to specially constituted riot police groups. The connotations of the latter are not conducive to police/public identification. It is at times of great public disorder that emphasis is placed on the strength of the British police service resting on its ties with the vast majority of the population.

The problem of a terrorist situation, in particular, is placed fairly and squarely on the shoulders of the police. On occasions (such as Balcombe Street) there may be some form of negotiation between the terrorists and the police and it is in this situation that the training the officer has received will reap rewards; and also that officer is aware of the intense public attention on him at the same time.

The police have always had a dual role of law enforcement and peace-keeping. Perhaps too much emphasis has been placed on enforcing laws and too little on keeping the peace. The media have much to answer for. They have highlighted conflict to such an extent that shock and horror has become the unit of exchange and shock and horror solutions are the only ones that appear acceptable. In relation to public disorder, the police have extensive powers by statute and common law. So law reform is not a priority, but it is none the less very important as being part of an overall need to strengthen the powers of law and order.

Before 1967, a separate and complementary form of riot existed under the *Riot Act, 1714*. Statutory riot was committed when 12 or more persons remained together for an hour after a magistrate had read a proclamation specified in the Act. It was repealed by the *Criminal Law Act, 1967*, but recent events resulted in calls for a similar provision to be re-enacted. After the Bristol disturbances the Police Federation suggested that the offence should be re-defined, and the correspondence columns of *The Times* carried letters advocating some provision making it an offence to fail to disperse when properly called upon. The common law offence of riot needs 5 elements — at least 3 persons; common purpose; lawful or unlawful; execution, or at least inception, of a common purpose; intention to help one another, by force, if necessary, against opposition in executing the common purpose; and force or violence, not merely in the common purpose but displayed in such manner as to alarm persons of reasonable courage.

The Law Commission Report No. 123 'Offences relating to Public Order' made various suggestions for reform of this area of law, including the creation of offences of 'violent disorder' by a group of 3 or more, and conduct intended or likely to cause fear or provoke violence. It is suggested that the offence of 'riot' should be retained in amended form. These suggestions have not yet been implemented; and currently there is a bill before Parliament called the Criminal Disorder Bill. Powers to act in respect of breaches of the peace are basically satisfactory, but the

154

language is old fashioned and more emphasis on preventive action is needed, and a statute required[21]. The intrusiveness of the legal system is accentuated by Britain's general policing philosophy, which puts emphasis on trying to prevent crimes from happening rather than reacting after the act.

Public order maintenance demands implementation of the basic requisite for members of a police force — absolute consistency and impartiality in the exercise of their professional duties[22]. It is vital in this context for police to be apolitical, although this is a very difficult situation. Any political influence would prejudice their impartiality, which must be the cornerstone of their professional activity. In every nation, and Britain is no exception, the police force is the foundation on which the orderly functioning of government rests.

The debate on law and order has been affected by the riots. Jim Jardine, leader of the Police Federation, described them as marking 'the threshold of a new era of public order'. The riots must not become an institutional part of British society — caused as some argue by the police, or as the majority argue by disaffected persons.

Disaffection in another way is helpful to the police, namely disaffected criminals in Ulster who have turned supergrass, i.e. men who have the power to help convict hundreds of terrorists. There is nothing new about the use of the evidence of accomplices in criminal trials. The law in England and Wales and Northern Ireland is the same. In both jurisdictions, where an accomplice gives evidence for the prosecution it is the duty of the judge to warn the jury that, although they may convict on his evidence, it is dangerous to do so unless it is corroborated. This old rule now has the force of a rule of law. A similar rule applies where a judge is trying a case without a jury. The judge must warn himself that, although he may convict on an accomplice's evidence, it is dangerous to do so unless it is corroborated. Subject to these rules the uncorroborated testimony of an accomplice is admissible in law and the tribunal of fact has the right to convict upon it. The decision in each supergrass case in reliance on the evidence of an accomplice as well as the decision to grant immunity to an accomplice — rests with the Northern Ireland D.P.P. (Director of Public Prosecutions) acting under the superintendence and subject to the directing of the Attorney General[23]. The Royal Ulster Constabulary is relying on the supergrass system in the long slog against terror. The terrorists will try to track down and kill an informer just so long as he is determined to betray the para-military organisation he once worked within. But if the supergrass betrays a second time by breaking his agreement with the police and finally refusing to go into the witness box he must be left well alone. There are not many supergrasses who have stopped short of sending their fellow terrorists to prison, while still holding on to the major prize they have secured for themselves: immunity from prosecution.

155

For the moment the Ulster Police have good reason to feel well satisfied with their supergrass system. But there have been other supergrass cases which have collapsed because the informers exploit the deals they have made with the police, and refuse to go through with their testimony in court[24]. The RUC themselves believe that they badly need the informers — 'converted terrorists' is the official police euphemism — because it is notoriously hard to secure evidence for the courts. Giving evidence against a terrorist organisation places one high on a hit list. During the late seventies, there was a spate of convictions based on admissions by suspects in police custody. But the interrogation methods inside Castlereagh and Gough Barracks which produced the confessions were discredited by Judge Bennett's report of 1979. Safeguards for the prisoner were introduced, the flow of confessions all but dried up; and pure forensic evidence proved scant and inconclusive. The only evidence which remains is that of the accomplice, the potential supergrass. It can be bought. Supergrasses have been used both in Great Britain and Northern Ireland before, but this time the inducements being offered are on a greater scale.

Although there are strong inducements to terrorists to turn supergrass there are also enormous pressures on them not to take that road. The IRA is operating an open-ended amnesty promising no harm to informers who retract their evidence before they harm the Provisionals. The police are content to point out that terrorist crime really has been sharply reduced in recent months precisely in those areas where supergrasses have emerged to demolish whole structures of men within the illegal organisations. The police have the backing of the government. The arguments over the use of supergrasses will continue in Northern Ireland, but so will the trials (viewed with mixed feelings by people). The supergrass system hardly epitomises the nature of the balance between coercion and consent. Society renegotiates the terms under which it likes to be policed. The long term repercussions of Scarman could mean the collapse into re-crimination, or lead to a reappraisal of what police need and how society should be policed.

While the police generally are in favour of capital punishment, they argue that it is no panacea. What is needed to beat the terrorists is a flexible and carefully co-ordinated programme of national measures. There is certainly no clear-cut evidence either way concerning the de-terrent value of the death penalty with regard to the hard-core terrorist. Any reintroduction would result in a sudden and severe escalation in terrorist violence at least in the short-term. An intelligence service of the highest quality is clearly a vital prerequisite for any effective counter insurgency campaign. Trends for greater police intelligence effectiveness have been improvements in techniques in intelligence gathering, in-filtration and surveillance, and in data computerisation.

The real dilemma facing the police today is that the pressures and strains imposed by terrorism and police-public confrontations in sensitive issue areas in the public order field, can work fairly dramatically to end the special relationship. There is no guarantee that the 'police advantage' will persist. The police task must be to maintain that advantage in spite of being baulked by the difficulty of maintaining adequate manpower coupled with the related problem of producing a continuity of highly trained, flexible and sophisticated command personnel for the police bureaucracy. The police maintain, with the support of many members of the public, that it was no easier to explain the riots than it was to predict them. Public order is now, and will continue to be, a major discussion point, and the role of the police in the community is being questioned.

The upsurge in terrorist activity and bombings in Ireland and the United Kingdom in 1982–83 have brought calls for the reintroduction of identity cards; the re-enactment of an Internment Act as existed for political undesirables and extremists during the Second World War; lodging registration to help monitor movements of possible terrorists; more specialised anti-terrorist units in the centres of major cities; security checks at entrances to public buildings and parking restrictions. Renewed public vigilance is required especially when police strength is being dissipated as a result of terrorism and public disorder, leaving some parts of the Metropolitan and provincial forces undermanned. The proscribing of extreme political parties such as the provisional IRA's political wing, Sinn Fein, is not the sole answer to the problems.

New anti-terrorist measures include round the clock mobile police squads, ready to respond to any threat plus an increase in the metropolis of C.I.D. and Special Branch officers, further Special Patrol Group units and 320 more officers on the beat, extra dog handlers and traffic officers. Two obstacles to effective security against terrorists in mainland U.K. as opposed to Ulster (which the police fully recognise) are firstly the denser distribution of population (London has 6.8 million people compared to 350,000 civilians in Belfast). This can result in the virtually unsolvable workload of dealing with millions of suspects; and secondly the international as well as the British problem of the apparent availability of bomb materials and other offensive weapons to those cold blooded enough to use them. In the absence of an international agreement among responsibly minded nations to boycott countries which harbour and train terrorists different nations can still pool their experience on the anti-terrorism front. Little practical co-operation in cases at police level has been forthcoming in spite of a growing and disparate terrorist threat.

In a democracy, terrorists have limitless opportunities with little risk to themselves. The question to be answered in the next year or so is how to limit these opportunities and increase risks to the men of violence, without changing the liberal nature of Britain. It is a bonus for any terrorist if the political and police authorities panic into reacting without thinking through the consequences of premature initiatives. The public's alertness is the best line of defence[25]. The aim of the terrorist is to have his way whatever the opposition. He creates a state of uncertainty among the public.

NOTES

1. For detailed discussion of Army-Police role see articles by J. R. Thackrah 'Army-Police Co-operation: A General Asessment', *Police and Society Research Centre Paper*, Vol. 1 No. 7, October 1982; and 'Army-Police Co-operation Against Terrorism', *Police Journal*, January–March 1983.
2. C. Dobson & R. Payne, *Terror! The West Fights Back* (Macmillan 1982), p. 62.
3. T. Bowden, 'Men in the Middle — the UK Police', *Conflict Studies No. 68,* February 1976, p. 14.
4. Dobson and Payne. *op. cit*, p.68.
5. Bowden, *op. cit*, p.13.
6. *Hunt Report* (Cmd 545, 1969)
7. F. Gregory, 'Protest and Violence: the Police Response', *Conflict Studies No.75*, September 1976.
8. P. Wilkinson, 'Terrorism versus Liberal Democracy: The Problems of Response', *Conflict Studies No.67*, January 1976 p.16.
9. P. Shipley, 'The Riots and the far Left', *New Community*, Vol.IX No.2, p.197.
10. Commentary on Riots, *Police Journal*, October 1981, pp 326–7.
11. 'Riots and the Aftermath', *Police Journal*, October–December 1981, pp 320–327.
12. F. Baddeley, 'Racial Insurrection on Liverpool — Merseyside Toxteth Summer Riots, 1981', *Constabulary Gazette*, January 1983, p.7.
13. P. J. Waller, 'The Riots in Toxteth, Liverpool: a Survey', *New Community*, Winter 1981/Spring 1982, p.344.
14. Waller, *op. cit*, p.348.
15. M. Kettle, 'Evolution of an Official Explanation', *New Society*, 3rd December 1981.
16. E. J. Mishan, 'A Sceptical View of Scarman', *New Society*, 10th December, 1981.
17. R. Mark, 'The Police of the Eighties', *Police Review*, 14th November, 1980.
18. *Yorkshire Post*, 11th August, 1983.
19. J. Alderson, *Policing Freedom*, (MacDonald & Evans 1979), p.206.

20. Shipley, *op. cit*, p.198
21. Alec Samuels, 'Public Disorder: The Police need more legal powers', *The Solicitors' Journal*, 29th October, 1982, Vol.126 No.43.
22. M. Gonzalez-Lopez, 'The changing role of the police in a developed society', *International Review of Criminal Policy*, No.33, 1977.
23. Attorney General Questioned, *Northern Ireland Information Service*, 24th October, 1983.
24. J. Robbins, 'The Men who have the power to help convict hundreds of terrorists', *Listener*, 11th August, 1983.
25. For general discussion of police-public relations see 'Evolution of Police-Public Relations', *Police World*, Winter 1982–83 by J. R. Thackrah

An introduction to aspects of public order and the police

C. VICK

Since their introduction in 1829 the British police have mediated in two separate demands made by different social classes in British society. The first demand, for democratic incorporation into the political process of government decision making, was made by groups previously excluded from such processes. These were the middle classes, working classes and women. The second demand, 'the demand for order' in working class communities, was made by the upper and propertied classes. Both demands, from these different social classes, resulted in social conflict and public disorder. The police role was different in each of these two processes. In policing the demands for democratic rights, the police can be seen to act as a buttress between the groups making the demands and the government of the day. In contrast, in response to the 'demand for order' in working class communities by the propertied classes, the police were the instrument of that very process. The 'demand for order' was inextricably linked to the acceptance of the idea of policing itself. Although the police were an instrument of the demand for order, they, nonetheless, can still be seen to act as a mediator in the demand for order in the working and lower classes made by the upper and propertied classes.

Historically it is possible to characterise the police function as a mediatory one between conflicting social classes, who have their respective demands of each other. Disenfranchised groups have demanded democratic rights from governing classes, and governing classes have demanded order within working class communities. The idea of the mediatory role of the police has been to reduce violence in society. First, by replacing the use of the military in inter class conflicts and disputes. Secondly, the police were designed to penetrate into society in a way impossible for the military. From such a position within working class communities, the police acted as mediators in intra community conflicts, being the sole legal agents of the use of violence in settling disputes.

The social and political circumstances in which the police were introduced in London in 1829 were not favourable for ensuring their public acceptance and support. It was a period of political and class conflict and an unreformed Parliament, and also the lower classes were more accustomed to customary notions of order than the juristic/legalistic notions of order demanded by the upper classes and represented by the police. If the police were to act as mediators in a class divided society, with different class demands, then it was necessary that they should be

161

seen to be impartial. The political demands of these classes; the 'demand for entry into politics' and the 'demand for order' or the extension of authority into society, have implications both for public order and the issue of the legitimacy and acceptance of the police.

THE DEMAND FOR 'ENTRY INTO POLITICS'

Critchley's study 'The Conquest of Violence'[1] details the process of democratisation or the demand for 'entry into politics'. He distinguishes a forward looking and modern form of violence that is associated with this process of democratisation. Such violence 'aspires to gain for a minority group rights and privileges which it has never before enjoyed. The Reform Bill rioters of 1831, demanding 'one man one vote', the Chartists, some of the insurrectionary strikes of 1911–1912, and all the 'Votes for Women' suffragettes had in common this forward-looking motivation'[2]. There are two points in Critchley's argument that are worthy of emphasis. First, he argues that since about 1820 British Governments have grown increasingly responsive to public opinion and democratic pressure, and have been more ready to alleviate conditions leading to discontent. In particular with regard to the demand for 'entry into politics', the spread of the franchise was one of the major reasons why 'the prime causes of public violence in Britain had, by about the year 1900, been largely (though not wholly) eliminated'[3]. Such an extension of democratic rights helped to ensure the legitimacy of government. Secondly, Critchley argues that it was the minimum use of force used by the police that helped to ensure their acceptance. Critchley argues that it was the British police force's deliberate policy to show restraint and to offer no provocation to violence. 'Experience shows that such a force (in contrast to a brutal or oppressive force) is likely to prevent the recurrence of outbreaks of violence rather than to encourage their repetition'[4]. Ultimately, however, the quality of policing depends upon the nature of government. 'Democracy merely imperils itself by being insensitive. When frustrated protest degenerates into violence and violence into counter-violence it is liberty that suffers in the long run, because authority feels obliged to intensify its measures of law enforcement. This, unhappily, does not seem to be as widely understood as it ought to be'[5]. Miller has drawn a direct link between the process of democratisation of society and the gradual acceptance of the London police force. He has argued that it was the political conflicts within a class divided society that were the formative influences upon London's police. For Miller the London police tradition cannot be explained as the result of a consensual society. Rather, the London police were introduced and developed in a period of intense social conflict. The London police were introduced in a period of constitutional crisis over parliamentary representation for disenfranchised middle and working classes. In such a political climate Miller argues that the police became the target of almost universal hostility from London citizens. The aristocracy managed this challenge to their political authority by separating the middle classes from the working classes through the electoral reform of 1832. In the process of doing so policemen were quickly to become accepted and enthusiastically supported by middle class Londoners. 'The Metropolitan Police Act of 1839, extending police powers beyond the original 1829 Act, was a ratification of middle class support'[6].

The working classes, who were still excluded from political representation, were less enthusiastic than the middle classes for a legal order they saw as resting on 'one law for the rich, another law for the poor'. Miller argues that the police were seen by the working classes to be upholding law and order in an undemocratic society. A more general acceptance of the police among the working classes had to await the political reform in 1867, which extended the franchise to the skilled urban working classes. It was the 1867 reform that helped to place the police on a firmer basis of public support among the working classes. However, although political inequalities may have grown less, social and economic inequalities remained. This meant that working class acceptance of the police continued to be fragile and ambivalent.

Miller has also argued that the London police image and strategy was formed during a period of serious political conflict and crisis. The London police were introduced in London in 1829 before the middle and working classes had the vote. The police were introduced in an effort to reduce and contain such challenges to the political order. Miller argues that the police role was fundamentally political. In such a political situation the police had to adopt a strategy and image that would not exacerbate attitudes and fuel conflict.

To avoid becoming 'identified as the cutting edge of the ruling minority's oppression', they adopted a strategy whereby they rose above conflict by adopting a non political, impartial and impersonal image. The removal of the police from partisan politics was a crucial element of this impartiality. Because the police were formed during a period of political conflict in Britain, when there was widespread hostility to the government which created them and widespread fear and suspicion of the police themselves, the police had to adopt strategies to ensure their acceptance by society at large. In addition to the image of impersonal authority, the London police adopted a strategy of restrained use of force in handling public disorder. The acceptance of the authority of the London policeman rested on his image as a 'bureaucratic professional'. Miller argues that it was a part of the police task to educate the public to an appreciation of impartial authority. Indeed it was the growing belief in the impartiality of the police that was the secret of their success in the nineteenth century. The legitimacy and acceptance of the police, through the extension of democratic rights and the adoption of an impartial image, was further underpinned by the police performing service functions for both the middle and working classes.

Miller's study of the London police is a part of a comparative study in which he also examines the New York police. He argues that it was the different political circumstances and nature of social conflict that were the main reasons for each police force developing its different traditions and image. The London police were introduced during a time of class conflict, when working men were disenfranchised and were hostile to both government and the police. The police were formed in a society where the authority of a small elite was challenged by the majority of the population.

However, the political situation and the nature of social conflict in America was different. The American working classes were not disenfranchised and the political order was founded on majority rule. The majority of the population supported the political order. While the English working classes were generally united in their opposition to government, the American working classes were divided amongst themselves. The 'native working classes saw a political order they valued threatened by irresponsible foreigners who did not appreciate democracy'[7]. Miller argues that it was this different political situation, and the existence of ethnic conflicts, that was crucial in shaping the development of New York policing. 'Since the New York police upheld the political institutions of representative democracy which most Americans valued, there was little pressure for them to transcend social conflict to insure their own survival. Instead of upholding the rule of a small elite which was challenged by the majority of the population, the police supported a political order founded on majority rule which seemed threatened by an alien minority. Along with most New Yorkers, the police were free to treat a large group in the community as outsiders. This groups' participation in disorder did not require the sort of sensitivity needed to uphold minority rule without alienating the majority'[8].

Because the New York police image was not being formed during a period of serious political crisis, the creators of the force were not under pressure to rise above conflict and develop an impersonal image. Unlike London's police, who had to gain the acceptance of the general public by acting in an apolitical, impartial, and impersonal manner, support for the government and the police in New York was already assured. Instead of rising above conflicts with an impersonal image, the New York police 'tended to reflect and act out community conflicts instead of trying to establish and maintain standards which transcended the conflicts'[9] The New York police responded to the demands for order from 'respectable' New Yorkers. The need for restraint and moderation in the use of force was not present as it was in London. Instead there was popular support for the use of violent means to be used to restore order. 'Respectable' New

Yorkers seemed to have 'expected and accepted "no fuss, few words, but action" against the immigrant "dangerous classes" who seemed to be a "volcano under the city"'[10].

Miller characterises American police authority as 'delegated vigilantism' — the patrolman did what most citizens would have done in his position. The consequence was a tradition of police violence. The late nineteenth century patterns of policing in London and New York, saw London moving away from violent repression, while New York police were setting a pattern of violence.

In Miller's analysis, the London police tradition of impartiality and minimum use of force is seen as a legacy of a particular historical period. The conditions which characterised that period, namely political conflict over parliamentary representation and general hostility towards government and the police have now changed. Today the social and political conditions in London are more akin to those found in New York at the foundation of their police force. The authority of the government is accepted by the general population. The British police are a highly respected institution in British society. The conflict in British society more closely resembles ethnic conflict than any fundamental conflict between government and people. The British police could now be said to be under the same pressures as the New York police at the time of their foundation. With the increase in crime and disorder during the 1970s and 1980s there has been a corresponding increase in the 'demand for order'. It is more likely that our present social conflicts are seen as ethnic conflicts, and are seen as a consequence of immigrants or aliens who threaten our social and political order. Given the majorities support for the political and social system, 'as in New York, many Londoners pressured the police to suppress disorder regardless of the means, demanding that bobbies be released from some of their traditional restraints'[11].

The 'demand for order' within the marginalised lower working classes is now made by the 'respectable' middle and working classes. Miller questions whether under such pressure the traditional restraint of the British police can survive.

THE DEMAND FOR ORDER IN A CLASS SOCIETY

The process of social change identified by Silver is what he has termed 'the demand for order in civil society'[12]. The social processes Silver considers could be seen to be the reverse of the process of democratic 'incorporation' or 'demand for entry into politics'. Violence was one means adopted by those groups seeking 'entry into politics' and incorporation into the political processes. Violence and protest was one means used against the state to ensure a part in the democratic political process. The police role was that of mediating in this process of political conflict and struggle. Silver, however, reverses the scenario and to illustrate how the State has extended both its moral authority and coercive powers into society with the introduction of the police force.

Bittner has also argued that the moral aspirations of Western democratic societies to the abolition of violence, and the desire to install peace as a stable and permanent condition of everyday life, required the introduction of the police service. The use of violence within the society could be limited and controlled if its exercise was vested in a 'corps of specially deputized officials endowed with the exclusive monopoly of using force contingently where limitations of foresight fail to provide alternatives'[13]. Bittner, like Silver, draws a sharp distinction between the military and the police. While both the military and the police have the use of force at the core of their function, the military use of force against external enemies, which can be ruthless in its application, is not the hallmark of the police use of force, 'Above all, force may not be used for any other purpose but to effect restraint'[14].

Silver writes that 'that police were designed to penetrate civil society in a way impossible for military formations and by doing so prevent crime and violence and to detect and apprehend criminals'[15]. He argues that the penetration of the police into civil society was both a simultaneous process of the extension of moral and political authority throughout daily life as well as the extension of state coercion. For Silver, the police mission is both a moral and coercive one:- 'The benefits of police organisation — continual pervasive moral display and lower long term costs of official coercion for the state and propertied classes — absolutely required the moral co-operation of civil society. Thus, the extension of moral consensus and of the police as an instrument of legitimate coercion go hand in hand'[16]. And, 'the police rely not only on a technique of graduated, discretionary, and ubiquitous coercion but also on a new and unprecedented extensive form of moral consensus'[17].

As the moral consensus has extended outwards from the 'centre' to the 'periphery' of society (or downwards from the elite or ruling classes, through the middle classes to the working classes) so too the demand for order within society has increased. The demand for 'law and order' has become a constitutional imperative. Not only are public expectations of public order higher than before amongst those 'peaceful', 'respectable', and propertied classes, but also the demand for 'law and order' is now heard most loudly amongst those groups, who at the introduction of the police, were seen as the very object of police concern, namely the working classes.

THE MEDIATING ROLE OF THE POLICE

In adopting a consensual model of society, Silver does not detail the extent of opposition to the introduction of the police force and the degree to which coercive as opposed to moral force was used by them to 'penetrate society'.

The extension of police authority into a class society met with the resistance of sections of the working classes to the imposition of new concepts of orderliness and discipline that reflected the ideals and aspirations of the middle and upper classes. Emsley has pointed out that two conflicting definitions of order can be identified; juristic and customary. '"Order" for the jurist was an ideal to be achieved; it embraced good behaviour, cleanliness, morality and sobriety, and it thus required the suppression, or tight regulation, of gaming, prostitution, vagabonds and alehouses or cabarets'[18].

This view of order, held by propertied classes, came into conflict with a more popular, customary view of order held by poorer classes. This customary view of order favoured the 'maintenance of local values, of traditional community behaviour, and the exclusion of poisonous local conflicts which the introduction of the "law" could bring'[19].

Storch[20] has documented how the working classes resisted police interventions into their daily lives and recreational activities. The response by the working classes to the attempted imposition of new standards of order into their communities, which attempted to transform their culture, was frequently one of stiff resistance in the form of anti-police riots. In areas where the police were newly implanted the aim was to drive them out altogether. In areas where the police were well established, anti-police protest was aimed at preserving popular recreations or customs. A state of armed truce between working class communities and the police resulted which broke down if it was felt that the police were becoming over watchful regarding recreational activities, or were behaving in a brutal or disrespectful manner. When the police became established in working class communities it was the quality of day to day police-public relations that determined whether there would be further anti-police riots.

The acceptance of the legitimacy of police authority was a gradual, piecemeal, pragmatic process of negotiation and accommodation between the police and these sections of society. It was the fact that the police were able to exercise their discretion in the matter of law enforcement that enabled them to mediate between those classes who led the 'demands for order' and the calls for the enforcement of the law, and the realities of a class divided society in which conceptions of what constituted 'good order' often conflicted.

Despite the fact that the police were given the role of 'domestic missionary', Storch has argued that 'Mayne acquired a pragmatic awareness of the resiliency of these popular institutions and became quite hesitant to dissipate the energies of his force in constant open warfare with them'[21]. Rather, 'police authorities of necessity had to engage in a cost-effective calculus, based upon disposable manpower, size of the district, and the extent of the pressure being exerted by moral-reform interest groups, magistrates, or watch committees'[22]. The police pursued a policy of increasing surveillance rather than one of intense and overt suppression of aspects of working class recreational life.

The use of discretion by the police in order to secure some degree of compliance from the community is described by Ignatieff. 'They often chose not to take their authority to the letter of the law, preferring not to "press their luck" in return for tacit compliance from the community. In each neighbourhood, and sometimes street by street, the police negotiated a complex, shifting, largely unspoken "contract". They defined the activities they would turn a blind eye to, and those which they would suppress, harass or control. This "tacit contract" between normal neighbourhood activities and police objectives, was sometimes oiled by corruption, but more often sealed by favours and friendship. This was the microscopic basis of police legitimacy, and it was a fragile basis at best'[23].

The police can be seen to play a mediating role between those classes who hold a jurist view of order and a highly legalistic view of the police function, who expect the law to be enforced without fear or favour, and those classes who had different conceptions of order, who resisted such an imposition of the 'law'. Whyte has described the 'buffer' role of the police as follows; 'The smoothest course for the officer is to conform to the social organisation with which he is in direct contact and at the same time to try to give the impression to the outside world that he is enforcing the law. He must play an elaborate role of make-believe, and, in so doing, he serves as a buffer between conflicting standards of conduct'[24].

Kinsey and Young have defended the use of police discretion and have argued that the ultimate source of their autonomy 'lies in the peculiar contradictory class position and role that the police find themselves in'[25].

The cultural autonomy of the police from the middle and upper classes undermines the strict application of bourgeois standards and shields certain sections of the poor from the dispassionate impact of the law. The police do not try to enforce middle class standards of order upon the respectable working classes. However, the police do reflect 'respectable' working class standards and conceptions of law and order and seek to impose them upon marginalised working classes (e.g. unemployed blacks, gypsies, 'problem' families etc.).

LAW OR ORDER

The apparently singular demand for 'law and order' can, on occasions, involve a choice between law or order. 'The ordinary practice of policing treats "law enforcement" and the "preservation of order" as coincident goals. It is no accident that "law and order" is one word in the consciousness of the police, and to a great extent of the public at large. Arresting lawbreakers is perceived as the sine qua non of policing and as naturally leading to the preservation of order. Ordinarily, this may be so, but when the consent on which policing is based breaks down it is not only possible but plausible that arresting law breakers will provoke or promote disorder'[26]. Field points out that ordinary law enforcement activities of the police could provoke disorder.

Given the choice between the enforcement of the law or the maintenance of order Scarman has written: 'His priorities are clear: the maintenance of public tranquillity comes first. If law enforcement puts at risk public tranquillity, he will have to make a difficult decision. Inevitably there there will be situations in which the public interest requires him to test the wisdom of law enforcement by its likely effect upon public order... The Conflict which can arise between the duty of the police to maintain order and their duty to enforce the law, and the priority which must be given to the former, have long been recognised by the police themselves...'[27].

Cohen has noted that the conflicting demands of enforcing the law and the maintenance of public order have become institutionalised in different policing departments. The contradiction between these two police functions has intensified. 'The more resources allocated to increasing the efficiency of repressive policing, the more manpower has to be poured into "community relations" to restabilise the public image of the force. The more technologically sophisticated, and hence impersonal, the systems of surveillance, the more home-beat coppers are needed on the ground'[28].

The two conflicting policing functions of peacekeeping and law enforcement have historically been embodied in the individual constable. It was his discretion that determined the balance between these functions. However, these functions have become differentiated and institutionalised. The two different styles of policing have been described by Sir Kenneth Newman: 'A neighbourhood policeman who does not see too much and does not interfere will be tolerated. But let him arrest someone for an offence and immediately a score or more of youths will surround him, assault him and release the prisoner. Perhaps he will call up reinforcements, in which case the number of youths will multiply to 100 or more and there will be a confrontation which could escalate into a full blooded riot... It is the rough, difficult and potentially violent aspects of multi-ethnic areas that oblige the police to supplement neighbourhood policing with police units having a more robust capability. In London this need is met by deploying police mobile support units, each manned by an Inspector and about 20 men, to provide a rapid response to spontaneous outbreaks of disorder'[29].

It is the militarisation of the police through the development of specialised units as described by Sir Kenneth Newman that Lea and Young believe has led to the further alienation of the community from the police[30].

I have emphasised from the start of this essay that the police organisation and its use of force is different from the military. The central difference is the use of discretion by individual police officers. Bordua has written that: 'In democratic societies the problem of assuring that the police are organised so as to be a reliable instrument for the maintenance of order and the suppression and prevention of crime, while at the same time assuring that they exhibit restraint and sensitivity to citizens' rights, means that organisation of the police cannot be like that of an assault battalion which on command can be relied upon to do its duty regardless of cost to itself, its enemies, or the surrounding social fabric'[31].

CONTINUING THE MEDIATING FUNCTION

The British police have mediated in two separate demands made by different social classes in British society. The demand for 'entry into politics' necessitated a fundamental reform towards a greater demo-cratisation of the processes of political decision making and government. Such a process of incorporation of the middle and working classes into the political decision making process, helped to secure the legitimacy not only of the authority of government, but also of the police. It is mainly among the 'marginalised' lower classes that the police are seen to represent social class interests different from their own. 'The Law', which the police enforce, can be seen as embodying the interests of those in authority over them. It is amongst the marginalised lower classes, that support for the police and the idea of policing by consent is most fragile.

The 'demand for order' required the introduction of the police service itself, and the acceptance by different social classes of the idea of a policed society. At the introduction of the police force the 'demand for order' was made in generalised terms about the whole of the working class who were seen as 'dangerous'. But as distinctions were made by those in authority, between the 'respectable' and 'rough' sections of the working classes, the 'demand for order' can be seen to have become concentrated upon the marginalised 'rough' sections of the working classes. The 'respectable' working classes have joined the middle classes in their demand for order as the focus of their concern has narrowed on to the 'marginalised' working classes. Brogden has written; 'Both major classes, as well as the solidary peer groups within the police institution, can unite against them (marginalised working classes)'[32].

The social and political context in which the police have traditionally ensured the priority of their peacekeeping/order maintenance functions over their law enforcement function has changed since their introduction. That social and political context is now one of a far higher degree of public support for the police, and a greater 'demand for order'.

The police could face possible difficulties if such a public 'demand for order' was understood as meaning that the law is to be enforced without fear or favour, thereby limiting the traditional discretion the police have had, and have used, to put order maintenance as a higher priority to the enforcement of the law. And, secondly, if such a 'demand for order' implies an acceptance of the greater use of force by the police in enforcing the law. Such a demand would jeopardize the traditional restraint of British policing. It is to be hoped that such an understanding of the demand for 'Law and Order' does not gain currency. If it does, then the mediatory function the police have historically played between different social classes will also be threatened. The police do 'find themselves buffeted one way and another by these opposing interests'[33], as Sir Kenneth Newman points out. But this is nothing new. They have traditionally mediated in the demands for order and the demands for democratic change of that social order. It is to be hoped that they can continue this tradition, difficult though this makes the job of policing.

REFERENCES

1. T. A. Critchley, *The Conquest of Violence*, Constable 1970.
2. T. A. Critchley, Ibid, p. 6.
3. T. A. Critchley, Ibid, p. 25.
4. T. A. Critchley, Ibid, p. 209.
5. T. A. Critchley, Ibid, p. 211.
6. W. R. Miller, *London's Police Tradition in a Changing Society* in 'British Police' ed. S. Holdaway (Arnold 1979), p. 14.
7. W. R. Miller, 'Cops and Bobbies' Police Authority in New York and London 1830–1870 University of Chicago 1977, p. 11.
8. W. R. Miller, Ibid, p. 11.
9. W. R. Miller, Ibid, p. 20.
10. W. R. Miller, Ibid, p. 23.
11. W. R. Miller, Ibid, p. 170.
12. A. Silver, 'The Demand for Order in Civil Society' in 'The Police: Six Sociological Essays' ed. D. J. Bordua, pp. 1–24.
13. E. Bittner, 'The Functions of the Police in Modern Society' National Institute of Mental Health (November 1970), p. 50.
14. E. Bittner, Ibid, p. 122.
15. A. Silver, Ibid, p. 12.

16. A. Silver, Ibid, p. 14.
17. A. Silver, Ibid, p. 15.
18. C. Emsley, *Policing and its Context 1750–1870*, Macmillan 1983, p. 132.
19. C. Emsley, Ibid, p. 132.
20. R. D. Storch, 'The Policeman as Domestic Missionary: Urban Discipline and Popular Culture in Northern England 1850–1880', Journal of Social History, Summer 1976, p. 486.
21. Ibid, p. 487.
22. M. Ignatieff, 'Police and People: The Birth of Mr. Peel's "Blue Locusts"', *New Society* 30th August 1979, pp. 443–445.
23. W. F. Whyte, quoted in, B. Chapman, *Police State* Macmillan 1970, p. 97.
24. R. Kinsey & J. Young, 'Police Autonomy and the Politics of Discretion' in D. Cowell, T. Jones, J. Young *Policing the Riots* Junction Books 1982, p. 125.
25. 'Public Disorder', Home Office Research Study No. 72 (1982), p. 20.
26. 'The Scarman Report — The Brixton Disorders', 10th–12th April 1981, Pelican 1982, p. 103.
27. P. Cohen, 'Policing the Working Class City' in M. Fitzgerald, G. McLennan, J. Pawson 'Crime and Society' Reading in History and Theory, Open University Press 1981, p. 128.
28. Sir Kenneth Newman, 'Fighting the Fear of Crime' in *Police* magazine Vol. XVI No. 1, September 1983, pp. 30–31.
29. J. Lea & J. Young, 'Urban Violence and Political Marginalisation' in 'Policing the Riots', p. 13.
   On 'militarization' of Police see also J. Lea & J. Young 'The Riots in Brixton 1981' in *Policing the Riots*, Junction Books 1982.
30. D. J. Bordua, 'Police' Encyclopeadia of Social Sciences, p. 178.
   See also E. Bittner 'Function of Police in Modern Society' chapter 'The Police' and 'War on Crime'.
31. M. Brogen, *The Police: Autonomy and Consent*, Academic Press 1983, p. 233.
32. J. Jardine, 'Jardine Tells Whitelaw', '*Police*' Vol. XIII No. 10, June 1981, p. 9.
33. Sir Kenneth Newman, 'Fighting the Fear of Crime', '*Police*' magazine Vol. XVI No. 1, September 1983, p. 26.

This essay is a selective review of some of the literature on public order and the police. Some readers may feel that I have placed undue emphasis on the mediating role of the police in intervening in social conflict between social classes, and the role the police might play in lessening social conflict by balancing the conflicting demands between the order maintenance function and the law enforcement function. The idea of the police acting as mediators in a class society is not beyond dispute and should not be understood as the only view of the police role presented at Bramshill.

Dilemmas of Police Management and Organisation
M. D. PLUMRIDGE

'Cost and efficiency, over the long run, *follow* from the emphasis on quality, service, innovativeness, result-sharing, participation, excitement, and an external problem-solving focus that is tailored to the customer' (Thomas J. Peters and Robert H. Waterman Jr. 'In Search of Excellence' Harper & Row, 1982, p.321).

The police manager in the 1980s is faced with a number of dilemmas foremost among which is that he is experiencing increasing pressure to account for the use of expensive resources when he is conscious that his control of those resources is, at best, tenuous and his mission unclear and controversial.

The scenario from which this dilemma springs consists of:
1. A rapidly changing society which presents a range of new policing problems. Among such changes are
   (a) the development of pluralism in society bringing an increased number of often vociferous minority groups into being
   (b) arising out of (a) a tendency for the traditional two-party approach to fragment and give rise to a wider spectrum of political opinion on many issues, including the role of police in society
   (c) the rapid increase in unemployment which has produced a large body of disaffected youth
   (d) the growth of tension and conflict within society accompanied by a readier use of violence
   (e) increasing pressure on public finance which demands the strategic deployment of limited resources, and the evaluation of the relationship between inputs and outputs, be it quantitative or qualitative
   (f) increasing pressure from the representatives of the public at a local level for more police accountability and more consultation over policing strategies.
2. The rapid development of information processing potential leading to a greatly enhanced research effort, both within and outside the service, which ensures a better informed public and demands research conscious police managers. Decisions taken intuitively or on the basis of experience alone are becoming increasingly vulnerable to both internal and external validation.

3. As problems become more complex, and as the body of knowledge grows, so the myth of the omniscient, omnipotent police managers evaporates. Police organisations become more differentiated and more complex and the role of the manager shifts from that of the unilateral decision-maker to that of the co-ordinator and team leader who can develop collaborative and creative decision-making.
4. As the volume and diversity of information penetrates all homes and workplaces through the medium of radio and television more and more police officers become drawn into the public debates on organisational and management effectiveness, and their knowledge of, and interest in managerial methods has been aroused.
5. The enhancement of the status of the police officer in recent years, coupled with the growth of unemployment in society, has created a highly favourable recruiting situation. The resultant selectivity is leading to the recruitment of a new generation of well-educated, questioning constables.

Such a scenario ensures that police management is becoming a challenge to the most gifted and socially skilled members of our society.

The public image of the police as crime-fighters, largely fostered by the police themselves, and encouraged by the mass-media, has usually been able to feed on public fears of a breakdown in law and order in order to gain both support and resources. Research and experimentation into resource deployment has steadily eroded that position and it has become clear that without the full co-operation of other social agencies and, indeed, of the public themselves, crimes are unlikely either to be prevented or to be solved.

We are still passing through the period of the great debate concerning reactive versus proactive policing. Reactive policing means that the officer is summoned to the scene of a crime by a member of the public, be he victim, witness or private security guard, who then gives evidence leading to the apprehension of the offender in 90% of all arrests made (Reiss, 1971)[1]. Proactive policing, on the other hand, means that the police themselves initiate some type of key activity designed to deter crime or to identify and apprehend law-breakers. Numerous pieces of research have failed to reveal a significant relationship between proactive methods and a reduction in crime. The Kansas City Patrol Experiment seriously questions the ability of the police to prevent crime by preventive patrolling (Kelling et al, 1974)[2]. On the other hand another study (Wilson and Boland, 1978)[3] concludes that when more units of patrol are deployed and the officers used an 'aggressive' police style, there is an increase in robbery arrests and a lowering of the robbery rate. In San Diego, California, the police, with the assistance of some 4,500 'Community Alert Groups' have reduced the incidence of burglary by 11% per annum for the past 3 years. Such a phenomenon serves to underline the fact that the police are at their most effective when acting as 'co-producers' with members of the public (Ostrom et al, 1978)[4], and does little to enhance the claim that police are professional crime-fighters.

Given these trends it seems that the police would do well to avoid the need to justify the use of their resources in terms of crime-fighting for, in the light of current evidence, they may well find themselves hoisted on their own petard. Rather they might heed that trend of opinion which sees them as an agency of central and local government whose role, as part of social planning, is primarily concerned with the handling of emergencies (Goldstein H., 1977)[5]. This service role is indicated by the research of Sandra Jones and Dr Michael Levi (1983)[6] who say, 'Our research has shown quite clearly that there is a major gap between police and public valuations of the service role and of routine human interaction skills. The problem is that the latter are not as easily measurable as are the more technical police goals (except in the negative, by the incidence of complaints against the police). The primary task must be to convince the police themselves (for the public already *are* convinced) that these service goals are *primary*, and that the police, in contrast to their self-image as omnipotent professionals, are merely dependent community aides'. Jones and Levi go on to say 'Their "professionalism" resides in their ability to maintain community confidence, to promote public solidarity (both against crime and for its own sake), to channel information, and to respond to public "wants" rather than to impose their concept of public "needs"'.

In this either/or debate Dr P. A. Waddington[7] makes a plea for a more balanced role under the title of 'peace officer'. He says 'What is common to the multifarious duties of the police is the exercise of authority. The police are empowered to intervene in virtually any emergency because they are the monopolists of legitimate coercion in civil society. They, and they alone, can tell people what to do (within extensive limits) and coerce compliance if those people refuse'. He goes on to say 'In the continuing debate as to how Britain should be policed in the last quarter of the 20th century, the police should seek, in my view, to convey these realities. They should say, without embarrassment or apology, that what the police do is to intervene authoritatively in circumstances with which ordinary people cannot cope. They should proudly proclaim that this is a task calling for considerable professional skill'.

Hence police work has to be seen along a continuum with the use of legitimate force (the law enforcement role) at one end and the use of subtle social and interactive skills at the other (the service role). Moreover, at any given moment, at the scene of any incident, the individual constable must be capable of responding in an appropriate manner. Such a role requires a very high level of versatility and social awareness, and the organisation which supports him must be capable of great

175

sensitivity and flexibility. To the constable 'on the ground' it all too often seems that his role requires great maturity and sensitivity and the wisdom of Solomon, whereas the organisation of which he is a part, in an insensitive punishment-centred manner, demands submissiveness, deference and immaturity. The recent A.C.P.O. report[8] on the incidence and sources of stress in the police service suggests that primary causes are management systems and management styles. Far from reducing the stress induced by the ambiguity of the role and traumatic incidents dealt with the latter greatly exacerbate the problem. It would appear that police organisations are designed upon the model of an army, whose function is to fight crime, when that function occupies at most 10% of its daily activity! The implications of such a situation are enormous and it is quite apparent that the roles and styles of police managers will need to undergo some fundamental changes.

On a recent visit by a group of senior British police officers from the Senior Command Course at Bramshill to San Diego Police Department in California one of the Commanders from that force, well-known for his innovative approach to police work, said, 'Of course I am no longer a police officer. The most senior operational policeman in this department is a Captain who is responsible for running police operations in a section of the city. My role is that of a police manager whose task it is to provide operational policemen with the wherewithal to carry out those operations as effectively and as efficiently as possible. If I could not move down the road and run that insurance company or that engineering factory I ought not to be in my present position'. These words had a considerable effect upon his British visitors in the light of all they were to see and experience in San Diego for, while they ran counter to the culture of the British police service, they seemed to them to epitomise a current trend which is inexorably influencing expectations of *them*. As the investment of national resources in the public services is squeezed, so the evaluation of their managers focuses increasingly on their capacity to use resources wisely and to extract maximum benefit from them. In order to do this managers in any organisation need a clear definition of its mission and objectives; in their absence what are to be the guidelines for resource deployment and the evaluation of the results of their strategy, and hence what is to be the level of future investment in their service? For this reason strategic planning and Policing by Objectives (P.B.O.)[9] are beginning to take hold of police organisations in a manner hitherto unknown. Pressure is being applied from government on to Chief Constables to manage strategically, and senior police officers are increasingly turning to managerial planning and evaluation techniques. Such techniques are highly seductive but they do not address the problems outlined above, indeed they may well exacerbate the stress if introduced into a 'top-down' punishment-centred organisation.[10] As was quoted above from Sandra Jones the human interaction skills required of the service role are not as easily measurable as are the more technical police goals such as arrest rates, clearance rates and response rates. Nevertheless, if those skills are to flourish they need to be carefully and strategically developed and nourished by the organisation. The police manager in an authoritarian organisation might harbour the illusion that he controls those interactive skills as closely as he believes that he controls the technical police goals. This *is* an illusion as research has shown in a wide variety of organisations. It is, in fact, much more likely to be an illusion in police organisations as police work is carried out almost entirely in a situation of non-visibility to managers and supervisors and, more often than not, to any witness. The main product of the organisation is the *behaviour* of its constables which management can seldom observe, let alone measure or control.

Herein, then, lies the dilemma to which we referred at the beginning of this chapter. If the police manager chooses to measure results according to technical police goals the results will not only be spurious but they will cover only a small proportion of police work. If, however, he chooses to measure the behavioural dimensions of the service role, not only is he likely to be short of information but that which is amenable to him is likely to be qualitative data obtainable only from his customers i.e. the public. Compounding this dilemma is the strong possibility that the more he preoccupies himself with rational management methods the more he may distance himself from his constables 'at the sharp end'. Elizabeth and Francis Ianni[11] have vividly portrayed the two competing cultures which they call 'Street Cops and Management Cops', admittedly in a United States setting, but with unmistakable parallels in the Institute of Policy Studies' report on the Metropolitan Police[12]. The Iannis give a full account of the 'cop's code' which includes a range of practices, including a mistrust of bosses, which run counter to the culture of the 'management cops' with its preoccupation with hierarchy, rules, predictability and evaluation; they conclude 'The two cultures no longer share a common vocabulary, a common set of work experiences, and increasingly have different objectives'. This phenomenon has been indicated by a number of researchers in the United States, Britain and the Netherlands[13].

The opening quotation to this chapter was taken from that best-seller by Peters and Waterman 'In Search of Excellence; Lessons from America's Best Run Companies'[14]. In order to qualify for a rating of 'best-run' they all had to demonstrate a capacity for survival, adaptation and results. The characteristics which they had in common, as the opening quotation tells us, were:

1. The emphasis on quality
2. Service
3. Innovativeness, habit-breaking, and a great capacity to learn
4. Result sharing

5. Participation
6. Excitement
7. An external problem-solving focus that is tailored to the customer.

How then, do British police managers match these characteristics? As Maurice Punch says '... there have been very few explicitly organisational studies of the police while the predilections of ethnographers and the politics of research access conspire to make lower level participants, the patrolman or the detective, the irresistible subjects of study'[15]. The Iannis, for example, whose work was quoted above, were denied research access to police headquarters. While Manning and Van Maanen argue that 'the essence of police work is to be located at ground level', in these times of increased managerial accountability the dearth of studies of police managers and police management needs to be corrected.

The author of this paper and Superintendent S. Males carried out two studies[16] in parallel of the roles of Divisional and Sub-Divisional Commanders..Each studied some 150 officers in 7 forces (i.e. 300 officers in 14 forces in all) but each used different methods. Males' study focused on:

1. The managerial tasks seen to be difficult, important and time-consuming.
2. The skills needed to perform those tasks as perceived by the role-holders, their bosses and their subordinates.
3. The variables affecting the perception of the role-holders (among these was a personality profile using the Myers-Brigges Type Indicator[17]).

Plumridge's study focused on the various ways in which the role-holders perceived and experienced their managerial tasks and, by the use of Repertory Grid[18] elicited:

1. The skills perceived to be necessary to carry ot the managerial tasks.
2. Ways in which tasks were associated in their minds.
3. The style and culture of police organisations.

The respondents in both studies identified two main clusters of tasks which were seen by them to be both highly significant and interrelated:

1. Those tasks constituting rational, scientific management such as planning, setting objectives, deploying resources, and measuring performance.
2. Those tasks concerned with the management of people such as team-building, developing subordinates, assessing and appraising, counselling subordinates, and managing conflict.

However the results showed that many of the basic conditions and skills required for the effective performance of these tasks were either missing or inadequate. Counselling, for example, was seen as a highly judgmental and prescriptive process, rather than one of helping reflective learning. The picture which emerged was one of an essentially top-down organisation which did not value highly listening, consultation or participation.

If we examine the results of this research in the light of the characteristics of the 'excellent' organisations portrayed by Peters and Waterman the following conclusions emerge:

1. *The Emphasis on Quality*: There was heavy emphasis on maintaining high standards of professional conduct in their area of command. However, given that there were many indications of a lack of openness in communication between levels in the hierarchy it is difficult to see how this was to be achieved. It was also interesting to find that care and accuracy were generally not highly rated.

2. *Service* (i.e. strenuous attempts to please the customer): Considering that the study was carried out after the publication of the Scarman report it was rather surprising to find that liaising with external representative bodies was not seen as particularly important and requires rather more skill at talking fluently than at listening; it was also perceived as needing high levels of judging and influencing skill. 'Developing his knowledge of his clientele/area of command' was seen as even less of a problem. Other studies have shown that the victims of crime often feel the need for psychological support from the police which is frequently not forthcoming, and that in spite of the fact that social surveys reveal high levels of public concern over rowdiness and vandalism such jobs are often perceived as demeaning by constables.

3. *Innovativeness and the Capacity to Learn*: While the respondents valued initiative and innovation highly Males and Adlam[19] have both found that the predominant personality type among police managers is not intuitive or innovative and prefers well-tried methods. Nor did the respondents value listening, consultation, the carrying out or sponsoring of research, or the use of specialist resources, either internal or external, all of them potential sources of learning.

4. *Result Sharing*: Less evidence on this score emerges from the research results but we do know that the results of police work are currently difficult to ascertain and that police organisations show few symptoms of openness.

5. *Participation*: The top-down nature of police organisations, the low value placed on listening to, and consulting with subordinates, combined with a generally poor view of meetings as potentially creative gatherings, suggest that the organisational culture is unlikely to encourage high levels of participation.

6. *Excitement*: While police work engenders much excitement its source appears to lie in the crime-fighting role. The service role which constitutes the bulk of police work, and is the one most valued by the public (Jones, 1983) is reported by many researchers to be dismissed as 'rubbish' in the 'street-cop' culture. Plumridge and Males found a high level of satisfaction among police managers but there was a preoccupation with 'motivating subordinates', which suggests lack of excitement.

7. *An External Problem-Solving Focus that is Tailored to the Customer*: The issues raised in sub-para 2 (above) do not suggest such a focus and, as discussed earlier in this paper, Jones and Levi say that police managers are more likely to give their customers what they think that they ought to need rather than what the public actually want.

This rather superficial comparative analysis evidently requires fuller treatment but, when added to a series of national reports on the police and governmental pressure for efficiency and effectiveness, it indicates that a considerable challenge faces the police manager during the remainder of this century. The emerging role requires that he be highly skilled in:

1. Helping those around him to set attainable goals and objectives.
2. Deploying his resources purposefully, economically, creatively and imaginatively.
3. Monitoring and measuring results using scientific research methods.
4. Managing change and organisational processes.
5. Analysing and appraising behaviour and performance.
6. Counselling and coaching in order to develop people.
7. Motivating subordinates by listening and securing commitment.
8. Building and maintaining an effective multi-skilled team.
9. Participating in corporate planning and in developing both a management philosophy and a learning climate.
10. Networking and liaising effectively with people, both inside and outside the organisation.
11. Developing his own capacity to learn and his self-awareness.

The research results of Plumridge and Males showed that divisional and sub-divisional commanders recognised both the importance and difficulty of 1–8 above but demonstrated a number of dysfunctional perspectives upon the manner in which they might be achieved and the appropriate skills and attitudes needed to carry them out; their perception of items 9–11, however, was that they are neither particularly important nor difficult. An overview of this research, coupled with the findings of those few research studies which provide us with insights into the nature of police management, produced a model whose main characteristics are:

1. It is pronouncedly hierarchical and values deference and conformity. This produces a monolithic culture which is uncomfortable with expressions of individuality.
2. Decision-making processes are 'top-down'[20] and speed, firmness and decisiveness are highly valued.
3. It believes in self-sufficiency, hence networking, sharing resources, and seeking help are regarded as symptoms of inadequacy. For this reason stress tends to be denied and is seen as 'losing one's bottle'. This makes it a closed system.
4. Conflict is perceived as dysfunctional and it has a need to paper over the cracks and demonstrate solidarity.

5. It is formal, reserved and suspicious; hence trust, openness and delegation cause it discomfort.

The combination of these organisational features indicates an organisation in which stress levels are likely to be high, as witnessed by the A.C.P.O. report on stress. As internal conflict and the expression of feelings tend to be taboo the outlets are likely to be found in alcoholism, disturbed families and aggressive sports; could it be also that the outlet is found in aggressive acts 'on the streets' in situations of low visibility? Distressing as the consequences of such acts are they beg even greater questions for the organisation itself. As Charles Handy has said 'Stress shortens time-horizons, polarizes issues, exaggerates the importance of the present, makes difficulties into crises and inhibits creativity'[21]. Furthermore it stunts the development of the individual, the group, and the organisation at a time when flexibility and adaptability are required.

At this stage of the argument we are in danger of presenting an over-simplified dichtomy of organisational types, on the one hand the control pyramid △

with its assumptions that the higher one goes the more omnipotence and omniscience one possesses, and hence the need for top-down control, which is apt to become a volcano of smouldering repressions, and/or the other the support pyramid (inverted) ▽

which assumes that the most important organisational members are those in the front line doing the work, and that the 'lower' one goes the greater the responsibility to provide them with the supportive wherewithal to accomplish their tasks effectively. The contrast here is between a hierarchy and a 'lowerarchy depicts a static organisation[22] in which:

1. The structure is rigid, much energy goes into preserving roles, departments, rules, procedures, committees and tradition. It is hierarchical, defines roles tightly, and adheres to the chain of command.
2. The atmosphere is impersonal, formal, reserved and suspicious, and is, above all, task-centred.
3. The management philosophy and attitudes are concerned with:
   (a) controlling personnel through the sanctions of coercive power
   (b) caution towards risks and errors; the latter are to be avoided and are punished
   (c) an emphasis on selecting the right man for the job
   (d) self-sufficiency and hence a closed system concerning the sharing of resources or seeking help
   (e) low tolerance for ambiguity and conflict, i.e. order must be imposed.

181

4. Decision-making and policy-making stem from the top with little participation from below. Decisions are not to be argued with and there is a clear distinction between policy-making and policy execution.
5. Communication is restricted in its flow, is downward (one-way), and feelings are hidden and repressed.

In the support pyramid, which typifies a creative, innovative organisation:
1. The structure is flexible and prepared to depart from tradition. There is much use of temporary task forces and organisational changes. There are multiple linkages based on collaboration between functions.
2. The atmosphere is people-centred, warm, informal, caring, intimate and trusting.
3. Management philosophy and attitudes are concerned with:
    (a) the function of management is to release the energy of personnel
    (b) power is used supportively
    (c) experiment and risk-taking
    (d) errors are to be learned from by debriefing, counselling, and reflective learning, and there is an emphasis on personal growth and development
    (e) interdependency, there are many and varied resources both inside and outside the organisation, hence it is an open system sharing resources
    (f) a high tolerance of ambiguity and conflict.
4. Decision-making and policy-making involve all those affected and there is collaborative policy-making and policy execution. Decisions are treated as hypotheses to be tested and are approached in a problem-solving manner.
5. Communication flows openly and multidirectionally. Feelings are shared and valued as imporant information to be acted upon.

While the need for increased potential to innovate in police organisations was indicated earlier in this paper it would nevertheless be unthinkable that they should become entirely innovative. Handy[23], among many others, has shown that an effective organisation needs an amalgam of several different management types and styles and that the bulk of the managers will be required in the 'steady state' part of the organisation i.e. that part which carries out the routine, everyday work of the organisation in which order, reliability and predictability are necessary. Margerison[24] also demonstrates the need for such variety when, in mapping managerial work preferences, he produced a paradigm based upon the Myers-Briggs Type Indicator (Fig.1.).

Fig. 1.

EXPLORERS

(1)   (2)

INNOVATIVE   DEVELOPER
TYPES   TYPES

Managers   18.2%   Managers 18.4%
Police   6%   Police   16.0%

ADVISERS   ORGANISERS
(Process   (Task centred)
 centred)

CO-ORDINATOR   OPERATOR
TYPES   TYPES

Managers   8.8%   Managers 54.6%
Police   6.5%   Police   71.7%
(4)   (3)

CONTROLLERS

In this model the percentage figures quoted are from:

1. A sample of 849 managers from industry and public
   services attending open courses at the Management
   Development Centre, Cranfield Institute of Technology.

2. A sample of 171 police "middle managers" from the
   rank of Chief Inspector to Chief Superintendent in 7
   police forces studied by Males (these percentages
   coincide almost exactly with those found by Adlam
   in a sample of some 850 police managers).

From this model significant factors affecting police organisations are as
follows:

1. They are very short of innovative types who like to turn their
   imagination loose on exploring connections between ideas and
   events (Quadrant 1).

183

2. They are rather short of co-ordinators, i.e. those who are skilled in working with people by negotiating, consulting, counselling, and managing conflict (Quadrant 4).
3. They have a reasonable proportion of developers i.e. those who can pick up new ideas from other sources and apply them to their own organisation (Quadrant 2).
4. They have an extremely high proportion of operators i.e. those who are reliable and predictable in carrying out the work of the organisation (Quadrant 3). These are the types needed in Handy's 'steady state' part of the organisation which performs its daily work; as Margerison says 'it is a major strength of operators that they do gather the facts, that they do persevere and seek to try and establish schedules so that work can be done'.
5. Quadrants 3 and 4 represent the traditionalists and conformists who are content with existing organisation, methods and style. Four out of five police managers are of this type compared with a little more than three out of five managers.
6. One in every five police managers is an explorer (Quadrants 1 and 2) compared with two in every five managers. These are the ones most willing to learn and change; between them they are the ones most likely to change organisation structure and methods, and style.
7. Almost one third of the managers are people and process centred, i.e. concerned about human relationships, human skills, and the *ways* in which decisions are made (what Douglas McGregor called 'The Human Side of Enterprise')[25]. They are the ones most likely to change the style of the organisation. Only one in eight police managers share those concerns.
8. Quadrants 2 and 3 represent the task centred people whose lack of concern for the quality of relationships means that they would tend to be impatient with, and unskilled at interpersonal skills necessary for effective consultation, counselling, team-building and the management of change. They would prefer rationality and decisiveness. While 76.1% of managers are in this category no less than 87.5% of police managers are — and they belong to an organisation which, it is suggested specializes in dealing with people and whose product is behaviour!

The dearth of managerial types on the left hand side (Quadrants 1 and 4), i.e. innovators and co-ordinators who are likely to be people-centred, socially skilled, and concerned with styles of interaction and decision-making processes (as opposed to the nature of the decision taken), is quite serious for police organisations in view of the various recent reports recommending more sensitive interactive behaviour both within the organisation and in relationships with members of the public. Such behaviour includes listening, counselling, consulting and harmonizing in conflict situations; those in Quadrants 2 and 3 are liable to be impatient with those who exhibit such skills and to resist or reject any attempt to develop them in themselves. Equally serious is the dearth of innovators at a time when pressure is mounting upon police organisations to learn new skills and to find more effective ways of deploying their resources for, as has been said earlier, it is those in Quadrants 1 and 2 who are the explorers, innovators, and learners; they are the catalysts of change. What is even more serious is the complete imbalance between the right hand side (Quadrants 2 and 3) and the left hand side (Quadrants 1 and 4) in the ratio of 8 to 1. This emphasizes the top-down control culture outlined by Plumridge and Males on pages 180–1 of this chapter and means that the support culture (page 182), in which openness, sensitivity and creativity are likely to be nurtured, will be totally swamped.

The problem starts with the image projected by the organisation. If that image is one of a crime-fighting organisation in which deference and conformity are highly valued it will not attract many potential innovators and co-ordinators in the first place. If, however, they do apply, in spite of the image, they are likely to be screened out by recruitment panels consisting mainly of operators, plus a few developers, who are highly likely to recruit those in their own image. However, should they be successful they still have to run the gauntlet of the initial recruit training, run, one assumes, mainly by operators, and their probationary service. As probationer constables life is likely to be very difficult for them as they experience the pressure of the group norms and expectations of their fellow constables, and the assessments of their sergeants, who are likely to be looking for different skills from those which they actually possess. The Special Course was devised in order to break this mould and to circumvent the culture, but the experiences of ex Special Course members, upon their return to operational duty, have invariably been, to say the least, difficult. However, to return to our main theme, should our potential innovators and co-ordinators emerge from these experiences unscathed, and should some perceptive senior officer find a home for their particular talents (often in a specialist role) it will not be long before pressure upon them mounts to 'get back to real police work and feel a few collars!' Thus when an organisation develops a particularly pronounced style and culture it has generated sufficiently powerful defence mechanisms to ward off potential threats imposed by intruders. So long as the policy of developing police managers from within its own ranks continues, and particularly the period of heavy socialization on the beat, this whole process is likely to be reinforced.

What is needed is evidently what Beckhard and Harris have called 'a large system change strategy' which they define as 'a *plan* defining what *interventions* to make *where*, by *whom*, and at what *time* in order to move the organisation to a state where it can optimally *transform* needs into results in a social environment that *nurtures people's worth and dignity* (my italics). Managerially this means defining the kinds of activities that need to be induced and *the kinds of expertise that need to be brought to bear to help with the change* (my italics again); identifying people in the organisation who need to become committed to the change; establishing a time-table and specifying priorities of changes and practices in procedures, rewards, policies, and behaviour; establishing a system of evaluating progress toward a new state; and *providing education in skills needed to both operate in the new condition and manage the change* (my italics again)'[26].

If such a system is to be practicable it has to be accompanied by a move to develop all organisational members into what Mumford has called 'self-directed learners'[27] as opposed to learners who are dependent upon being trained by the organisation. Such a stance, as defined by Mumford, involves the development of the following skills of learning:-

* the ability to establish effectiveness criteria for yourself
* the ability to measure your effectiveness
* the ability to identify your own learning needs
* the ability to plan personal learning
* the ability to take advantage of learning opportunities
* the ability to review your own learning processes
* the ability to listen to others
* the capacity to accept help
* the ability to face unwelcome information
* the ability to take risks and tolerate anxieties
* the ability to analyze what other successful performers do
* the ability to know yourself
* the ability to share information with others
* the ability to review what has been learned.

Returning to the analysis of police organisations it is unlikely that, given the power of the top-down culture identified, they will be able to generate internally either the large system change strategy or the development of self-directed learners. For such a phenomenon to occur would require much more of a balance between the four managerial styles in Fig. 1.; hence it is likely to occur only with the aid of outside intervention. As the introduction of a two-tier entry system appears to be both abhorrent and politically impracticable change is likely to occur only if and when the capacity of the organisation to cope with the pressures upon it cause so much pain in the form of internal conflict, a drop in commitment and morale, or high levels of stress; any of these factors may cause the organisation to seek outside help. There are, in fact many signs that this process is already beginning to occur in the face of governmental pressure and public criticism.

Change on a whole system scale will not occur by fragmented approaches; it needs a multifaceted and multilevel approach. The ingredients of such a strategy would include:-

1. A need for commitment to change by top management and a willingness on their part to seek the help of those skilled in the art of organisational change i.e. sufficient humility to learn.

2. A willingness, together with the development of appropriate skills, to enlist the help of all organisational members to redefine organisational objectives and to develop the skills needed to implement them; as Greiner[28] has said 'we must revise our egocentric notions that organisation change is heavily dependent on a master blueprint designed and executed in one fell swoop by an omniscient consultant or top manager' — the typical stance of the top-down culture of developers and operators.

3. The recruitment and nurture of more potential innovators and co-ordinators who are capable of attending to the *processes* of change.

4. The development of a new breed of internal consultants or change agents with a considerable leavening of innovation and co-ordination skills, who have a thorough knowledge of the dimensions of organisational effectiveness and the skills to influence it. It is of interest to note that the U.S. Army and the U.S. Navy have founded schools of organisational effectiveness at Monterey, California (the latter headed by Reuben Harris, quoted earlier in this chapter) which puts selected middle ranking officers through a six month development programme in consultancy skills prior to posting them as advisers on organisational effectiveness on the staffs of senior officers.

5. The development of all organisation members as self-directed learners. This would be most likely occur if all work teams at all levels in the organisation were helped to:
    (a) set their own objectives
    (b) develop the skills necessary to implement them
    (c) develop the skills necessary to monitor and review their own performance
    with the assistance of the consultants described in 4 above.

Hence, it is argued, the main dilemma facing police organisations is that, at a time when there are pressures on them to be more responsive to the needs of their clients and to provide value for money, the prevailing culture is incompatible with the apparent needs of those clients. Furthermore the imbalance between personality types within the organisation reinforces that incompatibility to the extent that it is difficult to foresee self-generated change, of the magnitude required, taking place without some form of outside intervention. This imbalance may be reduced in one or all of the following ways:-

1. By introducing more innovators and co-ordinators into the service and developing ways of encouraging and rewarding them.
2. As in each one of us the opposite characteristics lie dormant in varying degrees, a change in managerial style at the top of police organisations aimed at moving from a control to a support pyramid would serve to release more energy in the forms of innovation, openness and sensitivity.
3. By introducing a longer and more professional training period which focussed upon self-development, self-directed learning and self-esteem and autonomy i.e. self-discipline instead of imposed discipline and the expectation of conformity. In other words learned responses are liable to be much more sensitive, flexible and effective than trained responses.

A shift from a primarily crime fighting culture to a primarily service culture requires creative approaches both to the training and deployment of resources and to new ways of developing a dialogue with the organisation's clientèle. Such approaches are likely to require a wide range of skills which are not highly regarded or rewarded in the present culture. Moreover if the organisation is to be more effective and give value for money, each individual member has to be willing and able to set, monitor and achieve personal action plans which help to meet the goals and objectives of the organisation; all of which surely is another way of saying that he must be a self-regulating professional as opposed to being someone's subordinate. As his responsibilities rise through promotion he will need increasing levels of skill in co-ordinating the work of his team, helping them to set personal goals, counselling, coaching and managing inevitable conflicts between them.

REFERENCES

1. Reiss A. J., Jr. 1971, 'The Police and the Public', New Haven, Conn: Yale University Press.
2. Kelling G. L., Page T., Dieckman D. and Brown G. E., 1974, 'The Kansas City Preventive Patrol Experiment', Washington D.C.: Police Foundation.
3. Wilson J. Q. and Boland B., 1978, 'The Effect of the Police on Crime' — Law and Society Review 12: pp. 367–390.
4. Ostrom E., et al 1973, 'Community Organization and the Provision of Police Service', Beverley Hills, California, Sage Publications.

5. Goldstein H., 1977, 'Policing a Free Society', Cambridge, Massachusetts, Ballinger.
6. Sandra Jones and Dr. Michael Levi, 'The Police and the Majority: the Neglect of the Obvious?' — The *Police Journal* — December 1983, Vol. LVI, No. 4.
7. Dr. P. A. Waddington, 'The Acceptable Face of Policing' — *Police*, November 1983, Vol. XVI, No. 3.
8. Manolias M., 'Stress in the Police Service', August 1983 — Home Office.
9. Lubans V. and Edgar J. M., 'Policing by Objectives; a Handbook for Improving Police Management'. Social Development Corporation, Connecticut 1979.
10. Gouldner A., 1954, *'Patterns of Industrial Bureaucracy'*, New York, Free Press.
11. Elizabeth R. Ianni and Francis A. J. Ianni, 'Street Cops and Management Cops: The Two Cultures of Policing' in 'Control in the Police Organization' ed. Punch M., M.I.T. Press, Cambridge, Massachusetts, Chapter 13.
12. Smith D. J., 'The Police and People in London', Policy Studies Institute 1983.
13. For example in Britain, Manning P. K., 'The Social Organization of Police Work', pp. 145–151, 1977, M.I.T. Press, Cambridge, Massachusetts.
    And Chatterton M., 1975, 'Organizational Relationships and Processes in Police Work' unpublished Ph. D. thesis, University of Manchester.
    In the Netherlands, Punch M., 'Officers and Men: Occupational Culture, Inter-Rank Antagonism, and the Investigation of Corruption,' in 'Control in the Police Organization' ed. Punch M., Chapter 12, M.I.T. Press, Cambridge, Massachusetts, 1983.
14. Thomas J. Peters and Robert H. Waterman Jr., *'In Search of Excellence: Lessons from America's Best-Run Companies'*, Harper and Row 1982.
15. Punch M., 'Control in the Police Organization', ibid., p. 227.
16. Males S., 'Police Management on Division and Sub-Division', Police Research Services Unit 1983.
    Plumridge M. D., 'A Study of Police Management and Command Roles' Bramshill Police Staff College 1983.
17. Myers I. B., 'The Myers — Briggs Type Indicator', Princeton: Educational Testing Service 1962.
18. Smith J. M. and Stewart B. J. M., 'Repertory Grids: A Flexible Tool for Establishing the Content and Structure of a Manager's Thoughts', in Ashton D. (Ed.) 'Management Bibliographies and Reviews: Volume 3'. Bradford: M.C.B. Publications, 1977.

189

19. Adlam K.R.C., 'The Psychological Attributes of Police Officers: Empirical Findings and Some Comments Upon Their Implications', 1983 (see this volume).
20. Greiner L. E., 'Patterns of Organization Change', *Harvard Business Review* May–June 1967.
21. Handy C. B., '*Understanding Organizations*', Penguin 1979, p. 370.
22. Knowles M. S., 'Releasing the Energy of Others — Making Things Happen', in *Journal of Management Development*, Vol. 2, No. 2, 1983, pp. 26–35.
23. Handy C. B., Ibid, pp. 198–204 and '*Gods of Management*', Souvenir Press 1978.
24. Margerison C. and Lewis R., 'Mapping Managerial Styles' — 'International Journal of Manpower', Vol. 2, No. 1.
25. McGregor D., '*The Human Side of Enterprise*', McGraw-Hill, 1960.
26. Richard Beckhard and Reuben T. Harris, 'Organizational Transitions: Managing Complex Change' — Addison-Wesley, 1977, p. 15.
27. Alan Mumford, 'Making Experience Pay: Management Success Through Effective Learning', McGraw-Hill, 1980, pp. 81–97.
28. Greiner L. E., Ibid.

The State of the Police in the Eighties
J. R. THACKRAH

In a consensus-pervaded society, policing is a comparatively simple concept, but when a society begins to mount a challenge to authoritarianism, policing becomes more burdensome, particularly at the point where the challenge is rising but authoritarianism has not begun to recede. Many will argue that this turning point has been reached in the U.K. Our society presses for greater emancipation, and the police need to understand the forces of change in order to help society to attain its higher aspirations. In this lies a problem, for the police are culturally and professionally concerned with the status quo. Ideas of policing realignment need to be understood, taught and acted upon. The police are often only the scapegoats for the inability of society to make adjustments to ease these social tensions.

The police service today is under threat as never before, ironically from within itself as well as from outside. With the present community policing strategy, the service is on the right course for adapting to changes demanded by society, however, a more critically aware public is demanding a new professionalism coupled with increased accountability. Greater emphasis will be placed on localised policing, especially on the man on the beat but shortage of resources will continue to be a limiting factor as demands on the police are bound to increase and although the manpower position is unlikely to deteriorate, it would be unrealistic to expect dramatic improvement.

Problems of inner cities are likely to become even more intractable, with possibilities of increasing disorder — the events of 1981 perhaps being merely the tip of an iceberg. As the pattern of population shifts, the will to devote resources to these problems is likely to diminish. Increases in leisure activity must not be reflected in crime figures.

To most British people the law is the policeman. In the U.K. the police are in theory public servants, subject to common law and with no special arm — like the CRS in France or the Carabinieri in Italy — under direct government control. Instead of the 'third force' the only force in extremis is the Army. Nevertheless the police are also, as Lord Gardiner, a former Lord Chancellor, described them, 'the most powerful and least accountable of any in Western Europe. Nowhere else do they have the power to prosecute without any independent evaluation; and in other countries forces are accountable through a minister'. The power to prosecute without any independent evaluation is likely to be changed in the future (probably 1986) with the coming into operation of the new independent prosecution service.

The police's conduct has become much more exposed to debate, and they have moved much closer to the centre of the political stage.

Sir Robert Mark throughout his period as Commissioner of the Metropolitan Force from 1972 to 1977, insisted that the Yard should maintain its autonomy, and that the police should themselves look after complaints. Mark insisted that political or bureaucratic interference and the police did not go hand in hand. Independence was essential to their acceptability and to the preservation of democracy. Also, the Commissioner was not keen that complaints should be investigated by an independent body.

As crime has increased, criminals have become more organised and communications have quickened. More critics have demanded a national police force. The Willink Commission of 1962 recommended that chief constables should retain their powers, but the objections return with each scandal about local police forces — such as the prolonged failure to track down the Yorkshire Ripper.

Police centralisation involves much larger democratic issues, including the protection of individual rights against data banks and computers. Britain is one of the few European countries whose citizens have no identity number and need not carry any identification. The Lindop Committee on data protection believed centralised computers would enable the police to put together information about individuals much more efficiently but also more secretively. This situation calls for much closer scrutiny by parliament or its representatives. Overriding all these issues the public image of the police would benefit from greater openness and tactful explanations such as on matters of data protection and open government. The public need to be aware that while welcoming technology as an immensely powerful tool in police work it has created the opportunity for new and more sophisticated types of crime.

The last few years have seen the development by chief constables of more positive views on a wider scale of attitudes to policing and crime. The chiefs in the shires could afford to be more relaxed than those in the six Metropolitan areas who are faced with crumbling inner cities and rootless minorities whose problems were spotlighted by the riots. The Chief Constable of Greater Manchester, James Anderton, maintained his tough policies in the face of growing complaints of police brutality. Mr. Anderton also had little patience with his local council. When citizens complained about police brutality against rioters the council supported a local committee of inquiry, but the Chief responded pointedly by submitting his own report to the police committee. Conversely the then Chief Constable of Devon and Cornwall, John Alderson, argued that the police force had become too professionalised and divorced from the community. Police relations with their communities and tactics with rioters were wrong — and he proposed a committee of local councillors to supervise the Metropolitan Police. His views were considered to be 'softly, softly' and too liberal, by his colleagues, but they epitomised a healthy differing of views on policing matters between the chief constables.

The British compromise between local and central control has left, as in other spheres, a large unaccountable gap in the middle. It is clear that in the future only a stronger and more responsible system of local government can provide more effective say in police matters, without still further centralisation. The police are in the midst of society yet regarded as being right outside it — an ambivalence which has been in existence throughout the history of the police in the U.K.

The problems of democratic control — whether through town halls, Whitehall, parliament or the law courts — converge on the police. They are, as Mark put it 'the anvil on which society beats out the problems of political and social failure'.

In the light of such a situation, is a national police force required? Such a force would do nothing to improve police-public relations (some would argue it would worsen them), but on grounds of efficiency in a period of weakening respect for law and order the proposal has been revived, despite the rejection of the plan by the majority of the Willink Commission, over twenty years ago. Those who argue in favour of a national police force maintain that the present dispersal of police forces in the face of modern criminal methods is a disservice to the community — for example, five different squads supervise stretches of motorway in the Midlands, and delays and duplication of effort can be all too common. Secondly, a uniform pattern of recruitment, training and promotion would lead to improved *esprit de corps* and greater efficiency. At present there is the feeling that appointments go to local men without proper regard for finding the best men for the job. Police cadets' training varies widely with the authorities concerned and the resources they put at the disposal of the training officers. Thirdly, standardisation of equipment of all kinds must improve efficiency, speed up detection and ease collaboration within the regions, which would presumably still continue within the national force. A point which is often overlooked is that improved central direction from an overall leadership with less frequent intervention by the Home Secretary would diminish 'political' control. For instance, the Minister of Defence does not interfere with the day-to-day running of the Armed Forces. Lastly, if current local forces prove too weak to grapple with the increasing volume of crime, especially crimes of violence, there may well be a demand for 'vigilantes' as was demonstrated in 1974 and 1980 when several ex-service officers came out with plans to bolster up 'law and order' with what would have amounted to private armies; and in 1976 when a judge suggested anti-mugging patrols in parts of South London. Professor Goodhart (the dissenting member of the Willink Commission) said 'The danger to a democracy does not lie in a central police that is too strong, but in local forces that are too weak.'

Arguments against a national force are equally strong and unequivocal. Fears of a State police on the lines of the many totalitarian regimes are genuine. Secondly, many people fear that the last links between the community and the police constable would be destroyed, with the onset of a 'here today, gone tomorrow' image for the police. Thirdly, from the nostalgic and historical angle there is the long tradition of local control over the police, which began in medieval and Tudor times with the parish constables and the watchmen. Finally, it is a fact that the problems of police supervision and organisation are very different from those of forces designed to meet an attack from a foreign power. The local variations, the need to develop ties with the local community and to acquire knowledge of regional conditions all militate against heavily centralised control.

What can be made of policing contemporary society in the eighties, and what can be planned for the 1990s? Such consideration should not be too academic. In 1962 the Royal Commission on the Police recognised that the role of the police depended on the social context and that concepts of policing were bound to change as society itself changed. Since that time the essential purposes of the police have not changed; but the means by which these purposes are discharged, the demands made on the police and the shape and structure of the service have altered considerably. The last two decades have seen changes in society generally, and in this context in particular in public attitudes towards the police — for example, changes in the way police manpower has been deployed following the introduction of the pocket radio; and in recent years, a renewed emphasis on links with the community. With costs soaring and inflation seemingly a permanent feature, the need to use manpower efficiently and flexibly is vital. This will imply looking at the police service as a whole, and in particular reappraising the role of civilians in such areas as technical support; the requirement for senior officers of the right calibre, and their necessity to cope with the consequences of the 'bulge' created by high levels of recruitment. In technical areas a flexible approach to complementing and manning will be necessary.

The social role of the police has become more important and greater emphasis is placed on community policing. After the sad events of 1981 priority must be given to the problem of social breakdown and conflict and promoting ordinary community control. Relations with ethnic minority groups have to be improved — but while police have a major responsibility to promote good community relations they should not be made the scapegoats for the inner city problems. In relation to this matter and the need to recruit members of ethnic minority communities, consideration must be given to encouraging the recruitment of those with specialist skills.

In spite of the traditional independence of army and police roles in a true democracy, the prospects of a lengthy threat to public order should not be ruled out. Arrangements for mutual aid and co-operation with the armed forces must be kept under constant review.

The emergence of a society clearly disaffected with traditional standards and norms of behaviour would be a serious challenge for the police. Law enforcement must not be viewed as the priority to which inevitably scarce resources must be devoted to the exclusion of other aspects of policing. It will probably not be possible to rely simply on increasing police manpower in the traditional sense with the likely constraints on resources. Yet the need for an increasingly professional police service, if the demands of technological advance are to be absorbed, is patent, and already present. The service thus will be part of a new era and will benefit from its technology.

Alongside the technological age we have an affluent society with an increasing crime-rate, a liberal outlook which has effectively diluted the judicial and penal functions, and a law enforcement agency which is striving to keep abreast of change and simultaneously fulfil a traditional role.

What of the future? Does society really want law and order? There is little doubt that the vast majority of people do, but unfortunately the predominant voice is that of the clamorous minority, those who worship the sacred cow of social reform at all costs, and the politically-motivated men of the twilight zone whose aim is the downfall of law and order and the ultimate disintegration of society as we know it in the United Kingdom. On a practical scale there now prevails within the service, as well as in society as a whole, a very considerable intellectual dilemma as to the true objectives of a modern police service and this dilemma accounts in some way for the failure of the police to make a more challenging impact upon the more intellectually sensitive of our young people.

In their training the police need to be made proof against their own indignation, their own instinctive resentments. If society expects this kind of ideological detachment from its police, it owes them its protection and support in discharging their duties. The police need a full range of intellectual skills made available to them if they are to have a proper perception towards society. They need to be representative of the community. This development is specially necessary as the disorders in 1981 constituted a watershed in the development of a field of intersecting debates focusing on law and order, race, youth and the inner cities.

The time is now ripe for a re-statement and, if research finds it necessary, a redefining of the role of the police. Have the police of recent years removed themselves too far from the communities they should be policing? Are the police now looked upon as strangers in many areas, as an anonymous organisation which cannot be held to account to anyone?

195

Have the majority of police authorities failed to adequately ensure the efficiency of their forces?

Some people in all walks of life believe that police powers are increasing while individual protection is decreasing. Generally the crucial constitutional position of independence enjoyed by the police service has been maintained with the consent of its public. Traditional modes of policing rest on the premise of being carried out by locally-appointed citizens in constant contact with the public, thereby expressing and symbolising concern for the needs of the community.

The police service faces a paradox — namely how to manage increasing demands being made upon its limited resources and at the same time gauge the extent to which it should cling to the perceived traditional image still yearned for by so many sections of the public. The abandonment of the latter would diminish the unqualified support of the public. Total abandonment is inappropriate. The police will continue to rely upon the public for freely-given consent and support. Nevertheless, it would be naive to discard the use of recently established policing methods and technology to satisfy an outdated traditional image. The police service must harness its technical aids, use of firearms, group policing methods and other 'specialist' activities in a fashion which is consistent with the views of the public. This will enhance the continuum of a non-oppressive organisation, exercising legal authority fairly, efficiently and effectively on behalf of and with the consent of its public.

The demands for greater police accountability and effectiveness are the result of some public dissatisfaction with the declining success of the police service often reported by the media, e.g. the Stephen Waldorf incident in 1983. The Scarman Report perceived an encore of calls for a return to the perceived traditional image of policing. As Scarman suggested, Chief Officers of Police must find some means of more accurately measuring the climate of the community so as to exercise their prerogative in the allocation of resources. Unlike the economist in a free market a Chief Officer cannot rely on price rises as an indicator of social change.

Even today, people who do not conform in society are more likely to oppose the police, these people tend to see society ranged against them. These same people, whilst pleased to see more people from ethnic minorities in police, education and government ultimately require an even more radical change in society. A critical issue for discussion by government may be that the spread of social disadvantage is made worse by the way we deal with it — in other words by institutionally practising violence we breed violence. In this way there is a young body of bipartisan opinion which argues that the Brixtons and Toxteths could occur again. A Police Commander of one of the areas affected, accepted some of the criticisms which Scarman made of policing in his area — by stating that in the future the community would be involved more closely. On such matters the police face a major dilemma — to get the community to co-operate more closely with the police when, at the same time, decisions have to be made on the enforcement of law and order which people may not like. Police would prefer to do things on a voluntary basis rather than with a formal set up, because everything is more friendly.

Courts are seen as being handmaidens of vested interest leaving individuals to fend for themselves. The less freedoms we enjoy the greater the polarisation between libertarianism and authoritarianism. Although the law might be weighted in favour of police to catch up on their shortfall haul of crooks, juries are reluctant to convict just on police evidence from police questioning. Sexism and racism still have a high consideration among certain sections of the population when looking at police attitudes and performance.

Police are operating in a society with irredeemable poverty and much unemployment leading to greater violence when police powers obviously have to be strengthened. Police education in Britain is being designed for performance with people entering from a wider range of home and career backgrounds on whom high practical expectations are placed.

Dialogues have to occur between police and public on the nature of society to avoid dehumanising law and order. Practically, the balance between law enforcement and the avoidance of disorder needs to be redressed in response to Britain's troubled times. Government is faced with broad contradictory choices between law and order responses on the one hand and remedial responses cognitive of the underlying causes of violence on the other. In the eyes of many people the police were the political scapegoats for the riots. Yet riots and public disorder will always be around and the balance between liberty and enforcement is finely set.

Police effectiveness is growing in spite of limited decreases in the crime rate — but a more appropriate measure is the nature of public opinion towards the police. Impartial law enforcement is vital. The police pay an initial price in terms of their good name by the exposure and measurement of malpractices, but the report of the Policy Studies Institute on the Metropolitan Police, shows that the reputation of the police in the eyes of the public will benefit in the long run.

It is in many ways a false inference that prejudice on the part of the police is the cause of black hostility. The police are put, by the perform-ance of their duties, in a position where it is only too easy to exacerbate feelings of exclusion and where feelings may well be vented on them anyway. This is a recognised danger point in social control and even in the preservation of civil peace; and emphasises the value now placed on in-service training and the Metropolitan Police's interest in a 'multi-agency' approach. Such an approach concentrates on the definition of an objective and the adoption of co-ordinated measures to achieve it, in which police are one among several public and perhaps also voluntary agencies.

197

Competency is as important as style when police respond to incidents. The basis of the *Police and Criminal Evidence Act* is one of caution, whilst seemingly providing extra power to the police it was necessary not to offend particular interests and the need for accountability was paramount. The recent emphasis is seen in many areas, for example, consultative committees, independent investigation of complaints and the need to explain through the media the reasons behind certain actions.

The Act extends the power to stop and search and detain to the whole county. The period for which suspects may be detained at a police station is being statutorily defined for the first time. Under Common Law there is no fixed limit, though in practice limits have been imposed whilst at the same time maintaining flexibility. Detention without charge for up to 96 hours will only be permitted for very serious offences such as homicide, rape, kidnapping, terrorism, causing explosions and carrying firearms with criminal intent. Burglars, un-armed robbers and similar classes of offender will have to be brought before a court after 24 hours and a case made out for further de-tention.

The Act has further weakened other earlier proposals such as the right to examine by warrant the records of professional persons during the investigation of serious crime. It provides for 'excluded material', which includes solicitors records, medical records, journalists notes, records of Samaritans and social workers, priests and Citizen Advice Bureaux. The onus of deciding what is relevant and whether it should be considered as evidence is to be moved by law from police to professional individuals.

This whole trend suggests a general mistrust in the ability of the police to regulate themselves, a trend that can be partly explained by the reduced contact between police and society which has occurred to some extent over recent years. Public anxiety may also be explained by changes in our approach to policing. More selective recruiting, im-proved communications, transport and information recording, enhanced training and the use of management techniques in the deployment of personnel all help to provide a better service to the public. Most of the changes in the police service can by fully justified to a public which is still predominantly behind the police. Changes have combined to force the police service to review its methods on a continued basis in order to provide society with an effective form of policing. In the words of the current Commissioner of the Metropolitan Police:

'The public cannot have its cake and eat it. It cannot on the one hand demand a civilised power-restricted form of policing and on the other hand stand by passively, apathetically or critically and demand that the police alone solve the problems of the com-munity.'

In a wider context Sir Kenneth Newman's words were echoed decades earlier by C. P. Snow:

> 'Until this century social change was so slow that it could pass unnoticed in one person's lifetime. That is no longer true. The rate of change has increased so much that an imagination can't keep up.'

The police imagination must not only keep up with such change but, if possible, foresee it and plan for it. What a challenge for the eighties and nineties.

Contributors

JOHN RICHARD THACKRAH, B.A. Comb. (Hons), PG Cert Ed, M.A.
Has been a lecturer in History and Politics at Bramshill since 1977. His special interests are: the Effects of Terrorism on Democracies, Counter Insurgency, Public Order, Police History and Police-Public Relations. He has written articles in the Police Journal, Police and Society Research Papers, Police Studies and Police World.

IAN STUART, B.A.
After 6 years' lecturing in the Far East, Ian Stuart joined Bramshill in 1969, becoming Academic Director of the Inspectors' Course in 1978 and of the Junior Command Course in 1979. He lectures in Economics and in Statistics.

NEIL RICHARDS, B.Sc. (Econ), M.A., M.A.Ed.
Graduated from London University in 1967 and holds masters' degrees from the universities of Durham and Leicester. Before joining the Police Staff College he taught moral and educational philosophy at a variety of educational institutions including Leicester University and the College of St. Paul and St. Mary, Cheltenham. As an academic staff tutor, his special interest is in applied ethics and he has been concerned with developing police related ethics at the College.

BRIAN MASON, M.A., M.B.I.M., M.I.T.D.
Has been recently promoted to the Head of the Politics and Public Administration Department at the Police Staff College, Bramshill, which he joined in January 1978 following a career encompassing the Royal Air Force Education Branch and lecturing and teaching at a variety of educational and training institutions, from university, through Colleges of Technology to comprehensive schools.

JOHN M. BRINDLEY, B.Sc.
Graduated from the University of Bristol with first Class Honours in Psychology. He was appointed to the Police Staff College, Bramshill in 1975. Since that time, he has applied psychological understanding to many aspects of police work, concentrating particularly upon interpersonal perception, stress and psychological assessment.

ROBERT ADLAM, B.Sc.

A psychologist who has specialised in personality studies. Currently he is developing his studies into personal construct psychology and has begun to analyse police phenomenology. His other interests include the work of Marcel Proust and 19th Century French Art.

DAVID WATTS POPE, B.COMM (Hons), DIP.Ed. (Hons), A.C.P.
(Senior Staff Tutor, Police Staff College, Bramshill)

Has had a variety of experience in schools, colleges and the Open University but has specialised, since joining the Staff College, in Community and Race Relations training. He has acted as adviser to a number of forces in setting up their Community Relations systems, helped in the establishing of national courses for Community Relations Staff and lectured throughout the country on such matters. His publications include '*Community Relations, The Police Response*' (Runnymede Trust, 1976) and '*Modern Policing*' (Croom Helm 1981).

NORMAN GREENHILL, B.A.

Senior Lecturer and sociologist. Joined Bramshill staff from Bristol University Extra-Mural Studies Department in 1969. Has been principally concerned with developing studies in the spheres of race relations, police-community relations and preventive policing.

COLIN VICK, B.Soc.Sc., M.Sc.

Graduated in sociology as an external student of London University in 1970. He joined the Police Staff College in 1975. He was a part-time tutor with the Open University from 1978–83. His thesis for an M.Sc. (Educational Studies) at Surrey University (1983) was entitled 'Higher Education and the Police'. His interests remain in the field of higher education for the police.

MICHAEL D. PLUMRIDGE, B.A., F.B.I.M., F.I.I.M., M.I.P.M.

Came to the Police Staff College in 1971 from a background of R.A.F. Education Officer, works manager in the boot and shoe industry, tutor and research worker at Roffey Park Management College, and Senior Lecturer in Personnel Management and Organisational Behaviour at Brighton Polytechnic. He is a Fellow of the Anglian Regional Management Centre and a member of the executive committee of the Association of Teachers of Management.